Paris Was Yesterday

PARIS WAS YESTERDAY

1925–1939

JANET FLANNER

(GENÊT)

Edited by Irving Drutman

A HARVEST/HBJ BOOK
HARCOURT BRACE JOVANOVICH, PUBLISHERS
SAN DIEGO NEW YORK LONDON

First published in the USA in 1972 by The Viking Press

"Murder in Le Mans" and "Murder among the Love Birds" originally appeared in *Vanity Fair*. "Mme. Lydia Stahl" and "Mata Hari" originally appeared in *Harper's Bazaar*. All other material originally appeared in *The New Yorker*.

LIBRARY OF CONGRESS CATALOGING-IN-PUBLICATION DATA
Flanner, Janet, 1892–
Paris was yesterday : 1925–1939 / Janet Flanner (Genêt) ; edited
by Irving Drutman.
p. cm.
"A Harvest/HBJ book."
Reprint. Previously published: New York : Viking Press, 1972.
Includes index.
ISBN 0-15-670990-2 (pbk.)
1. Paris (France)—Intellectual life—20th century. 2. Paris
(France)—Social life and customs—20th century. I. Drutman,
Irving. II. Title.
DC737.F555 1988
944'.360815—dc19   87-29617

Printed in the United States of America

First Harvest edition 1988

A B C D E

Prefatory Note

The material in this volume has been selected mainly from Janet Flanner's fortnightly "Letter from Paris" in *The New Yorker*, which she started transmitting in October 1925, signed, then as now, with her *nom de correspondance*, Genêt. The period covered is from 1925 to 1939. Several chapters from *An American in Paris*, published in 1940, have also been included.

The original text has been slightly amended here and there to clarify topical allusions otherwise lost in time.

Where moved by memory, Janet Flanner has made occasional additional comments, which are set within brackets.

I.D.

Introduction

Memories are the specific invisible remains in our lives of what belongs in the past tense. It is now more than a half century ago, back in the opening 1920s, that for the first time Paris began being included in the memories of a small contingent of youngish American expatriates, richer than most in creative ambition and rather modest in purse. For the most part we had recently shipped third class to France across the Atlantic, at that date still not yet flown over except by migratory sea birds. We had settled in the small hotels on the Paris Left Bank near the Place Saint-Germain-des-Prés, itself perfectly equipped with a large corner café called Les Deux Magots and an impressive twelfth-century Romanesque church, with its small garden of old trees, from whose branches the metropolitan blackbirds sang at dawn, audible to me in my bed close by in the rue Bonaparte. Though unacquainted with each other, as compatriots we soon discovered our chance similarity. We were a literary lot.

Each of us aspired to become a famous writer as soon as possible. After the New York publication of Ernest Hemingway's *The Sun Also Rises*, he became that first and foremost famous expatriate American writer. When I look back on the stir created by his individual style of writing, what stands out in my memory is the fact that his heroes, like Ernest himself, were of outsized masculinity even in small matters. In his writing, his descriptions of the color of deep sea water beside his boat or of the trout's fins in the pool where he angled were like reports from the pupil of his eyes transferred by his pen onto his paper. As a special gift Ernest had a physical style of writing with his senses that was uniquely his own literary creation yet which soon influenced American male fiction-writing. He had introduced European nature in its grand scale in his novels, then fallen in love with Spanish bullfights and consorted with bullfighters; and later on in Africa he took to big-game hunting, for which he had a bloody passion. In a letter he wrote to me he said he liked to hunt because he liked to kill. By temperament he was professionally excessive, like a form of generosity. Married four times, he had taught each of his wives how to shoot and survive on safaris. When he finally killed himself with a gun, it was the ultimate melodrama of his spectacular existence. Ernest's father had also been a suicide and so had mine, both of the deaths occurring at about the same period of our young lives (I was older than Ernest by seven years), when we were in our twenties. This was a piece of personal duplicate history that he and I had discovered accidentally one day and had discussed with exploratory interest at a quiet back table in the Deux Magots café, which he always favored for serious talk, such as his reading aloud in a rumbling whisper the first poetry he had written after the war. I recall how as an agnostic I had taken a more rationalist view than he of suicide as an act for freedom—in my mind and conscience a possible permissible act of liberation from whatever humiliating bondage on earth could no longer be borne with self-respect—and our talk ended with the mutual declaration that if either of us ever killed ourself, the other was not to grieve but to remember that liberty could be as important in the act of dying as in the acts of living. So, years later, I did not believe that Ernest's death in Idaho from that grotesque gunshot, was an accident, as officially reported at first and only a year later officially denied in favor of the more profound truth. I had automatically recognized that fatal gunshot as his mortal act of gaining liberty. But I grieved deeply when the pitiful facts of his final bondage were made public, such as those unbearable bouts of maladive suffering of a man who as I knew (because he had told me) was a stoic in relation to the pain he had frequently undergone in his accident-prone life; and what was worse, his realization, at the last, of his tottering faculties and the threatened loss of his reason. At Ernest's death, I grieved most because he died in a state of ruin.

The hearth and home of the Left Bank American literary colony after 1920 turned out to be Shakespeare and Company, the extraordinary rue de l'Odéon bookstore founded by the American Sylvia Beach. She had gone to Paris in 1917 during the worst war in French history because, as she said, she "had a particular interest in contemporary French writing." Her father, Reverend Sylvester Woodbridge Beach, D.D., was pastor of the First Presbyterian Church in Princeton, New Jersey, of whose congregation Woodrow Wilson was a member while president of Princeton University and considered himself and family still members even after he became President of the United States. Settling her bookshop in the rue de l'Odéon, Sylvia was able to learn how such an establishment should be run from her close friend Mlle. Adrienne Monnier, owner of the Maison des Amis des Livres, just across the street, a French literary center not only for the most superior contemporary French writing but for its authors as well, such writers as André Gide, Jean Schlumberger, the poets Paul Valéry and Jean-Paul Fargue, and the novelists Valéry Larbaud and Jules Romain. At all hours they frequented the Monnier shop and on special days held reverent sessions there, attended by Sylvia and occasionally by a few of us American writers as well, in which they read aloud from their unpublished manuscripts. The immediate compatibility of these two extraordinary women shopkeepers, opposite numbers in what became a cultural Franco-English language stream flowing down their street, visibly added to its picturesque quality. Adrienne was mildly spectacular. Buxom as a handsome abbess, she was a placidly eccentric neighborhood figure in a costume she had invented for herself and permanently adopted. It consisted of a full long gray skirt and a sleeveless velveteen waistcoat worn over a white blouse. Sylvia, thin as a schoolgirl, dressed like one, in a juvenile short skirt and jacket over a white blouse with a big white turndown collar, like one of Colette's young heroines, and a big colored bowknot at the throat. Adrienne, however, looked like some character actress from the Théâtre de l'Odéon at the head of their street, who had strolled out from a dress rehearsal in full stage costume.

Shortly after Sylvia had opened her shop, she received the visit (as she later told me) of two American women. "One of them, with a very fine face, was stout, wore a long robe and on her head a most becoming top of a basket. She was accompanied by a slim, dark, whimsical woman; she reminded me of a gypsy." They were, of course, Gertrude Stein and Miss Alice B. Toklas. Miss Stein was the first subscriber to Sylvia's lending library, for which she wrote a jocular little advertisement, sent to the rest of us Americans in the quarter, to incite us also to subscribe, which most of us did. It read, "Rich and Poor in English to Subscribers in French and Other Latin Tongues," and concluded with a cogent statement of Sylvia's book-rental terms. The three ladies became neighborhood friends, though always at swords' points in their differing opinions on writing. Sylvia disagreed with Gertrude's rather disrespectful notion that French writing consisted of "fanfare" and Gertrude was so outraged when Sylvia began the publication of James Joyce's *Ulysses*—she would certainly have been horrified at its bordello section from the Dublin nights—that she called at Shakespeare and Company to inform Sylvia that thereafter she and Miss Toklas would withdraw their patronage in book-borrowing and in future borrow only from the eminently respectable official American Library on the Right Bank.

The publication *in toto* of *Ulysses* in 1922 was indubitably the most exciting, important, historic single literary event of the early Paris expatriate literary colony. Through portions of it that we had seen in New York printed in their *Little Review* by Margaret Anderson and Jane Heap, many of us in Paris knew the scope of the opus—that chaotic fictional masterpiece-mixture of single Celtic genius, of Anglican erudition, of Irish character analyses and Dublin night-and-day thoughts and events, culminating in the final revelatory concupiscent monologue by Molly Bloom, linear ancestress for the merely monotonous permissive lubricity that has been printed in our time in the recent 1960s. It has been a commonplace to say that *Ulysses* was the great isolating novel in the English language that was published in the first segment of our twentieth century, an isolating novel in that it was itself isolated from all other great fiction in our tongue. In its unique qualities, in 1922 it burst over us, young in Paris, like an explosion in print whose words and phrases fell upon us like a gift of tongues, like a less than holy Pentecostal experience. Over the years, *Ulysses*, though read only in its early fractions, had established itself as part of our literary life to come, when and if eventually completed and published. Thus long before our eyes had ever seen Sylvia Beach's entire printed text in Paris and before our hands had ever lifted the full weight of its 730 pages, Joyce's *Ulysses* had become part of the library of our minds. As we learned by listening to and watching Sylvia in her bookshop, to accomplish her publishing feat she became Joyce's secretary, editor, impresario, and banker, and had to hire outsiders to run her shop. She organized international and local subscription lists for the book to help finance its printing. After typesetting had begun at Dijon, in a kind of postscript ecstasy of creation, Joyce scribbled some ninety thousand words more on the costly, repeatedly reset proofs, making a four-hundred-thousand word volume, of which Sylvia managed to have two copies printed for his fortieth birthday on February 2, 1922—one for him, one for her.

By the eighth edition, despite lost sales in England and the United States, where it was banned and seized and had earlier been pirated, Joyce was living luxuriously. When we minor Left Bankers occasionally went to dance in the evening in Montparnasse at Les Trianons, we could peer into its elegant restaurant and see the Joyces still at dinner, he being served royally. But we never saw Sylvia dining with them. We also used to see him often in front of Sylvia's shop. He was a frail-looking figure to have caused such an international commotion—with his black hat cocked on the back of his head, twirling his cane and wearing not very clean white sneakers. As Sylvia herself apologetically said, "There was always something a little shabby about Mr. Joyce." She thought him handsome, with his deep-blue eyes, one badly damaged by glaucoma, which had half blinded him. The strain of proofreading his almost illegible handwriting helped ruin her eyesight, too.

Ulysses was the paying investment of his lifetime after years of penury, Sylvia said, while hardly acknowledging the fact that the publishing costs almost wiped out her Shakespeare and Company. The peak of his prosperity came in 1932 with the news of his sale of the book to Random House in New York for a forty-five-thousand-dollar advance, which, she confessed he failed to announce to her and of which, as was later known, he never even offered her a penny. "I understood from the first that, working with or for Mr. Joyce, the pleasure was mine—an infinite pleasure: the profits were for him," she wrote gently in her book of memoirs. "All that was available from his work, and I managed to keep it available, was his." What she mostly gained, besides fame, were unwelcome offers—and she a minister's daughter—to publish erotica as a steady thing, such as *Lady Chatterley's Lover,* at the request of Aldous Huxley, and the spicy memoirs of a maître d'hôtel at Maxim's.

Does anyone read *Ulysses* now, read it entire, word by word, with the impetus we did fifty years ago? I wonder. And I disbelieve.

Still strong today are the memories of the good new taste of Paris food that I was eating for the first time precisely in that long *Ulysses* publishing period. With my stomach stirred to hitherto unexperienced satisfactions, with my palate even now able to recall the sudden pleasure of drinking a tumbler of more than ordinary red or white French wine, I can recall the sensual satisfaction of first chewing the mixture in my mouth of a bite of meat and a crust of fresh French bread and then the following swallow of the wine itself, like the dominant liquid guide leading my nourishment down through my gullet into my insides. Eating in France was a new body experience.

My preferred small restaurant was located in the rue Jacob, just below the Place Saint-Germain. It was called La Quatrième République. Since at that moment France was still living under the Third Republic of President Poincaré, I early asked M. Chuzeville, the restaurant owner, who was also its cook, why he had projected himself forward in history into a republic which as yet did not even exist. Chuzeville, who wore luxuriant mustachios and was probably a disgruntled socialist, said that at the rate the Third Republic government of France was running downhill, a Fourth Republic would soon be unavoidable, so he had named his bistro for it in advance, to be readied for the future without having to paint a new sign over his door, which would cost money. He was a polite, taciturn mountain man from the Jura, a district noted for its odd *pelure d'oignon* wine, so named (logically enough) because of its onionskin color, in taste a little hard and calcareous, ordinarily difficult to procure in Paris and doubtless a product from the vineyard of a Chuzeville cousin, who sold it to him cheap.

The bistro itself was very avant-garde in décor. The Russian

Georges Hoyningen-Huene, at that time just starting his career as a photographer for *Vogue* magazine, had been a painter. On the wall of the restaurant's narrow circular staircase, which like the newel of a snail's shell wound upstairs to the second floor, he had painted a series of false steps in a Cubist design, very striking as a lesson in abstract distortion and also very treacherous, since if you looked at the wall's false painted treads while going up or down, you were likely to miss the reality of the shallow wooden steps beneath your feet. In a Russian pun he had nicknamed Yvonne, the young waitress, Yvonne the Terrible, because he said she was such a terrible waitress, which was palpably untrue as she never once fell down the steps during the years I lunched there. The lunch was fixed in price and in its lack of surprises. There was a plate of hors d'oeuvres including a slice of Jura paté, flavored with wild thyme, and as the main dish, a succulent stew or an escallop of veal and a salad with goat's cheese, plus a small carafe of the onionskin and, of course, a demitasse of black French coffee which tasted like death. It was a civilized, countrified, appetizing inexpensive French meal. It probably cost me about thirty cents, plus a ten-cent tip for Yvonne the Terrible.

Up to the 1930s I mostly lunched in my rue Jacob restaurant in the company of some minor Surrealists, Surrealism having become the latest Paris intellectual revolutionary aesthetic movement such as Paris always foments when the cerebral sap of the Gallic mind runs in two opposite directions at once, one aiming at the destruction of a present society and the other at setting up a utopia on which nobody can agree. Surrealism, which was a bastard descendant of Dada, was basically founded on the premise that art must not be beautiful but should on the contrary shock and dismay the eye of the beholder. Another of its concepts was violent anti-Catholicism, usually demonstrated by the Surrealists insulting priests and spitting on nuns on the Saint-Germain streets. Interest in the ancient study of dreams, or oneirology, was also a Surrealist fundamental, as was devotion to Leon Trotsky and Freud, and, in Surrealism's sadistic physical practices, street brawling was considered an essential. The Surrealists had their own club table facing the door of the Deux Magots, from which vantage point a seated Surrealist could conveniently insult any newcomer with whom he happened to be feuding, or discuss his plan to horsewhip an editor of some belligerent anti-Surrealist newspaper for having mentioned his name or, worse, for having failed to mention it, in the latest Surrealist gossip notes on the bitter power struggle between the devotees of Surrealism's founder, André Breton, and their rivals, who had shifted to the leadership of Louis Aragon, Surrealism's greatest novelist and prince of poets.

Nancy Cunard, who had just begun her well-known liaison with Aragon, often lunched with me at the Fourth Republic. Another Surrealist habitué was Pierre de Massot, a fairly good poet and a roaring Communist (the only political faith the Surrealists approved of). He was also passionately pro-American on all international questions and for his breakfast each morning drank a bottle of Coca-Cola instead of a cup of *café au lait*, which he despised as being old-fashioned and chauvinist.

A minor and mannerly Surrealist table companion was the young writer René Crevel, whose novel *Les Pieds dans la Plat* (*Your Feet Are in Your Plate*)—its title indicated an individual at cross purposes with society—had been an intellectual success. Crevel lisped slightly, rather like a child, and had innocent, large childish eyes that always shone when he was telling absurd fantastic tales, which he would make up ad lib, convulsing us by their ludicrous disconnected plots, whose lack of logic was a mark of pure Surrealistic creation at that time. After the Second World War René developed tuberculosis, and his widowed mother, by selling some of her late husband's investments at a sacrifice, was able to send her son to Switzerland for two years, where his lungs were cured. But back in Paris, he became part of the band of young men surrounding the eccentric Princesse Violette Murat (in a strange lack of visible proportions, she had nearly no neck—"she looks more like a truffle than a violet," Marcel Proust said of her as he saw her for the first time one night at the Ritz). She eventually went down to Toulon, where she lived at the dockside in an abandoned submarine and took to smoking opium intemperately, in which René joined her. For him, it was fatal.

o o o

The French painters in Paris frequented Montparnasse and sat on the terraces of the Dôme and the Select. André Derain was the only artist I knew who frequented the Deux Magots. He was a big, well-dressed, countrified fellow who always wore a citified felt hat which he would ceremoniously lift to me, with a bow, as he passed my table. The beautiful Max Ernst and his beautiful wife also occasionally graced the Deux Magots terrace. The really great artist visitor to the Saint-Germain quarter was Picasso, but much later. After 1945, he began coming to the Café de Flore at night. He always sat at the second table in front of the main door, with Spanish friends. I would sit where, without seeming to, I could view his remarkably mobile face with its amazingly watchful eyes. He never did anything except sip his one small bottle of mineral water, speak with his Spanish friends, and look at all the people who were not looking directly at him. When he had finished his libation, he left for home, invariably before eleven. One of the waiters was a Spaniard, and he said to me, "Señor Picasso always walks home to his apartment in the Rue des Grand Augustins by exactly the same route each night; it never varies. He is a genius, and a man of fixed habits." Everyone respected the isolation Picasso had established for himself there at the Flore.

About fifteen years ago I happened to be in Cannes, where, on the Croisette, I met the young artist son of an old New York friend of mine, who spoke to me and gave me his news. He was married, and newly a father, and as a favor Picasso, whom he knew, had drawn a vague sketch of the young artist's infant son, which he had promised to sign and dedicate if the father would go to Picasso's villa, La Californie, that very day at noon. Did I want to drive up with him? I stipulated I would like to take the drive but would not get out of the car. When we arrived at the gate of La Californie, the young father went inside with his invaluable drawing, a moment later emerging to say, "Picasso says to come in," which I did not wish to do, as an intrusion was the last thing I had intended. When Picasso sent a second pressing demand, I was forced to accept. As I walked into the salon, which was as crowded with varied art works as an auction room, Picasso turned to me with his hand outstretched in greeting, and then, with a loud cry of astonishment, shouted,

"You! Why didn't you ever speak to me in the old days at the Flore? For years we saw each other and never spoke, until now. Are you just the same as you were? You look it!" By this time he had his arms around me and was thumping me enthusiastically on the shoulders. "You look fine; not a day older," and I said, "Nor do you," and he said, "That's true; that's the way you and I are. We don't get older, we just get riper. Do you still love life the way you used to, and love people the way you did? I watched you and always wanted to know what you were thinking. . . . Tell me, do you still love the human race, especially your best friends? Do you still love love?" "I do," I said, astonished at the turn the monologue was taking. "And so do I!" he shouted, laughing. "Oh, we're great ones for that, you and I. Isn't love the greatest refreshment in life?" And he embraced me with his strong arms, in farewell.

Saint-Germain was always the literary quarter and, until the American influx of the early 1920s, quiet and bourgeois. Each year the increasing number of us there assumed a sort of outpost quality. We were the Americans who for one reason or another chose to dwell in Paris—for writing, for work, for career, for the amenities of French living, which was cheaper and more agreeable than life in the United States. My satisfaction in living there was double: I felt I was living both at home and abroad —living surrounded with the human familiarity of American friends and acquaintances, and the constant, shifting stimulation that came from the native French. The local American colony was the largest of any in Europe. Its literary flavor had continued to predominate in the early years. Those belonging to it whom I saw most frequently included Louis Bromfield, who lived outside the city in the cathedral town of Senlis, and whose Sunday luncheons were noted for the extraordinary bouquets he concocted in perfect imitations of the flower paintings by the sixteenth-century painter Brueghel. Louis had the greenest thumb and maintained the finest flower garden of any American in the Ile-de-France territory, except Mrs. Edith Wharton, whose white garden was celebrated.

Ernest Hemingway was, of course, in and out constantly, often in the company of Ezra Pound, who seemed an odd friend for him to have, since Ernest was always the champion sportsman in every café he entered and Pound, with his little beard, looked and was conscientiously aesthetic. Ernest was fond of him and regarded him as an excellent literary critic. They used to talk about writing at the Closerie de Lilas café across from the old Bal Bullier dance hall. I liked neither Pound's arbitrary historicity, nor his condensed violence, nor his floating Chinese quotations such as marked the poetry he wrote for the *Little Review,* nor all his weighty, ancient, mixed linguistics, like stony chips whacked off with *hauteur* from the old statuary of the scholarly mind.

Djuna Barnes was the most important woman writer we had in Paris. She was famous among us for her great short story, "A Night among the Horses." Within a short time after the publication of her novel *Nightwood* (brought out in London before publication in New York) it became available in a paperback edition and attained enormous popularity among young European intellectuals all the way from Rome to Berlin. I wrote of it at the time as "a difficult book to describe, since the only proper way of dealing with its strange, nocturnal elements is to have written it in the first place, which surely no one but Miss Barnes could have done." Djuna was tall, quite handsome, bold-voiced, and a remarkable talker, full of reminiscences of her Washington Square New York life and her eccentric childhood somewhere up the Hudson. My favorite story of hers dealt with a period when her father, who entertained odd ideas of nourishment, decided that since chickens ate pebbles to aid their digestion, a few pebbles in the diet of his children might be equally salubrious. I was devoted to Djuna and she was quite fond of me, too, in her superior way. She wrote a chapbook called *The Little Ladies' Almanac,* and illustrated it boldly. It was a take-off of many ladies in the American colony, published privately, I think by Miss Natalie Barney, *doyenne* of the Left Bank, who appeared in it as a leading character under the guise of Dame Musset. I was one of a pair of journalists called Nip and Tuck. Djuna wrote a play that she showed to T. S. Eliot; he told her that it contained the most splendid archaic language he had ever had the pleasure of reading but that, frankly, he couldn't make head or tail of its drama. She gave it to me to read, and I told her, with equal candor, that it was the most sonorous vocabulary I had ever read but that I did not understand jot or tittle of what it was saying. With withering scorn, she said, "I never expected to find that you were as stupid as Tom Eliot." I thanked her for the only compliment she had ever given me.

In our expatriate colony were the poet Archibald MacLeish, whose wife sang—she had a pretty voice and sometimes gave concerts, John Dos Passos, popular and esteemed by all the other male writers in Paris (the French regarded him as the most normal, typical American), E. E. Cummings and his wife Marion Morehouse, both of them civilized and handsome, Hart Crane, whom I only met once at dinner, when he became so intoxicated and created such a scene in the Montparnasse restaurant over a mislaid overcoat that I hoped never to see him again, and did not, a squeamishness I later regretted, Kay Boyle, with her variegated brood of children, who was for a writer a rare domestic center, Glenway Wescott, who always seemed fresh from his Harper Prize for *The Grandmothers*, and was already regarded as a handsome, formal literary figure, and his friend Monroe Wheeler, who set up the private bibliophile press called Harrison of Paris, which brought out a *rarissime* edition of Aesop's *Fables*, with original drawings by Alexander Calder.

Of these littérateurs, George Davis was the only one who lived in my hotel. George had come from the Middle West and was writing a novel which he obstinately wished to call *Like Bronze Cows*, a title sensibly changed by his publishers to *The Opening of a Door*. The book was a great critical success, but he was unable to write more than two chapters on his second novel. He was a sulky, ultra-sensitive, brilliant character and a deadly wit, who developed into the unique editor of the entire expatriate literary crew, first as an assistant to Frank Crowninshield at *Vanity Fair*, then as fiction editor of *Harper's Bazaar* under the inspired, Irish-born editor-in-chief Carmel Snow, where he was the first to put serious fiction into a fashion magazine and helped develop two new, amazing young American writers, Carson McCullers and Truman Capote.

Scott and Zelda Fitzgerald had made a special social category of themselves and their pleasures, always more in the south of France than in Paris, though their famous dinner party on the houseboat anchored in the Seine was the only social American event that achieved a kind of historical importance, almost as if it had been French. When Scott was in Paris he had an eccentric, friendly habit of coming to my hotel to discuss literature at two o'clock in the morning, either with me or with Margaret Anderson, if she happened to be stopping there at the time. He would stumble up the staircase, in which the night light invariably went out before he achieved the fourth or fifth floors, and tap at any door until he received a welcome. The most rarefied of any of the young literary figures there, he seemed always to be suffering under the strain of his own genius, which did not burgeon fully until he wrote *The Great Gatsby*. Only Scott had realized that the bootlegger Gatsby represented the perfect picaresque American figure in that extraordinary alcoholic era. In his writing, Scott had the true tragic sense. To my mind, he alone created the pure and perfect anti-hero, the criminal lover defrauded of his love.

Scott's face was beautiful, like the visage of a poet. In his manner he was remote, set apart by his elegance. He was the only one of my writer friends who ever gave me the mutual identification of my having any literary sensibilities. I had earlier written an unsuccessful first novel, called *The Cubical City*, for which I had been mentioned by critics as possibly a successor to Rose Macaulay, providing I stuck at my labors, and Virgil Thomson had roundly declared that I should cease being apologetic about my book. In September 1925 I started the fortnightly "Letter from Paris" in *The New Yorker*. The only specific guidance I had received from the editor, Harold Ross, was his statement that he wanted to know what the French thought was going on in France, not what I thought was going on. This was a new type of journalistic foreign correspondence, which I had to integrate and develop, since there was no antecedent for it. *The New Yorker*, at its beginnings, was also like an oversized minnow learning to swim. It had not yet found its style, and it was to take me some time before I began to find my own, which instinctively leaned toward comments with a critical edge, indeed a double edge, if possible. Criticism, to be valid, in my opinion, demanded a certain personal aspect or slant of the writer's mind. At the time, this was a practice far more popular in London journalism than in that of New York. Also, New York journalistic reportage was not so much merely flatly chaste in its descriptions but in many ways arid in its thinking. All I really knew about what Ross wished me to write, and what I wished for me to write, was that it must be precisely accurate, highly personal, colorful, and ocularly descriptive; and that for sentence style, Gibbon was as good a model as I could bring to mind, he having been the master of antithesis, at once both enriching and economical through his use of opposites.

Since my assignment was to tell what the French thought was going on, my only obvious, complete, facile source of information was the French press. At that time, as I remember, there were eight daily secular Paris newspapers, divergent in political loyalties, and there was as well a theatrical paper called *Comœdia*, which covered every aspect of Parisian entertainment, from the Comédie-Française (including occasional professional notes on the career of Molière) to what was new and nude (in the Folies-Bergère).

Fortunately for me, a completely new type of American theatrical entertainment, with a new imported coloring, had just opened at the Théâtre des Champs-Élysées. It was called *La Revue Nègre*. I wrote about it timidly, uncertainly, and like a dullard. As a matter of fact, it was so incomparably novel an element in French public pleasures that its star, hitherto unknown, named Josephine Baker, remains to me now like a still-fresh vision, sensual, exciting and isolated in my memory today, almost fifty years later. So here follows what I should have written then about her appearance, as a belated tribute.

She made her entry entirely nude except for a pink flamingo feather between her limbs; she was being carried upside down and doing the split on the shoulder of a black giant. Midstage he paused, and with his long fingers holding her basket-wise around the waist, swung her in a slow cartwheel to the stage floor, where she stood, like his magnificent discarded burden, in an instant of complete silence. She was an unforgettable female ebony statue. A scream of salutation spread through the theater. Whatever happened next was unimportant. The two specific elements had been established and were unforgettable —her magnificent dark body, a new model that to the French proved for the first time that black was beautiful, and the acute response of the white masculine public in the capital of hedonism of all Europe—Paris. Within a half hour of the final curtain on opening night, the news and meaning of her arrival had spread by the grapevine up to the cafés on the Champs-Élysées, where the witnesses of her triumph sat over their drinks excitedly repeating their report of what they had just seen—themselves unsatiated in the retelling, the listeners hungry for further fantastic truths. So tremendous was the public acclaim that for the first week's run the cast and the routine of the performance were completely disorganized. Drunken on the appreciation they had received, and on champagne, to which they were not accustomed, the Negro choruses split up into single acts consisting of whichever males or females could still keep their feet, or had not lost their voices from the fatigues of pleasure, all of them nevertheless alive and creative with the integral talent of their race and training. Most of us in Paris who had seen the opening night went back for the next two or three nights as well; they were never twice alike. Somewhere along the development, either then or it might have been a year or so later, as Josephine's career ripened, she appeared with her famous festoon of bananas worn like a savage skirt around her hips. She was the established new American star for Europe.

Each June the inexpensive Left Bank hotels began being booked up in advance for the whole summer by new Americans who would settle down for a couple of weeks there as if the quarter were a kind of summer resort and then pass on, full of memories and satisfactions. Paris was still a beautiful, alluring, satisfying city. It was a city of charm and enticement, to foreigners and even to the French themselves. Its charm lay in its being in no way international—not as yet. There were no skyscrapers. The charm still came from the *démodé* eighteenth- and nineteenth-century architecture that marked the façades of the private dwellings and the old-fashioned apartment houses.

On the streets the public-school children wore their black aprons with fresh white collars wrapped around their small necks. They wore high wooden-soled boots—usually bought secondhand from the corner shoe cobbler and made indiscriminately for an undetermined foot, neither right nor left—that created a great loose clatter as the children hurried down the sidewalks from school en route for home and a piece of bread and a square of chocolate, then the traditional afternoon snack for them.

On warm summer days the *bateaux mouches*, the Seine's small excursion boats, took one out as far as Saint-Cloud and brought one back to the Louvre. Seated on their hard, uncomfortable outdoor benches, one felt that one was traveling on a nineteenth-century picnic. On hot afternoons the French women on the café terraces quietly drank lemonades and the French men consumed their inferior French beers. In winter the big terraces like that of the Deux Magots were heated by large *bracieri*, filled with coals.

Over in the Luxembourg district, in a winding street leading down from the Panthéon, final home of the French illustrious dead, there were a series of *bals musettes* where we used to go and dance at night. They were modest neighborhood dance halls, invariably small, such as had traditionally flourished in the last century in Montmartre, then the territory of the Impressionist painters. When modern art became the vogue and the bohemian quarter shifted to Montparnasse, the *bals musettes* followed.

They were noisy and economical. The young men paid a few sous each time they stepped out with a partner onto the dance floor, which was also economical in the use of its space. It offered little room for anything but dancing. The tables where one sat for drinking were pushed against the wall, though the crowd was too young and too inexperienced to drink much. As for the orchestra, which consisted of a violin and an accordion, it was roosted out of everyone's way up on top of a platform built on a pole. Friday and Saturday nights were the big nights, and one saw some fine waltzing and fancy dancing. The java, to special music, contained four stamping rhythmic steps in its performance, and was passionately popular. *Le fox*, the fox trot, a recent importation from America, was also beginning to catch on contagiously. As you never conversed with your partner, which was considered an invasion of privacy, you never knew who he was, except that he was perhaps a Sorbonne student or more likely a superior young workman, dressed in his best, well shaved and gallantly scented after his weekly bath. Though operating in the so-called students' bohemian quarter, the *bals mu-*

settes were always extremely respectable, whereas the small *boîtes*, such as the Jungle, on the Boulevard Montparnasse, were brazen, gay, and licentious in their atmosphere, as were later their social and financial opposites, the new smart champagne *clubs de nuit* in the Champs-Élysées district.

It was on the Champs-Élysées that Paris set in on its change, just before the early thirties. Like Fifth Avenue in New York, that once quiet domestic beating heart of the exclusive residential organism, the Champs-Élysées suddenly burst out with a rash of colored cinema signs which proved that what had been quiet mansions underneath had become transmogrified as movie houses, always the first intruders. Of all the luxurious private residences that once made that elegant short French *parcours* of wealth and domestic usage, finally only what was called the Travellers Club survived, as it still does today. It was formerly the residence of the great cocotte Cora Pearl. It was rumored to contain gold faucets with swans' heads on its bathtubs. It was known to have been perfumed at one time during her heyday by the daily offering, from an enamored admirer, of a sufficient number of bouquets of violets to carpet her small reception salon, which featured no other visible floor covering. Her visitors walked only upon purple flowers. The Travellers Club is today the most exclusive costly residential club in Europe. Its façade is what visibly remains, and behind it the gentlemen temporarily live in their suitcases. *Sic transit.* Like any great elderly capital Paris has accommodated itself to improvement and to destruction by modernization, and of loss through change.

At any season, and all year long, in the evening the view of the city from the bridges was always exquisitely pictorial. One's eyes became the eyes of a painter, because the sight itself approximated art, with the narrow, pallid façades of the buildings lining the river; with the tall trees growing down by the water's edge; with, behind them, the vast chiaroscuro of the palatial Louvre, lightened by the luminous lemon color of the Paris sunset off toward the west; with the great square, pale stone silhouette of Notre-Dame to the east. The stance from which to see Paris was any one of its bridges at the close of the day. The

Pont Neuf still looked as we had known it on the canvases of Sisley and Pissarro.

Paris then seemed immutably French. The quasi-American atmosphere which we had tentatively established around Saint-Germain had not yet infringed onto the rest of the city. In the early twenties, when I was new there, Paris was still yesterday.

JANET FLANNER

Paris Was Yesterday

1925

Josephine Baker

Josephine Baker has arrived at the Théâtre des Champs-Élysées in *La Revue Nègre* and the result has been unanimous. Paris has never drawn a color line. Covarrubias did the sets, pink drops with cornucopias of hams and watermelons, and the Civil War did the rest, aided by Miss Baker. The music is tuneless and stunningly orchestrated, and the end of the show is dull, but never Miss Baker's part. It was even less dull the first night, when she did what used to be, what indeed still should be called, a stomach dance (later deleted).

Tristan Tzara

Tristan Tzara, founder of the Dada movement, which most people seem to think has something to do with bad taste in modern pictures, has just married the daughter of a rich Swedish industrialist. Too rarely poor poets marry well. Tzara is probably the most sensitive and original French poet today, aside from being not French at all, but Rumanian. No one has written more foolishly at times, but many have written almost as foolishly and never once so well. He and his wife, on what the French law now probably calls his money, are building a huge modernist house in Montmartre. Tzara is a great man of small stature and wears a monocle.

La Cuisine

Two great servers of the French palate are gone. Émile Prunier is dead—famous Prunier, whose sea-food restaurant was the Friday home of all good gourmets in Paris. His Portuguese oysters were one of the modest-priced tasty traditions of France, and his American clientele so numerous that he planted for them local beds of Cape Cod clams and blue points so that Yankees could feel at home at his bar. His death comes on the heels of that of the famous Mother Soret of Lyons, whose "chicken in half-mourning"—the sable color was achieved by the inclusion of truffles—was one of the great dishes of the land. She died with a knife in her hand in her kitchen, where she had cooked for fifty years, and her death was solemnly listed in the newspaper *Comœdia* as that of an artist.

Anatole France (1844–1924)

As a literary note, it must be commented that the anniversary of Anatole France's death passed absolutely ignored. A year ago, his funeral furnished one of the biggest, most pretentious spectacles modern Paris has ever seen, with its vast display of flowers and a detachment of troops assembled on the Quai Malaquais outside the house where he had been born. Victor Hugo's famous cortege was a family affair beside the thousands that followed France. But in his grave a twelvemonth, he failed to get a line in most of the daily papers. His books even failed to sell better on that day than any other in the year. The truth is, he is infinitely more popular in the United States than in his own land.

[*Anatole France's literary reputation and personality now seem to have sunk completely into oblivion. Ironically enough, if his name is mentioned at all today it is in relation to Proust's novelist character Bergotte, a writer remembered by another writer and without much praise. I recall that at France's funeral procession, the first of these official honorary ceremonies that I had ever seen, the cortege was followed through the streets by a group of disrespectful Surrealists, who despised his popularity and his literary style, and who shouted insults to his memory ("Un cadavre littéraire!") in unison every step of the way. This was possibly the first of their sadistic street manifestations and was considered a scandal, since Paris has so long been noted as a great appreciator of its intellectual figures. J. F.*]

Henri Rousseau

The best canvas show of the moment is at the Grand Magazin de Blanc, now displaying on the third floor Some Selected Works of the ex-Customs Official Henri Rousseau. He who laughs last laughs longest, and it is a pity he is dead. In the nineties, he couldn't give his pictures away, not even to the janitress for a Christmas present. Once he sold one and made a large note of it in his laundry-list book. "Sold to Madame X, a Beautiful Mexican Landscape with Monkeys in it, price one hundred francs." He had never been to Mexico, of course, but had seen monkeys in the Paris zoo. The museum at Prague paid one hundred and forty thousand francs (about $3000) * for one of his canvases last year. For a long time the French took him for a fool, but the German art critics took him for a good investment. Most of his canvases are now in Berlin.

* The official rate of exchange in 1925 was 21.25 francs to the dollar. During the period covered in this volume, the rate fluctuated from a high of 15.15 (in 1935) to a low (in 1939) of 39.83.

1926

Brillat-Savarin (1755–1820), **Madame de Sévigné** (1626–1696)

Anniversaries are natural to an old capital, but Paris at the moment is indulging in a recollective orgy. Two immortals are being revived. Anthelme Brillat-Savarin, who died a hundred years ago, only three weeks after his *Physiology of Taste* was printed, this being the first book ever to make a hero of the palate, and Madame de Sévigné (1626), whose endless polite, intelligent correspondence with her daughter is included in part nowadays in the curriculum of upper-class prep schools, as classics in courtesy and psychology. Of the two, Brillat-Savarin, the world's perfect gourmet and a spicy philosopher, easily wins first place in the public eye. The best of his classic aphorisms are still repeated as gospel today: "To eat is a necessity: to eat well is an art." "Dessert without cheese is like a pretty girl with only one eye." It is said that he never talked during his famous dinner parties and went to sleep at table immediately after. One of his dinner menus is to be repeated as part of the government's official festivities in his honor.

But famous as the gourmet was, it is Madame de Sévigné who really wins the momentary palm. Last month the Chamber of Deputies sat up all one night, figuring on how they could cut the national budget. By dawn thirty-five thousand francs' worth of coffee, sandwiches, and brandy had been consumed gratis from the state bar, and statesmen, still patriotically determined to cut expenses somewhere, fortunately went home before deliberation cost any more. But a few days later they voted thirty thousand francs to help celebrate de Sévigné's anniversary without even asking for a glass of water.

Maurice Rostand

Maurice Rostand, son of the immortal Edmond, is one of the most amusing young men in Parisian literary or, to be more exact, aesthetic circles. He is truly the *poète fatal*, although short with squarish shoulders; he is always a study in black and white, he wears very high heels, he rarely covers his long black hair with a hat, and he tosses his locks much in the manner of our own Edna Millay. He also is one of the few people alive who can wear a flowing tie and give the impression that it is the most natural sort of thing to do. When he recites his poetry, he slips out onto the stage almost surreptitiously and stands quite at one side before a blue-bordered, gray velvet curtain, clasping the drapery with his wan, pale hands. Now, young Rostand has finally opened in his romantic blank-verse play, *La Déserteuse*, wherein he plays the principal role. Like father, unlike son. This piece is as loud as *Chanticler* with none of its fine feathers.

Love Letters to Hugo

Fifteen thousand love letters written on the Isle of Jersey by poor Juliette Drouet to Victor Hugo have just been sold at auction for eighteen thousand francs. And now, so Francis de Miomandre remarks in *Les Nouvelles Littéraires*, this pitiable Juliette, regarded by her envious generation as the swooning, daring mistress of the sublime bohemian, turns out to be only a self-sacrificing supplementary wife who, doomed to spend years of exile in company of an egotist with whom she breakfasted, lunched, teaed, and dined, meekly wrote him a few letters a day, whether she had anything left to say or not. Fifteen thousand love letters would make a rough average of a love letter a day for forty-three years, but Juliette spent with Hugo a little less than twenty, which raises her average to martyrdom.

The Steins

Leo Stein, Gertrude Stein's brother, is finishing a book called *Aesthetic Responses,* and she, after the intellectual success of her *The Making of Americans,* is at work on *Portraits and Prayers.* A new verbal picture of Carl Van Vechten is to be included. No American writer is taken more seriously than Miss Stein by the Paris modernists.

Art (Semantics)

The art merchant Leonce Rosenberg is opening a show of Bad Taste, to prove his aesthetic theory that taste is largely whim.

Art (Commerce)

The John Quinn collection, which should be in a state museum, is now up for resale, its magnificent unity destroyed in the Parisian auction rooms of the Hôtel Drouot. These canvases were collected here for Mr. Quinn, of New York, by M. Pierre Roché, of Paris. Sent to Manhattan, where the pictures were sold and returned to France, now they will be resold and returned to New York. These voyages doubtless make up what is called the history of art.

Modern art, supposedly painted only to annoy the bourgeoisie, succeeded finally in annoying the artists assembled for the Quinn auction. The ugliness of the many Rouault items, particularly "The Man with the Spectacles," started jeers, encouraged someone in the back rows to bid thirty centimes for a Matisse nude (sold at one hundred and one thousand francs—about thirty-two hundred dollars), and culminated in cries of exasperation when "The Sleeping Bohemian," by the customs-officer Rousseau, went under the hammer at a half million. "This is not art but commerce," a bearded old artist in shabby velveteens cried. "Rousseau died in poverty. What was he paid for this silly canvas?" "Four hundred francs," a merchant replied; and the bidding went on to Derain's "Self Portrait," very fine at forty thousand francs. For forty-eight hours Mr. Quinn was better known in Paris than he had ever been known in New York. Rousseau, who gave many of his canvases to his concierge friends, would have been proud to see his "Bohemian" finally reproduced in *Le Petit Parisien*, known as the concierge's favored reading matter. It was Rousseau's final triumph and the first art note that newspaper ever carried.

Seurat's "Circus," as a gift of Quinn, has now been hung in the Louvre. Seurat died at thirty-two. By dint of huge labor he succeeded in selling two canvases before his death. The "Circus" was not one of them.

Art (Commerce)

CONTINUED

Marcel Duchamp's sale of Picabias is being widely discussed. Duchamp must be recalled in America for his "Nude Descending a Staircase": since then he has never painted another canvas. He received about eighty-nine thousand francs for his entire collection of eighty Picabias, the famous "Mind the Paint" bringing only three hundred and twenty francs. Today a good hat from a smart modiste costs more.

Charles Cros (1842–1888)

The eightieth birthday of Thomas Edison has brought to light again the old Parisian complaint that a Parisian poet, Charles Cros, invented the phonograph. This genial unfortunate, Paris claims, later effected the synthesis of precious stones, sketched out the telephone of Bell, discovered the principle of color photography (but was fifteen minutes late in patenting it because a rival beat him to the patent office), devised systems of musical stenography, autographic telegraphy and of interplanetary signals, and, at forty-six, too impoverished, too busy, too talented ever to have realized on his invention of Edison's phonograph, died, "in a corner."

Duchesse de Rohan (1853–1926)

The recent death of the dowager Duchesse de Rohan brought her for the last time before the notice of Paris, which had noticed her so often during her lifetime and had received from her so many benefits—almost as many as it had given her. She was the prejudiced and energetic head of one of the greatest families in France, and her long life and her salon in the Boulevard des Invalides were arenas where the aristocratic old and democratic new traditions fought, and the old tradition, like the old Duchesse, died. She was the last of a milieu where men were not men but dukes. She was christened Herminie, married a noble, bore handsome children, and then, her duties over, wrote four books of so-called poetry and dominated conventional Paris society. Then came the war and a new generation. She lost a son in Flanders, turned her salon into a hospital, became a Red Cross nurse. She wrote no more verse. She took to prose. But the end was not yet for this old aristocrat. Wife and mother of dukes, and mother-in-law of princes and Talleyrands, she suffered the indignity of a shop, opened one month ago by one of her daughters.

My Life and Loves

If the action of the courts in Nice against Mr. Frank Harris, charged with offending public morals by the publication of the second volume of *My Life and Loves*, for which he must stand trial in October, is sustained, Miss Sylvia Beach, proud publisher of James Joyce's *Ulysses*, may also be forced to call in legal counsel.

The Harris case, which is the first instance of a book by a foreign writer printed in English being questioned in France, is thus of more than academic interest to the realists of the ultra-stark school, publishing in Paris what their own countries would never permit. A little light is thrown upon the present state of affairs by the fact that after the appearance of *Ulysses* Mr. Harris sounded out Miss Beach as the most likely publisher for a biography upholstered with the red-plush detail of passion. Miss Beach is reported to have written, quite definitely, that she was not interested.

The Sun Also Rises

The appearance here of Ernest Hemingway's *roman à clef*, *The Sun Also Rises*, has stirred Montparnasse, where, it is asserted, all of the four leading characters are local and easily identifiable.° The titled British declassée and her Scottish friend, the American Frances and her unlucky *Robert Cohn* with his art magazine which, like a new broom, was to sweep aesthetics clean—all these personages are, it is maintained, to be seen just where Hemingway so often placed them at the Select. Not being amorously identified with the tale, it should be safe to say that Donald Ogden Stewart is taken to be the stuffed-bird-loving Bill. Under the flimsy disguise of Braddocks, certainly Ford Madox Ford is visible as the Briton who gives, as Mr. Ford does, dancing parties in the *bal musette* behind the Panthéon.

Baronne de Rothschild ?–1926)

The sudden death of the Baronne Henri de Rothschild, *née* Mathilde de Weisweiller, whose charity fetes gratified the ambition of so many women to go through the pompous Rothschild palace and win social distinction by the purchase, for five hundred francs, of one bottle of the Rothschild perfume, marked the end of the most progressive member of that inestimably rich, wildly conservative family; and even she, the avant-garde, replied "Certainly not" to a critic who had asked permission to visit her seldom shown and never written about collections of art treasures.

° Lady Duff Twysden, Pat Guthrie, Kitty Cannell, Harold Loeb.

De Max (1869–1924)

The reinterment of Édouard de Max was impressively held in the rain at Montparnasse cemetery, which overflowed with wreaths, speeches, and representatives from the Comédie-Française to which, though a Rumanian, he belonged. De Max was a great boulevard personality, handsome, a fine actor, egotist, and wit. Friend and leading man to Sarah Bernhardt, he believed in theatricality even in the grave, which he entered, by his own orders, painted as if to walk on the stage and dressed in the tinsel of robes he had worn in his favorite role of Nero.

Liane de Pougy

The announcement in journals here that Liane de Pougy—the Princess Ghika—is to divorce has stirred society and memories here. Today she is a beautiful sixty. Under the first days of the Third Republic she was its young shock and delight. She was launched at the Folies-Bergère by Edward VII, then Prince of Wales, to whom, though he did not know her, she sent a note saying, "Sire: Tonight I make my debut. Deign to appear and applaud me and I am made." He did and she was. Shortly after this, men began dying for her. She made suicide fashionable. Every Parisian who could afford it fell in love with her. For her feet, which were lovely, she soon had emerald rings which she wore only when in bed. Her other jewels were fabulous. Unable to wear them all at once and in order to humble a rival, she once entered the Opéra bare of any gem except the flashing of her eyes and teeth. But she was followed by her maid, her shoulders sagging beneath her mistress's necklaces: in her hands on a red cushion lay all the tiaras, brooches, rings, and other jewelry the lady had decided not to wear. A tentative admirer, in sending her a few roses, placed them in a silver vase, tied the vase in a victoria, added cobs, silver harness, coachman, and groom. Catulle Mendès loaded her with poems. She was a heroine for Marcel Schwob and Jean Lorrain. Now at sixty and still rich, for she guarded her gems, she will divorce her prince, whom she met and captivated one night in the Moulin Rouge, where, because she had been mistakenly given his box by the usher, she threatened to take off every blue garment she wore —including her silken stays—and which she enumerated, all of which she promised to throw at his head if he tried to make her move. As her explanation for her legal process now, she only remarks, "I have always been a victim of love." She has already filled eighty small volumes with the history of her life. These have not been printed, but have been accepted as a legacy by the Bibliothèque Nationale.

1927

Claude Monet (1840–1926)

The death of Claude Monet, first Impressionist, marks the end of a period. He was what remained of nineteenth-century art. He outlived all of his intellectual generation except Georges Clemenceau, in whose presence he died, as if to use all his friendly contemporaries to the bitter end. It was in Zola's presence that Monet first saw Manet's works. Manet inspired Monet; Monet inspired Zola, then a poor journalist. The Batignolles war of words was thus begun. Monet, who fought all his life for his art, suffered the ignominy of dying appreciated. Persistently refused by the Academy salons, he took part in the great 1876 Impressionist show, where critics and public laughed themselves into fits. Even the government officially snickered.

It was the greatest aesthetic and financial blunder critics ever made, if one excepts the one they made a few years later in regard to Cézanne and would probably make today if another great innovator appeared. But the public and the government suffered most. In 1921 the Beaux-Arts paid through its nose for Monet's "Les Femmes au Jardin." Had they not been so busy laughing, they could have had it in '76 for a song. Monet's coffin was placed on a village handcart and two peasants in Sunday clothes pushed him to his grave in Giverny. Clemenceau followed on foot.

Art (Commerce)

CONTINUED

One reads in the press that the art merchant Marcel Bernheim is being sued by an angry baker lady from the provinces. Well, it seems that Mme. Boy, of Seine-Inférieure, had long had a couple of old pictures in her attic. Recently, needing cash more than art, owing to the high price of flour, she came to Paris with her canvases and shrewdly showed them to Bernheim. He shrewdly said they were by a chap named Rousseau who was dead and for whose works there was no demand. But, being a kind merchant, Bernheim offered Mme. B. ten thousand francs for the pair. Having expected to get nothing for them, the lady at once demanded fifteen thousand. Angry French words flew, but after heated argument, the bargainers agreed on twelve thousand five hundred francs as being satisfactory to both sides. A few months later, Mme. Boy, back to baking again, picked up a provincial journal and read that a painting of a gypsy by her Rousseau had fetched a half million francs. When she came to her senses she was halfway to Paris again. There she found that Bernheim had sold her two canvases for two hundred and fifty thousand and one hundred and fifty thousand francs, respectively. Having met an art dealer on her first trip to town, she now became acquainted with a lawyer. At present the court has adjourned the case for investigation. Mme. Boy, who is an emotional woman, feels that if she loses her suit her life will be ruined. It may well be.

Georges Rème

One of the most popular citizens who ever caught the Parisian eye has just been sentenced to ten years in a Lyonnais prison and ten in exile. This is Georges Rème, who has already escaped from six of the best French jails. "Fortunately, *Monsieur le juge*," he murmured with a winning smile, "I am young. However," he added later to his advocate, "I doubt if I stay in prison at all. The climate of Lyons does not agree with me. I fancy that my sentence of ten years is an idle theory on the part of the bench." He may be right. "Despoiled of your silken robe," he is quoted as saying to the judge, "do we differ so much, you and I, if one judges the man beneath?" . . . "I have always had two charming weaknesses," he told the jury, "ladies and gambling." His advocate in defending him (Rème has already been convicted seventeen times for theft) argued in part that his client was "a character in the best French tradition, on account of his elegance, his imagination and wit. In certain circumstances a man such as Rème has to be invented if he doesn't exist, because in sad periods he is one of those who help to amuse the masses and distract them from the preoccupations of their mind." Of all the criminals of recent years, only the murderer Landru was more popular at distracting the preoccupied masses, a dozen or more of whom (female) he had previously amused to death in his country retreat.

The hotel servant girl who found the Condé rose diamond Rème had stolen—by biting into its hiding place in an apple belonging to one of the hotel's guests—was promptly sacked for her dishonesty by the management.

Colette Willy, Paul Poiret

At the Théâtre de l'Avenue, Colette Willy and the *couturier* Paul Poiret have opened in *La Vagabonde*, a play made from one of Colette's earlier books. She and Poiret have been barnstorming with it in inns before fashionable crowds who followed them through the Riviera. His Parisian debut proved that M. Poiret is not a bad actor. Nor is Mme. Colette. However, an efficiency expert could point out that Poiret might have greater talent for, let us say, dressmaking, and that Colette was wasting her time at being anything except a novelist. *La Vagabonde* should not run long. Its present production calls to mind the tastes Marie Antoinette once had for pretending that she was a dairymaid.

Ulysses

Sylvia Beach, Parisian publisher of Joyce's *Ulysses*, has collected a protest against Samuel Roth's pirating of her unprotected bookrights in America. The list of signatures is amazing in its literary dignity and length. Already over two hundred of the most important intellectual names of Europe, England, and sometimes the United States have rallied to her aid. Many of the names call up the old generation and the older animosities practiced before Joyce was even known to be alive. W. B. Yeats,

Arthur Pinero, "Æ", Lennox Robinson, Jules Romains, Arthur Symons, Frank Swinnerton, Jacob Wassermann, Arnold Bennett, Robert Bridges, Benedetto Croce, A. Kouprine, Ivan Bunin, Havelock Ellis, Norman Douglas, Somerset Maugham, Knut Hamsun, Maurice Maeterlinck, H. G. Wells, and Rebecca West are only a few. One day this protest, with annexed signatures, will be a bibliophile's item. Today it is a grand gesture to Joyce and Miss Beach and to the writing craft's spirited solidarity.

L'Aiglon

A great deal of historical hysteria is being shown over the possible transfer of the ashes of the little Duc de Reichstadt from Schönbrunn to the Invalides where, according to General Mariaux, its director, L'Aiglon should rest beside Napoleon, his father. Pelletier-Doisy and Sadi Lecointe, France's two leading aces, are named to bring back the Little Eagle through the air. The only definite statement the poor youth is known to have made was, "Let me die in peace." Alas! that he should not be allowed to rest in it.

Marie Duplessis (1824–1847)

The eightieth anniversary of the death of Alphonsine Duplessis, immortalized for our parents by Alexandre Dumas *fils* as Marie Duplessis, *la Dame aux Camélias*, has brought to light facts far less well known than her public use of flowers, red and white. In private life—what little she had—she was the Vicomtesse de Perregaux for a few days, her husband at once deserting the lovely bride whom every other husband in Paris coveted. At twenty-two she was already dying, but still beautiful. The health she sought at every fashionable spa in Europe could not be recovered. Her last spring on earth she spent in Paris, trailing her white face and white flowers to the Opéra. "Dying," remarked one admirer, "she had no more lovers, but she never had so many friends." The bitter truth seems to be that she died alone, save for the presence of a hired nurse to whose hand she clung her last three days and nights. "That hand," says Théophile Gautier, "she quitted only for the hand of death. With youth's last effort to resist destruction, she suddenly lifted herself erect, uttered three cries and fell back forever on her funereal sheets." Her obituary notice referred to her as Alphonsine Plessis, "inhabitant of the rue de la Madeleine, woman of property and celibate." Nothing in the obituary was true except that the famous Camille was dead. Dumas was in Marseilles when he heard of the loss of the woman he loved. Returning to Paris, he rushed to her bedroom, but it was empty except for the trellis that made its walls, where the camellias, uncared for, had already turned black. Camille is buried in the cemetery of Montmartre. A special fund has been raised to care for her grave, most of the money going to erase signatures of unhappy lovers who scrawl their names on her tomb.

Comtesse de Noailles

The most important book of the spring is doubtless the latest volume of verse from the pen of the Comtesse de Noailles, *L'Honneur de Souffrir*. Mme. de Noailles represents one of the oldest families in France: town squares in the Midi are named after it. She also represents one of the oldest forms of art, being a beautiful woman, and she writes one of the oldest forms of verse—passionate lyric poetry, melancholic, materialistic, exalted. In modern France her position as a grand poet is unique. Though still alive, she is regarded as immortal. It is supposed that the new book is addressed to the late Maurice Barrès, for whom her friendship supplied one of the literary legends of this decade. "It is thy death," one of her poems concludes, "that has made me faithful."

Honors

CoCo, clown from the Cirque de Paris, has just received the *palmes académiques* from the grateful government and will in future be entitled to wear purple in his buttonhole. Also the late Marie Harel, eighteenth-century farmwife of the town of

Camembert, has been glorified as inventor of that cheese (from which her widower later cleared his fortune). Mme. Harel's monument, a stone shaft, unfortunately resembles a slice of Gruyère. There is no justice.

Family Affairs

A frightening new legal precedent has just been set by the Paris Court of Appeals in upholding the decree that the Duc de Clermont-Tonnerre and his wife, the Duchesse de Gramont, must each pay a monthly allowance of fifteen hundred francs to their daughter, Mme. Béatrix Clermont-Tonnerre. She recently sued her parents for support, which, according to the journals, they protested on the grounds of disapproving of her life. The Duc and Duchesse were willing to finance their daughter provided *she* led the life to which they were accustomed. The court's decision strikes a blow at what is left of faubourg tyranny and pride.

transition

transition, the new magazine edited here by Elliot Paul and Eugène Jolas, in its initial number contains, if not a feast, some good food for thought, the tastiest plate being the German Carl Sternheim's "Busekow," an excellent story of an amorous Potsdammerplatz policeman—this in despite of excerpts from Ludwig Lewisohn's *The Defeated* and "Opening Pages of a Work in Progress," by James Joyce, the latter in the most extreme jabberwocky. Its first page reads thus: "riverrun brings us back to Howth Castle & Environs. Sir Tristram, violer d'amores, fr' over the short sea, had passencore rearrived from North Armorica on this side the scraggy isthmus of Europe Minor to wielderfight his penisolate war."

For those to whom punning is no punishment, it may be stated that Armorica is a coast of France notable for its excellent oysters from which, perhaps, are pried the following pearls also collected by Joyce: "not yet, though all's fair in vanessy, were sosie sesthers wroth with twone nathandjoe. Rot a peck of pa's malt had Jhem or Shen brewed by arclight and rory end to the regginbrow was to be seen ringsome on the waterface." If everyone lives, the entire Joyce manuscript, for which the civilized half of a half-civilized world has long been humbly waiting, will be printed. Alas, that Ulysses were not still among the Phæacians!

Eve Lavallière

After threatening him with lawsuits, Eve Lavallière, famed Offenbach singer and comédienne of the Second Empire, has finally consented that M. Marcerou put the mysterious and mystical story of her life into print. A few years ago, Mlle. Lavallière, who was born Mlle. Fenoglio, provincial child of a provincial suicide who had jealously murdered his provincial wife, went into a convent. Religion as well as the theater had always had a strange fascination for her since she ran away from her first convent when she was ten. It was shortly after having exchanged the cloisters for the flies of the old Variété, where *La Belle Hélène* and other tuneful successes of the last century were sung by her, that she became the hit of Paris and one of its most lovely public figures. Her eyes were coal-black, her adventures were many. Her husband was one M. Samuel, manager of Variété, to whom she bore a child.

Lavallière, so named for her penchant for those necklaces of a still royaler and earlier decadent decade, was on the boards as late as 1914, when she created the title role in *Ma Tante d'Honfleur*. She was ready to enter into a long engagement in the United States "when," as her biographer remarks, "God called her." So she retired to the château of Chanceaux-sur-Choisilles. Shortly after, Lavallière was accused of being a spy, perhaps because of her friendship with the Baron von Lucius, then first attaché at the German Embassy.

"Much chagrined by this," Marcerou adds, "she felt herself being drawn toward God again"; and so it went until, after being denied retreat by the Carmelites of Avignon, Lavallière declared a return engagement at the old Variété, as a sacrifice to heaven, and on top of it went on a pilgrimage to dark Africa. For several years now she has been a member of l'Ordre des

Tertiaires Franciscains in a little conventual town in the Vosges. Hers has been a great story.

Anent the original Mlle. de la Vallière (1644–1710), who in her later years also became a nun, Sainte-Beuve remarked sagaciously: "One may retire from the world on condition that the world knows it." As to this century's Lavallière, may we remark that M. Marcerou seems to be seeing to that?

Hugo *Père*, Hugo *Fils*

A centenary of Victor Hugo is being celebrated under the title of One Hundred Years of Romanticism, the preface to his *Cromwell* (1827) having propelled him to the head of that movement. Hugo's struggles were more painful than his final glory led us to believe. His success came only at sixty with *Les Misérables,* first entitled Les Misères, Jean Valjean having been named Jean Tréjean, then Jean Vlajean, before the familiar patronymic was finally selected. Hugo wrote three distinct handwritings. His son, Charles, also wrote three distinct spirit-writings, as M. Gustave Simon's *Victor Hugo et les tables tournantes à Jersey* proves. During these mediumistic fits, young Charles wrote alexandrines in the spirit of Shakespeare, Corneille, and Dante. However, this happened exclusively in Jersey and was never allowed to go any farther.

Captain Charles Lindbergh

The night (May 21, 1927) a young tourist named Captain Charles Lindbergh landed his plane *The Spirit of St. Louis* at Le Bourget, concluding his historic flight across the Atlantic Ocean, the Paris news vendors screamed through the streets, "*Bonnes nouvelles!* The American has arrived."

At their Montmartre night clubs Zelli and Florence stood champagne to the Americans, as did excited patrons in humble bars, gallantly offering bad brandy to their Yankee clients. The prettiness of French journalism the next morning must also be noted. Of Lindbergh, *L'Intransigeant* wrote, "He has a heart of steel in the body of a bird. He is a carrier pigeon." The dear

Paris *Herald* here accidentally pied its Mrs. Lindbergh story slightly so that its best paragraph read, "Downstairs a family had a larger self than most boys. He was never a angora cat." The Ministry of Foreign Affairs flew the Stars and Stripes, as did most of the tramcars.

Among the ambassadors and chic flying officers lending color and confusion to Le Bourget that night was also a vast, orderly contingent of apaches from La Villette. Their costumes were accurate—velveteen pantaloons, slouch caps, mufflers, cigarette butts. As Lindbergh swung through the sky, their comments were accurate also: "We'd have preferred it had been a Frenchman—*mais qu'est-ce-que tu veux? C'est un brav ga', ce type-là. Vive! Vive!*" In more exalted vein was young Maurice Rostand's poem, printed the next morning in *Le Journal* and beginning,

> *Tu avais dansé toute cette nuit,*
> *Et tu es porti, dans l'aube inquiète,*
> *Comme Alan Seeger, moins enfant que lui,*
>   *Mais aussi poète!*

The poem is thirteen stanzas long and is dated 21 *Mai, 1927, onze heures du soir.* Lindbergh did not arrive until 10:22, which is an average for the poet of three minutes a stanza or one minute a line, or almost as speedy as *The Spirit of St. Louis.*

       ＊ ＊ ＊ ＊ ＊

With Lindbergh's flight a fortnight old, the international pride and excitement remain. In his honor, English and near-English lard the French public prints. One of the tougher sporting papers, bursting with adulation, in one paragraph managed to refer to him as *le boy* who was seen giving *le shake-hand* to the President of the Republic with whom he would *lunchera* that noon. At the charity auction of the Société des Écrivains Anciens Combattants de la Guerre, Lindbergh's autograph sold for 700 francs when affixed to the written praise of the Comtesse de Noailles, who referred to him as *enfant sublime qui nous rappelle à tous notre médiocre condition humaine,* adding, "more generous than Christopher Columbus, he has delivered to us the continent of the sky."

       ＊ ＊ ＊ ＊ ＊

The two first bits of cloth from the airplane used by the gallant Charles Lindbergh in his great flight from New York to Paris, offered by the C.I.D.NA.A. (the company which effected the repairs upon his famous *Spirit of St. Louis*), sold at a charity auction for twenty-one thousand and twenty-five thousand francs, respectively, the third bit going to Henry Bernstein, dramatist, for twenty thousand and the fourth to the Count de Chavagnac for ten thousand francs. In all, seventy-six thousand francs, fallen, as you might say, out of the sky.

Diaghilev's Russian Ballet

The twentieth anniversary of the founding of Diaghilev's Russian Ballet, with Stravinsky as tonic and dominant, has just been held here at the Théâtre Sarah-Bernhardt. Its program includes three novelties as the major attractions that the present Ballet season offers Paris.

The first novelty, *The Triumph of Neptune*, with music by Lord Berners, has been adapted by Prince Schervachidze, with the ballet created by George Balanchine. The second, *La Chatte*, drawn from Aesop's tale of the cat, with music by Henri Sauguet, a young French composer, had two great commodities in its favor. These were Lifar, who danced with the bouncing verve of gutta-percha, and a lovely décor of isinglass by Gabo and Pevsner, two Russians once featured in New York by Jane Heap's Little Review Gallery.

The third Ballet novelty, *Oedipus Rex*, by Stravinsky, was presented under the patronage of the sewing machine heiress Princess Edmond de Polignac (for thus do born Singers and musicians arrange). There in brass and winds was the settled work of a master musician, one who has left his violent youthful *Noces* and *Printemps* behind and, in his middling years, turns to Bach as if finally coming to rational terms with all great musical minds. Anticipated, perhaps feverishly, as a ballet with a sung text by Cocteau, translated into Latin, with costumes by Picasso and sets by Stravinsky's brother's son, the opening of this much-heralded work dwindled, on presentation, to an oratorio in dress suits. The Latin was sung, with Italian pronunciation, to the French audience by Russians. Sophocles' name was on the *Oedipus* program because it seems he once wrote the thing in Greek. The language problem, however, did not count, as no one understood the singers, nor indeed ever does. And perhaps few understood Stravinsky, who, having once struck his century's new creative high C, in his latest work returned to the old and lower B major—Bach.

Mlle. Louise Breslau (1857–1927)

Louise Breslau is dead. Marie Bashkirtseff, whose famous diary was filled with studio jealousies of Mlle. Breslau's increasing success in the early salons, died, perhaps of artistic envy, at the age of twenty-four. Breslau, superior painter, perhaps superior person, lived on for half a century and has just died at seventy, remembered only because she was envied by the young Bashkirtseff, years and years ago. *Sic gloria.*

Émile Zola (1840–1902)

The recent celebration of the twenty-fifth anniversary of the death of Émile Zola, because it recalls his wretched life, is a sad literary French affair. Placidly accepted by us Anglo-Saxons as a library classic, his compatriots find him still living enough to redissect, and the agony begins afresh. His general influence on French writers today is null, Flaubert and Maupassant having won the disciples where naturalism failed. Today Zola is read only as a bargain by workmen picking up his novels for a few sous from the *bouquinistes* on the quais. "I shall be appreciated twenty years after my death," he cried with hope. His prophecy missed its accuracy by a margin of two years: in 1920 a reprint of his works was effected without much comment. "Never," remarks the Paris literary critic Marius Boisson, "was a writer so insulted, so covered with odium and caricature." After his famous *Confession de Claude*, Zola was called "the sewage of literature." Cartoons on walls and journals showed him as a pig wallowing in a sty. He was nicknamed "the boar of Médan," that being the name of the small town beyond St. Germain, harboring the avant-garde literary colony which he dominated.

In '98 a publicist well-named Le Bourgeois printed at his own expense and distributed thirty thousand cartoons showing Zola miming all the sad brutal postures from the lives of the Rougon-Macquart clan. On the publication of *La Terre*, five of his friends hastily printed a pamphlet of their defection, in which they referred to the "collapse of his mind, the morbid depravation of a chaste man turned foul." His entry into the Dreyfus Affair only added to the violence. The criminologist Lombroso was drawn into an opinion, declaring of Zola that "the contraction of his orbicular, the lateral obtusion of his sense centers, his night fears, his stomach trouble, the polyencephalitic condition of his youth, and above all the heredity of his old father and young mother, combined to make of him an hysterico-epileptic type, traceable in the paranoiac psychoses evident in all he wrote." As last straw and proof of Zola's ill-balance, Lombroso cited his "giddiness after long hours of intellectual overwork": Zola who cried, "The only sweet joy of my life has been my work," "I live only for my work"—and "by it," he might have added, being poor. Finally in despair: "To give oneself up to one's work, to the annihilation of all other things, is the superb futility of the intelligent man."

There is little danger Zola's ashes will be transferred to the Panthéon after his having knocked twenty-five times at the Academy and being twenty-five times refused. "What shall we do with Zola?" M. Boisson goes on to enquire. "Proscribed by his own generation, demodé in the eye of youth, disdained by the literary sharpshooters of today, what shall we make of him —apostle, martyr or saint? Still he preserves some sort of mystical ascendancy in the hearts of the working-classes he so cruelly painted." Then he adds as if for the reader's information: "Zola wrote *Nana, L'Assommoir, La Joie de Vivre, Germinal* and that really fine book *Son Excellence Eugène Rougon.*" It will be recalled that Zola died of an accident. Judging by M. Boisson, if his literary reputation lives it will be an accident as well.

Art (World of)

In the past Van Gogh shot himself, Gauguin's mortal malady was impolite, the etcher Meryon went mad, Ingres was continually contagiously ill, Manet was paralyzed—and what of the life and manners of their successors today? A conciliatory interview is recorded by the well-known art critic Fels in one of the recent periodicals. It is between Vlaminck and Vollard, the merchant of the nineties, known as a discoverer of Cézanne, Degas, Renoir, Rousseau, and Derain. Vollard had not spoken to Vlaminck for six years. The colloquy seems to prove that no matter how sane their patrons, French artists are still as mad as hatters, and much richer.

Vlaminck drives his fine motorcar at one hundred and twenty kilometers an hour. "And I'm a little upset about my automobile," he adds. "My chauffeur just killed a cyclist. The rear wheel barely touched him." "He was probably only waiting a good chance to die," remarks Vollard gloomily. Moreover, Vlaminck's insurance company had to pay one hundred thousand francs for the victim's death—"a great deal for a man who only rode a bicycle," Vlaminck opines.

The luncheon for three consisted of ten pounds of boiled potatoes, twelve artichokes, three chickens, and a side of beef cut into great chunks. The brutality and wit continued. "Renoir used to say," remarks the host, in old-fashioned peasant style serving himself first, "that he was the only one who knew when one of his pictures were finished. When he'd stopped painting a woman's back and felt he wanted to slap it, he said he knew the picture was done. . . .

"Women are comical. One came to me once and asked me to expertise a picture she said she had at home. There were rocks in it, she said, and trees and water. Would I please give her a signed guarantee that it was a genuine Courbet? . . .

"I knew a woman whose son was feeble-minded," Vollard countered. "Her friends said, 'If he falls in love he may recover his reason.' So she gave tea parties, invited nice girls, but the son threw the cakes on the floor and remained idiotic, from drink. 'Turn him into a painter,' I told her; 'he'll be just the thing and might make your fortune.' She did. He did."

Paris artists maliciously believe they know the son to whom Vollard referred. Could it have been anyone else except Utrillo?

Isadora (1878–1927)

In the summer of 1926, like a ghost from the grave, Isadora Duncan began dancing again in Nice. Two decades before, her art, animated by her extraordinary public personality, came as close to founding an aesthetic renaissance as American morality would allow, and the provinces especially had a narrow escape. But in the postwar European years her body, whose Attic splendor once brought Greece to Kansas and Kalamazoo, was approaching its half-century mark. Her spirit was still green as a bay tree, but her flesh was worn, perhaps by the weight of laurels. She was the last of the trilogy of great female personalities our century cherished. Two of them, Duse and Bernhardt, had already gone to their elaborate national tombs. Only Isadora Duncan, the youngest, the American, remained wandering the foreign earth.

No one had taken Isadora's place in her own country and she was not missed. Of that fervor for the classic dance which she was the first to bring to a land bred on "Turkey in the Straw," beneficial signs remained from which she alone had not benefited. Eurythmic movements were appearing in the curriculums of girls' schools. Vestal virgins formed a frieze about the altar fire of Saint Marks-in-the-Bouwerie on Sabbath afternoons. As a cross between gymnasiums and God, Greek-dance camps flourished in the Catskills, where under the summer spruce, metaphysics and muscles were welded in an Ilissan hocus-pocus for the female young. Lisa, one of her first pupils, was teaching in the studio of the Théâtre des Champs-Élysées. Isadora's sister Elizabeth, to whom Greek might still be Greek if it had not been for Isadora, had a toga school in Berlin. Her brother Raymond, who operated a modern craft school in Paris, wore sandals and Socratic robes as if they were a family coat of arms. Isadora alone had neither sandals nor school. Most grandiose of all her influences, Diaghilev's Russian Ballet—which ironically owed its national rebirth to the inspiration of Isadora, then dancing with new terpsichorean ideals in Moscow—was still seasoning as an exotic spectacle in London and Monte Carlo. Only Isadora, animator of all these forces, had become obscure. Only she, with her heroic sculptural movements, had dropped by the wayside, where she lay inert like one of those beautiful battered pagan tombs that still line the Sacred Way between Eleusis and the city of the Parthenon.

As an artist, Isadora made her appearance in our plain and tasteless republic before the era of the half-nude revue, before the discovery of what is now called our Native Literary School, even before the era of the celluloid sophistication of the cinema, which by its ubiquity does so much to unite the cosmopolitanisms of Terre Haute and New York. What America now has, and gorges on in the way of sophistication, it then hungered for. Repressed by generations of Puritanism, it longed for bright, visible, and blatant beauty presented in a public form the simple citizenry could understand. Isadora appeared as a half-clothed Greek. . . .

A Paris *couturier* once said woman's modern freedom in dress is largely due to Isadora. She was the first artist to appear uncinctured, barefooted, and free. She arrived like a glorious bounding Minerva in the midst of a cautious corseted decade. The clergy, hearing of (though supposedly without ever seeing) her bare calf, denounced it as violently as if it had been golden. Despite its longings, for a moment America hesitated, Puritanism rather than poetry coupling lewd with nude in rhyme. But Isadora, originally from California and by then from Berlin, Paris, and other points, arrived bearing her gifts as a Greek. She came like a figure from the Elgin marbles. The world over, and in America particularly, Greek sculpture was recognized to be almost notorious for its purity. The overpowering sentiment for Hellenic culture, even in the unschooled United States, silenced the outcries. Isadora had come as antique art and with such backing she became a cult.

Those were Isadora's great years. Not only in New York and Chicago but in the smaller, harder towns, when she moved across the stage, head reared, eyes mad, scarlet kirtle flying to the music of the "Marseillaise," she lifted from their seats people who had never left theater seats before except to get up and go home. Whatever she danced to, whether it was France's revolutionary hymn, or the pure salon passion of Chopin's waltzes, or the unbearable heat of Brahms' German mode, she conspired to make the atmosphere Greek, fusing *Zeitgeists* and national sounds into one immortal Platonic pantomime.

Thus she inspired people who had never been inspired in their lives before, and to whom inspiration was exhilarating, useless, and unbecoming. Exalted at the concert hall by her display of Greek beauty, limbs, and drapes which though they were two thousand years old she seemed to make excitingly modern, her followers, dazzled, filled with Phidianisms, went home to Fords, big hats, and the theory of Bull Moose, the more real items of their progressive age.

Dancing appeals less to the public than the other two original theatrical forms, drama and opera (unless, like the Russian Ballet, dancing manages to partake of all three). Nevertheless, Isadora not only danced but was demanded all over America and Europe. On the Continent she was more widely known than any other American of that decade, including Woodrow Wilson and excepting only Chaplin and Fairbanks, both of whom, via a strip of celluloid, could penetrate to remote hamlets without ever leaving Hollywood. But Isadora went everywhere in the flesh. She danced before kings and peasants. She danced from the Pacific to London, from Petrograd to the Black Sea, from Athens to Paris and Berlin.

She penetrated to the Georgian states of the Caucasus, riding third-class amid fleas and disease, performing in obscure halls before yokels and princes whom she left astonished, slightly enlightened, and somehow altered by the vision. For thirty years her life was more exciting and fantastic than anything Zola or Defoe ever fabricated for their heroines. Her companions were the great public talent of our generation—Duse, D'Annunzio, Bakst, Bernhardt, Picabia, Brancusi, Anatole France, Comtesse Anna de Noailles, Sardou, Ellen Terry.

Three of the greatest sculptors of her day at this time took Isadora's body as a permanent model and influence on their work though, alas, left no record in marble. Maillol alone made over five hundred drawings of Isadora dancing to Beethoven's Seventh Symphony; Rodin followed her all over Europe and literally made thousands of drawings, many still in the Musée Rodin in Paris. One of his most beautiful *gouaches,* now in the Metropolitan Museum, is *La Naissance d'un Vase Grecque,* in which he used Isadora's torso as his inspiration. Bourdelle also used Isadora as the main typical figure in his Théâtre des Champs-Élysées frescoes. These artists made the likeness of Isadora's limbs and the loveliness of her small face immortal. This was the great, gay, successful period of life. Her friends ran the gamut from starving poets down to millionaires. She was prodigal of herself, her art, illusions, work, emotions, and everybody's funds. She spent fortunes. After the war was over in France, her Sunday-night suppers in the Rue de la Pompe were banquets where guests strolled in, strolled out, and from low divans supped principally on champagne and strawberry tarts, while Isadora, barely clad in chiffon robes, rose when the spirit moved her to dance exquisitely. Week after week came obscure people whose names she never even knew. They were like moths. She once gave a house party that started in Paris, gathered force in Venice, and culminated weeks later on a houseboat on the Nile. She was a nomad de luxe.

In order to promulgate her pedagogic theories of beauty and education for the young, she legally adopted and supported some thirty or forty children during her life, one group being the little Slavs who afterward danced in Soviet Russia. During her famous season at the New York Century Theatre where she gave a classic Greek cycle, *Oedipus Rex, Antigone*, and the like, she bought up every Easter lily in Manhattan to decorate the theater the night she opened in Berlioz's *L'Enfance du Christ*, which was her Easter program. The lilies, whose perfume suffocated the spectators, cost two thousand dollars. Isadora had, at the moment, three thousand dollars to her name. And at midnight, long after all good lily-selling florists were in bed, she gave a champagne supper. It cost the other thousand.

Isadora, who had an un-American genius for art, for organizing love, maternity, politics, and pedagogy on a great personal scale, had also an un-American genius for grandeur.

After the lilies faded, Isadora and her school sat amid their luggage on the pier where the ship was about to sail for France. They had neither tickets nor money. But they had a classic faith in fate and a determination to go back to Europe, where art was understood. Just before the boat sailed, there appeared a schoolteacher. Isadora had never seen her before. The teacher gave Isadora the savings of years and Isadora sailed away. Herself grand, she could inspire grandeur in others, a tragic and tiring gift. There were always schoolteachers and lilies in Isadora's life.

Those three summer programs which Isadora gave in 1926 at her studio in Nice were her last performances on earth. At the end of the next summer she was dead. One of the soirées was given with the concordance of Leo Tecktonius, the pianist, and the other two with Jean Cocteau, who accompanied her dancing with his spoken verse. In all three performances her art was seen to have changed. She treaded the boards but little, she stood almost immobile or in slow splendid steps with slow splendid arms moved to music, seeking, hunting, finding. Across her face, tilting this way and that, fled the mortal looks of tragedy, knowledge, love, scorn, pain. Posing through the works of Wagner, through the tales of Dante, through the touching legend of St. Francis feeding crumbs and wisdom to his birds, Isadora was still great. By an economy (her first) she had arrived at elimination. As if the movements of dancing had become too redundant for her spirit, she had saved from dancing only its shape.

In one of her periodic fits of extravagant poverty and although needing the big sum offered, she once refused to dance in Wanamaker's Auditorium, disdaining for her art such a "scene of suspenders." She refused to appear in certain Continental theaters because they contained restaurants where dining might distract the spectators from her art. She early refused (though she and her family were starving in Berlin) to dance at the Wintergarten for one thousand gold marks a night because there were animal acts on the bill. During the worst of her final financial predicaments in Paris, when few theaters were offering her anything at all, she refused to dance at the Théâtre des Champs-Élysées because it was a music hall. Yet her image in sculpture adorned the theater's façade, where Bourdelle had chiseled her likeness for all times and passers-by. She talked vaguely of consenting to dance in Catalonia. To anyone who knew her it seemed natural that Isadora would like to dance in a castle in Spain.

The lack of money, which never worried Isadora as much as it anguished her devoted friends, became more acute during the last years of her life. Nevertheless she refused a legacy of over a quarter of a million francs from the estate of her stormy young husband, Yessenine, the Russian revolutionary poet whom she had married late and unhappily. At the worst of her final picturesque poverty, when, as Isadora gallantly declared, she hardly knew where the next bottle of champagne was coming from (champagne was the only libation she loved), it was decided by her friends that she should write her memoirs. At this time she was living in a small studio hotel in the Rue Delambre, behind the Café du Dôme in Paris. Isadora's handwriting was characteristic; it was large, handsome, illegible, with two or three words to a line and four or five lines to a page. During her authorship the scantly scribbled pages accumulated like white leaves, left to drift over her littered studio floor. Then, as in all the frequent crises in her life, her friends rallied around her with scenes, jealousies, memories, quarrels, recriminations, good cases of wine, fine conversation, threats of farewell, new leases of affection—all the dramatics of loyalty, disillusion, hero worship, duty, fatigue, patience, and devotion which animated even her Platonic associations—all the humorous and painful disorders which genius, as if to prove its exceptional chemistry, catalyzes in commoner lives. The book, called *My Life*, finally appeared posthumously. It was to have furnished money for her to live.

As her autobiography made clear, an integral part of Isadora's nature died young when her two adored little children, Deirdre and Patrick, were tragically drowned in 1913 at Neuilly; the automobile in which they were waiting alone slipped its brakes and plunged into the Seine. The children had been the offspring of free unions, in which Isadora spiritedly believed. She believed, too, in polyandry and that each child thus benefited eugenically by having a different and carefully chosen father. She also attributed the loss of her third child, born the day war was declared, to what she called the curse of the machine. At the wild report that the Germans were advancing by motor on Paris, the old Bois de Boulogne gates were closed, her doctor and his automobile, amidst thousands of cars, were caught behind the grill, and by the time he arrived at her bedside it was too late. The child had been born dead. "Machines have been my enemy," she once said. "They killed my three children. Machines are the opposite of, since they are the invention of, man.

Perhaps a machine will one day kill me."

In a moment of melancholy her friend Duse prophesied that Isadora would die like Jocasta. Both prophecies were fulfilled. On August 13, 1927, while driving on the Promenade des Anglais at Nice, Isadora Duncan met her death. She was strangled by her colored shawl, which became tangled in the wheel of the automobile.

A few days later in Paris great good-natured crowds had gathered in the Rue de Rivoli to watch the passing of the American Legion, then holding their initial postwar jollification and parade in France. By a solemn chance, what the crowd saw first, coming down the flag-strewn, gaily decorated thoroughfare, was the little funeral cortege of Isadora Duncan, treading its way to the cemetery of Père-Lachaise. Her coffin was covered by her famous purple dancing cape serving as a pall. On the back of the hearse, her family, though unsympathetic to her radical views, had loyally placed her most imposing floral tribute, a great mauve wreath from the Soviet Union with a banner that read "*Le Cœur de Russie Pleure Isadora.*" Though she had once rented the Metropolitan Opera House to plead the cause of France before we went into the war, though she had given her Neuilly château as a hospital, though she had been a warm and active friend to France, the French government sent nothing. Nor did her great French friends, who had once eagerly drunk her fame and champagne, walk behind dead Isadora.

Of all the famous personages she had loved and known and who had hailed her genius and hospitality, only two went to Passy, where she lay in state, to sign the mourners' books—Yvette Guilbert and the actor Lugné-Poë. Hundreds of others scrawled their signatures on the pages, but they were casuals, common, loyal, unknown. Since Isadora was an American, it was regrettable that both the Paris American newspapers, the Paris *Herald* and the Chicago *Tribune*, busy doubtless with the gayer Legion matters, did not send reporters to follow her funeral cortege to its destination. Thus Americans next morning read that Isadora was followed to her grave by a pitiful handful. Only five carriages made up the official procession; but four thousand people—men, women, old, young, and of all nationalities—waited in the rain for the arrival of her body at Père-Lachaise.

Of earthly possessions, Isadora had little enough to leave. Still she had made a will—and forgot to sign it.

All her life Isadora had been a practical idealist. She had put into practice certain ideals of art, maternity, and political liberty which people prefer to read as theories on paper. Her ideals of human liberty were not unsimilar to those of Plato, to those of Shelley, to those of Lord Byron, which led him to die dramatically in Greece. All they gained for Isadora were the loss of her passport and the presence of the constabulary on the stage of the Indianapolis Opera House, where the chief of police watched for sedition in the movement of Isadora's knees.

Denounced as a Russian Bolshevik sympathizer, Isadora said she never even received a postal card from the Soviet government to give her news of her school which she housed in its capital. For Isadora had a fancy for facts. As she once told Boston it was tasteless and dull, so, when they were feting her in triumph in Moscow, she told the Communists she found them bourgeois. She had a wayward truthful streak in her and a fancy for paradox. "Everything antique Greek," she once said to an American woman friend, "is supposed to be noble. Did you ever notice how easily the Greeks became Roman?"

Great artists are tragic. Genius is too large, and it may have been grandeur that proved Isadora's undoing—the grandeur of temporary luxury, the grandeur of permanent ideals.

She was too expansive for personal salvation. She had thousands of friends. What she needed was an organized government. She had had checkbooks. Her scope called for a national treasury. It was not for nothing that she was hailed by her first name only, as queens have been, were they great Catherines or Marie Antoinettes.

As she stepped into the machine that was to be her final enemy, Isadora's last spoken words were, by chance, "*Je vais à la gloire!*"

Loie Fuller

Loie Fuller's ballet has opened a ten weeks' engagement at the Moulin Rouge at a price (and this is a real novelty in French music-hall annals) of twenty-five thousand francs a week. In her private *hôtel* in the Boulevard de la Saussaye, within calling distance of the Rumanian Prince Carol—housed across the street—and in constant telegraphic communication with her intimate friend Queen Marie at Bucharest, Miss Fuller, between politics, has been directing a fantasy film. Ironically her cinema is drawn from one of Hoffmann's tales—"The Man Who Lost His Eyes." Her own eyesight having been injured by her long laboratory experiments with her electrical ballet devices and by her perfections in color photography (she has obtained a new control of red and green), Miss Fuller directs her films from behind dark glasses and from her bed. One of the most recent is a formless, objectless exposition of chromatics.

Her household consists of four secretaries, two chefs—one French, one Japanese—and a series of underlings, including the children of the concierge, once ordered by Miss Fuller to make their mud pies in her salon "because it's too wet for them to play outside." One of her ballet groups is reported scheduled for New York consumption, another will play Egypt, Morocco, and Monte Carlo during the winter season. It is a matter of common knowledge that Miss Fuller has no difficulty filling her ballets. Her girls are reported engaged at a fixed salary of three thousand francs a month whether they are dancing or not. In case of Miss Fuller's sudden death, bonds in London assure each dancer of an inheritance. All her life she has displayed the same genius for kindness and generosity.

Walter Berry (1859–1927)

As part of Paris life has come the death of Walter Van Rensselaer Berry, Parisian figure to Americans, American figure to Parisians. Between fluctuating national ranks he spent his long, fashionable expatriation in his private *hôtel* in the Rue de Varenne. French law forbidding that his ashes be cast to the winds of his country château, as had been his desire, his urban obsequies became a noble faubourg gathering suitable to an international gentleman whose energies had been patriotic, commercial and public, but worldly always. He had been president of the Paris American Chamber of Commerce. At his instigation

Belleau Wood was purchased as a national memorial to the Second, Third, and Twenty-sixth Divisions. And as tribute the country mayor of Belleau represented his little community at the American's last public function, which was his funeral, in the Pro-Cathedral in the Avenue George V, where there were assembled representatives of the President of the Republic, and of the Military Governor of Paris, Generals Foch and Gouraud. Present also was his lifelong friend Mrs. Edith Wharton. From the American colony were Mrs. Rutherford Stuyvesant, Mr. Henry Peartree, Mr. Blythe Branch, and Colonel Drake. From the French were Paul Valéry, M. and Mme. Paul Morand, M. and Mme. Henry Bernstein, Princesse Lucien Murat, M. Jean Cocteau, Duc de Gramont, Comtesse de Beaumont, Marquis de Castellane, Comte and Comtesse de Chambrun, Comte and Comtesse de la Rochefoucauld.

The ceremonies of death are precisely graded in France. There are seven classes of funerals, depending on the purse, and *un enterrement de première classe* has even three divisions of subdividing magnificence, which make in all nine fashions in which humans may say good-by to pomp forever. The plume-decked, broidered catafalque with its flowing curtains and silver insignia and its four plume-decked black horses with their somber caparisons and white reins, headed a procession in Mr. Berry's last honor whose magnificence is rarely seen in France today.

Marcel Proust (1871–1922)

In this month has passed the fifth anniversary of Marcel Proust's death. The final two volumes of Le Temps Retrouvé, along with *Chronique*, rather tiresome reprints of his *Figaro* contributory days, are now available. In Le Temps Retrouvé one finds that the glory of the Guermantes has passed. Gilberte is presented as the widow of St. Loup, killed in the war; Charlus is déclassé; Mme. Verdurin has married the old prince; Oriane and the duke are divorced. The glamorous style with which Proust established his dynasty and theirs is lacking in his arid descriptions of their decline. Himself dying as he wrote of their end, he was too weak to ornament their epitaphs. Proust has been dead since 1922, yet the annual appearance of his posthumous printed works has left him, to the reader, alive. Now there is nothing left to publish. Five years after his interment, Proust seems dead for the first time.

1928

Baroness von Freytag-Loringhoven (1875–1927)

The recent demise is announced in Paris of the Baroness Elsa von Freytag-Loringhoven, aged fifty-two. By birth a great Danish lady, by marriage various nationalities, she was known for her poesies ten years ago in New York by the *Little Review*, Sherwood Anderson, Carlos Williams, and others.

She was also notable for the perfection of her torso, used by Glackens, Henri, Bellows, Genthe, and friendly painters for whom she represented the consummate model. Her life, whether in Greenwich Village, Paris, or Berlin, was spent in poverty, adventures, liberty, logic, and eccentricities.

When modern art first came to Fifth Avenue she shaved, painted and varnished her handsome head as part of the new movement. Not long ago she appeared on the terrace of the Café des Deux Magots in a hat trimmed with a large watch and chain.

Always pro-French, she once called, in honor of her birthday, on the French consul in Berlin with her birthday cake and its lighted candles poised on her superb skull. A woman reared to epicureanism, after the Bolshevik Revolution and the loss of what was left of her fortune, she sold newspapers in Unter den Linden. Installed, through the kindness of Parisian friends, in the first comfortable quarters she had recently known, she and her little dog were asphyxiated by gas in the night, both victims of a luxury they had gone too long without.

The Italian Straw Hat

With the French cinematographers' threat to force by law a rationed exchange between the importation of Hollywood reels and the exportation of their own films, considerable curiosity settled around the recent showing of what was presented as France's big bid for film popularity—*Le Chapeau de Paille d'Italie*. For their sake, we trust you may later see it in New York as *The Italian Straw Hat*. This farce of plush, whiskers, and long skirts has been perfectly re-created from documents or perhaps from the original stage production of 1895. It is the work of René Clair, the white hope of Paris producers and maker along with Picabia and Satie of *Entr'acte*, the first and still the best of the early Gallic modernisms. While *The Italian Straw Hat* is not, as touted, the funniest comedy in Europe today, it is the funniest comedy about a straw hat to be seen on the boulevards.

Loie Fuller (1870–1928)

La Loie Fuller was born in 1870 in Illinois, in the town of Fullersville, named for her family who founded it, and lived for the last thirty-five years in Paris, where her death has certainly aroused more widespread homage and regret than if it had taken place in her native land. Here she made her first success at the Folies-Bergère with her flame and serpent dances, here she trained her world-famous ballets, here she knew Rodin, Sarah Bernhardt, Flammarion, Alexandre Dumas, and Anatole France, who described her as "a dazzling artist, a woman of delicate and refined feeling." It was also here, or so the pretty fable goes, that she first conceived her ideas for colored lights, inspired by the nuances dropping from the great rose windows of Notre-Dame upon her handkerchief, spread (since in her discouragement she had been weeping) upon her knees to dry. Her life was eccentric, but as correct as her feeling. Her existence was emotionally and physically austere. In her youth she welcomed friendship but never admitted love. In her maturity she gave great confused dinners for gourmet friends at which she nibbled only fruit and cucumbers, for which she had an odd passion.

She was scrupulous in her contracts, once living with her mother in penury to pay off an illegally pressed obligation of four hundred thousand francs. Simply and untheatrically dressed, enthusiastic, speaking execrable French, plump—in later years she looked, as she said, more like a visiting *Professorin* than a dancer. Second only to Isadora Duncan, Miss Fuller was the most widely known American woman in France. Her death drew from the French press such tender phrases as "a magician is dead"; "a butterfly has folded its wings."

Antiquities (World of)

With the authenticity of the Glozel "prehistoric" potteries now entering a million years late into the legal arena, a geyser of lawsuits is relieving the venom of all the gentle old professors involved. First, the peasant Fradins, on whose Vichy farm the disputed bisexual idols were found, are suing M. Dussaud, member of the Institute, for saying that these rather sensual objects were fabricated by them, the Fradins, a respectable family, in their leisure hours. Second, Dr. Morlet, a violent Glozelian, is suing the archaeologue Seymour-Ricci for having said that he, Morlet, pulled a prehistoric hatchet out of his cuff and not out of the Fradin field where, if any place, it should have been professionally found. Next, the Count de Begouen, prehistory professor of Toulouse and a violent anti-Glozelian (who would have thought these old men had so much blood in them?) is suing Dr. Roth, Glozelian, for being Glozelian and saying so in his lecture at the Sorbonne where the Sorbonne students, neutrally Glozelian, threw asafetida bombs at the doctor and would have thrown them at the Count except that he was still in Toulouse. As a result the bombs intended for him were used on the police, who are suing the students for breach of the peace.

Jacques Hennessy (1839–1928)

Jacques Hennessy, chief of the family noted for its *fine champagne* with its constellation of three stars, has disappeared from his vast circle of friends. For eighty-nine years he inhabited Paris as a bachelor and bon viveur. He died as he lived, in the best of health. His heart, which he boasted had never failed to accelerate when in the presence of a pretty woman, finally refused to continue its gallant function. Possessed of rents from

Cognac (Charente) which afforded him seven hundred thousand francs a month for pocket money alone, he spent his time and fortune generously rewarding those who had been the favorites of his prime, and men and women who had once been younger than he grew antique on the largesse of this sprightly octogenarian who died looking younger than they. Hennessy never took any exercise, despised sports, never walked if the effort took him away from carpets, and hated fresh air. His town house was equipped with double windows which were never opened, and on his daily sorties he was rushed from his door into a limousine through whose hermetic glass he took his view of the city, which, though he owned various country estates, he never left for the last twenty years. His eyesight remained remarkable: he never wore spectacles, claiming to be able to distinguish naturally between a blonde and a brunette. For two hundred years the Hennessys, once *immigrés* from Ireland in that rush of loyalty which carried many Celts to France in the wake of James II, have inhabited the Charente, where grow the coarse heady grapes from which their produce is made. Owing to the family's early thrift and labor, the town of Cognac and its tipple, both of which had fallen into desuetude, were revived, rebuilt, and rebottled.

Le Lapin Agile

Le Lapin Agile, last of the tree-shaded Montmartre taverns and once patronized by men since grown great, like Guillaume Apollinaire, Max Jacob, Pierre MacOrlan, and André Salmon, is to be closed. Old Frédéric, bearded and velvet-bonneted, a patron who has drunk with the best of them, strummed his guitar, given poets credit, and made the rich pay through their noses, cannot meet the Butte's new night taxes. It was at his table that Picasso proclaimed the first tenets of Cubism and added his mot, "When you paint a landscape it should look like a plate." Frédéric's painter-drinkers were those who broke from Impressionism and founded modern art; his writer-drinkers, those who seceded from Le Chat Noir, first became *les symbolistes* and then eventually whatever they are today—living or dead but famous either way. Le Lapin Agile housed the revolutionaries who rebelled against George Moore's once rebellious Nouvelles Athènes. Both mutinies succeeded indefinitely. The closing of their taverns marks the exact demise of the formulative artistic epoch.

Duchesse de Clermont-Tonnerre

The *Mémoires au Temps des Équipages,* of the Duchesse de Clermont-Tonnerre, is rousing comment in circles which, if restricted, are nevertheless far-reaching. Daughter of the Duc de Gramont, granddaughter of the old Beauveau, whose second wife was one of twenty-one noble brothers and sisters; as a child saluted as princess by peasants on her farm who begged her not to clean her shoes before entering their houses, as a woman related by marriage and inheritance to titled personages her republicanisms scandalized, Mme. de Clermont-Tonnerre takes advantage, in her book, of both forms of political thought flowing in her blood and brain. Few memoirs written by French aristocrats bewail aught except the good old times. This lady is valuable in having been modern and accurate before either were the style.

She looks backward with a shrug rather than a sigh. Avoiding ideas and offering in their place facts, her pen describes late nineteenth- and early twentieth-century faubourg French society—voyaging duchesses who sent no postal cards but whose secretaries cabled, to a limited list of friends, "The duchess is now crossing the Rocky Mountains"; aristocratic matrons who were in bed by ten and had never dined in public; old beaux who were proud to have relatives, but no friends; husbands who refused to give their wives postage stamps, having given them some the week before; country châteaux at which there were never less than forty guests; marriages proposed because the bridegroom would inherit fine tapestries "with borders"; hostesses who, like her parents, entertained ninety thousand guests and none of them intellectuals, in the course of their Parisian lives. It is such information and dry comment that Mme. de Clermont-Tonnerre offers. Lacking the delicacy, secrecy, and reverie of great eighteenth-century female documents, her book does not fail of their accuracy and malice. It is timely to an age when great ladies of all Western lands lend their portraits to advertisements of cold cream.

Flea Market

We grieve to announce the passing of the old Flea Market. This superb rubbish-vending agglomeration was founded in the thirteenth century when Paris was the pride of Christendom, and six hundred years later is abolished in an atheistic century for infringing on the Sabbath selling laws. Among the various city-gate weekly rag marts, the Kremlin-Bicêtre at the Porte d'Italie, the Montreuil at the Porte de Vincennes, the Fleas at Clignancourt will remain in memory as the most famous and satisfying. Among its fields of black mud was always to be found the choicest rubbish—the better cracked-ivory miniatures, the daintiest slightly broken Venetian glass pitchers, the smartest almost new single riding boots (usually lefts). From the Fleas sprang the present cult for the fine floral Louis-Philippe glass paperweights, to be had before the war for ten sous and now selling around two hundred francs. Here were to be found occasional and rare lemon-wood tables, sought for their sweet color by strolling connoisseurs. Here, in fine, was anything you wanted, from old radio sets to brand-new fourteenth-century antiques. A month ago an effort was made to oust the Fleas and utilize their space for skyscraper flats. Now the invoking of the Sunday selling law has turned the trick. During both these crises we cite the sentiment and sympathy of the Paris edition of the New York *Herald,* which worked as passionately for the Fleas as if they belonged to the Fourth instead of to the lowest estate.

Yussupoffs

The failure of Irfé, Prince Yussupoff's London dress shop, has added another lamentable item to the Parisian history of this extraordinary young Russian, who admits responsibility for the murder of Rasputin. Proprietor for years, it was said, of the Maisonnette Russe, an expensive singing restaurant in the Rue du

Mont-Thabor, where he and his wife were familiar figures—he slim and elegant in dinner jacket, she lovely and sad, wearing at last the famous Yussupoff pearls which her husband in bachelor days used as his own decoration—he was always much in the public eye. His book—written in French, published here a few years ago—in which he detailed step by step how the murder was committed, describing even the final kicks, blood, and blows passing between his royal feet and the drugged body of the peasant priest, caused an angry rift in the Russian Royalist party centered here, and the Grand Duke, his patriotic accomplice in arranging the plot, ceased communication with the Prince for his authorship. A few months ago, a series of fantastic underground stories, which finally reached the yellow journals, involved His Highness in reported melodramas consisting of, according to the first version, a check forgery, then the murder of a girl plus an embezzlement, and finally the ownership of a room in which a woman was murdered, although he took no part in the crime. His flight and exile from Paris were authentically announced by the most serious journals and then politely retracted, due to the menace of a defamation suit threatened by the Prince through the local Russian press. Then Rasputin's daughter arrived, bringing her suit against her father's confessed murderer and her demands for a half million dollars' damages. The suit will not be fought until the opening of the autumn courts. Until the publishing of his book, rather childishly styled, naïve, and frightening in its details, but lacking utterly the somber note customarily supposed to darken the memories of a royalist become criminal for his kind, the Prince enjoyed an aura of mystery. Authenticity put an end to it. He now appears as one of the most tragic, unromantic figures of the Slavic refugee colony.

Gene Tunney

Gene Tunney broke up the shop at Lipp's when he recently entered there one night with Mr. Thornton Wilder. The heavyweight champion ordered and obtained a schooner of light beer; Mr. Wilder, because he was with Mr. Tunney, also received something to drink, doubtless not what he ordered, for service was paralyzed. The cashier, ordinarily a creature of discretion, ceased making her change; the waiters rallied round Tunney's table shamelessly. All the French women stared, whispering, "*Comme il est beau!*" "*Quel homme magnifique!*" their escorts murmured without jealousy. It was a triumph which the champion accepted without too much grace. Nervously doffing and donning his hat as if the bay leaves irked him, he talked loudly, intelligently, for a half hour, and left.

Erik Satie (1866–1925)

A small advance-guard concert, featuring the briefer works of the American Virgil Thomson and the French composer Cliquet-Pleyel, was given lately in the Salle Majestic. These two represent almost all that is left of the Groupe d'Accueil. The final number on the program was properly Satie's "Death of Socrates," rarely heard here.

It is now only three years since Satie departed from his suburban attic, where, with a hammock, a candle, an enormous collection of the old umbrellas, new shoes, and derby hats which were his passions, he lived for twenty-four years and died as he had lived, in poverty; writing, though with little to laugh at, the first modern humorous French music. The Groupe d'Accueil, formed by his disciples, still deserves the praise given to persistence.

1929

Harry Lehr (1869–1929)

The recent death here of Harry Lehr, Gilded Age court jester to the Four Hundred, passed unnoticed in the Parisian papers. Though an expatriate in France for almost a quarter of a century, he lived out all those years as a New York legend. Years ago he had given a dinner in Manhattan in honor of a monkey. This had given him no social standing in France. Later he married a rich American wife. In recent years he lived in her superb eighteenth-century private hotel in the Rue des Saints-Pères, whose park was illuminated at dinner parties by a pair of theatrical spotlights, operated by liveried servants, which relieved guests of the necessity of appreciating the shrubbery on foot. Mr. Lehr passed his time in a routine that consisted of alternating isolation and tea parties. He had matured in Baltimore at a period when buggies were the rage. Though vehicles altered, he did not change, and in Paris rounded out his life by starting each afternoon in his wife's limousine for what, to the end, he called his "buggy-ride in the Bois."

Although he was for more than a decade one of the most familiar luncheon figures at the Ritz, his recently slender personal finances no longer warranted an expenditure for what was still the breath of life to him—observation and conversation in a smart public place. An emissary of his family was therefore dispatched to warn Ollivier, the maître-d'hôtel at the Ritz. The reply remains the most gracious personal tribute to Mr. Lehr's many years abroad. "Monsieur Lehr," said Ollivier, "will continue to be, as he always has been, welcome at the Ritz, where I shall be honored, in the future, if he would consider himself as my guest. Please inform Monsieur Lehr that his favorite table by the window will be reserved for him tomorrow, as usual."

The Well of Loneliness

It may be interesting to know that Radclyffe Hall's novel about Lesbians, *The Well of Loneliness*, though banned in England and under fire in New York, has escaped condemnation in France, where it now enjoys a local printing. Its biggest daily sale takes place from the news vendor's cart serving the de luxe train for London, La Flèche d'Or, at the Gare du Nord. The price is one hundred and twenty-five francs a copy. For first English editions, dealers in the Rue de Castiglione offer to buy for as high as six thousand francs, and to sell at as high as anything you are silly enough to pay.

[*Miss Radclyffe Hall was a strange but impressive-looking woman, short of stature, with a disproportionately large but handsomely shaped head and always with a perfect haircut. Her hands and feet were also large, as were the beautiful sapphires which she wore, one as a finger ring and one each as a cuff link. She wore beautifully tailored English suits, tight-fitting across the bosom and shoulders. In her tailoring, she was indeed une grande dame. The Paris Latin Quarter denizens first met her at a tea (with wonderful cucumber sandwiches) at Miss Natalie Barney's, heavily attended, since* The Well of Loneliness *had aroused a great deal of curiosity, if very little admiration as a literary or psychological study. As I recall, her whole analysis was false and based upon the fact that the heroine's mother, when expecting her, had hoped for a boy baby, which as a daughter, Miss Hall interpreted literally. This rather innocent and confused book was the first of the Sapphic interpretations in modern life. Today it seems unlikely it could ever have created a popular literary social scandal of such proportions.   J. F.*]

La Goulue (1869–1929)

The death in misery of La Goulue, one of the great *demi-mondaines* of the nineties, petted cancan-dancer of the then devilish

Moulin Rouge, model for Toulouse-Lautrec in some of his most famous cabaret canvases, and general toast of the whiskered town, afforded her a press she had not enjoyed since her palmiest days. La Goulue (Greedy Gal) was born Louise Weber, daughter of a cab-driver; she was a pretty, full-fleshed blonde of the mortal Olympian type popular with the gay Edwardians the world over. Rising by natural stages from the sidewalk to the ballet of the Moulin Rouge, her triumph came when bankers and Impressionists drank champagne from her shoe. She did the split amidst the sixty yards of lace trimming her stylish long skirt, and starred in the quadrilles in the arms of her famous partners: Valentin-le-Désossé (the Boneless Wonder), Grille-d'Égout (Sewer Gate—and very popular in his period), and a lady known as Nini Patte-en-l'Air. La Goulue achieved a private *hôtel* in the Avenue du Bois and even lived in what had once been the property of her famous predecessor, Païva, fashionable mistress of Napoleon III. It was from this discreet mansion that La Goulue was invited to dance before a gentleman who afterward literally covered her with banknotes and turned out to be the Grand Duke Alexis. She had charm, a dazzling complexion, and wit. It was the last great heyday for courtesans, and she made hay.

Then came her fall. She went to jail after some lark. She became a lion-tamer in a street fair. She became a dancer in a wagon show; Toulouse-Lautrec painted curtains for her, but she forgot them in some barn and the rats gnawed at them.° Then she became a laundress. Then she became nothing.

A month ago she reappeared; fat, old, and dancing drunkenly in a few feet of a remarkable documentary film about the ragpickers of Paris—called, after their neighborhood of wagon shanties, *The Zone*. Her last interview was given to the weekly *Vu*. After the first glass of brandy of the interview she took out a cracked mirror; after the third glass she recalled her cab-driving father. After the fourth she remembered the Grand Duke Alexis and, on the promise of a box of face powder, even remembered her son, who had died in a gambling den. A few weeks later her ragpickers took her to a city clinic, where she too died, murmur-

° They later turned up, cut into salable sections, in the shop of a dealer; purchased by the Louvre, reassembled and restored, they now hang in the Jeu de Paume.

ing as if declining a last and eternal invitation, "I do not want to go to hell."

Eugène Atget (1856–1927)

After seventy years of obscure living and dying, Eugène Atget, the most remarkable photographic documentor of his day, is now featured in all the avant-garde European reviews—his plates having been saved from destruction by the American photographer Berenice Abbott. Atget was a cabin boy, an actor (he played villains), and for the last fifty years a photographer. The last twenty years he lived exclusively on bread, milk, and sugar —from principle and poverty. The greater portion of his documentation was of street life—beggars, hand-organ players, shopfronts of literally all the *métiers,* horses, women's hats, shoes, fashions in fish, in civic and military uniforms—life as it was modestly or sinfully lived in every quarter and suburb of the entire city of Paris. He made a complete camera investigation of the roots in the medical-herb garden in the Jardin des Plantes, of the treetops in Versailles; he did the holiday crowds, obtaining poses and types as characteristic as the race-track and ballet documents of Degas. He was the first to utilize the beauty of the empty street before Utrillo made it fashionable, though Utrillo supposedly used Atget's streets in his own canvases (and complained of their lack of perspective).

The Hours Press

An item of exceptional interest to New York bibliophiles is the Hours Press, just set up by Nancy Cunard in her country place, Puits-Carré, at Chapelle-Réanville, in the nearby Eure. The hand press is Belgian, eighteenth-century Elzevir type is used, and the book list includes only rare, modern, and new items, in limited editions signed by the authors. The first issue is a revised version of George Moore's *Peronnik the Fool,* to be followed by *The Eaten Heart,* by Richard Aldington; *One Day,* by Norman Douglas; *A Plaquette of Poems,* by Iris Tree; *Canto,* by Ezra Pound; and *La Chasse au Snark* (Carroll's famous *The*

Hunting of the Snark), translated into French by Louis Aragon.

Miss Cunard is one of England's best, if most infrequent, poets, and is a daughter of Lady Cunard, one of London's greatest American hostesses. With Wyndham Lewis of *Blast* fame and others of the early *Wheel* group, Miss Cunard has long been an intransigent hub of modern literary interests, has a small and severe collection of great modern paintings and an enormous collection of African art, is still beautiful, a tireless traveler, and a remarkable letter-writer.

Yussupoffs

CONTINUED

The noble Yussupoff family seems born for common hard luck. Since his arrival in France the present prince has already been identified with a losing lawsuit over some Rembrandts, with the bankruptcy of a dressmaking shop, with the murder of Rasputin, and with a subsequent small scandal that threatened deportation. He is now up to his ears again, but this time it is poison. It seems that his valet encouraged another valet to put scopolamine in the tea of the latter's masters and their guests, of whom the poor Yussupoff was occasionally one. The polite poisoning has been going on for months, according to the Comtesse de Larcinty-Tholozan, born Princess Demidoff and therefore kin to Yussupoff, whose hereditary hard luck the poor lady is now beginning to share. In interviews to the press, read by a delighted, incredulous countryside, the lady explains the state of gagaism which scopolamine produced on her noble family and all their tea-drinking friends—a state of complete stupidity which none of these aristocrats found strange. Memory vanished, general conversation lagged, the two children dropped behind in their studies and became unable to add two and two without exciting comment from their proud parents. Casual guests popping in for *le five-o'clock* were led back to their limousines in a state of complete imbecility; and an aunt, the Duchesse de Luynes ("born d'Uzès," the Comtesse interpolated for the benefit of a democratic public) fell flat on her face after having sipped a cup of weak Orange Pekoe ("which was abnormal for Her Grace"). And "broke her arm owing to her sudden inability to stand on one leg," the Comtesse added in a statement of sweeping lucidity. Also, the unfortunate Comte de Lareinty-Tholozan, who has been imbibing from the scopolamine bottle steadily since last November, "each day lost a little more sense," according to his admiring spouse. The hilarity among red-blooded mortals caused by these blue-blood disclosures has been as good as a revolution.

Marshal Foch (1851–1929)

The funeral of Marshal Foch, Commander-in-Chief of the Allied Armies in France during the last year of the war, was the greatest mourning event held in Paris since the nationalization of the death of Victor Hugo. Pasteur was given an official interment, but a less spectacular one than the semi-governmental cortege recently accorded the less important Anatole France. The French populace clings to poets and soldiers, when alive or dead, and instinctively buries them with the greatest tenderness and grief. As proof, among the signatures of princes and kings in the Foch visitors' book were interspersed the illiterate autographs of peasants who had left the plow idle in distant spring fields in order to pay their homage. "Come all the way specially from Sables-d'Olonne," one poor farmer scrawled after his name, thus signalizing his first and doubtless last trip to Paris. One working girl, after standing from dawn to noon in the queue before the Marshal's magnificent eighteenth-century mansion, was able to add after her name, "In memory of my papa, killed by the enemy in 1917," and went back to her factory. Clemenceau furnished the most touching remarks. One by one the Grand Old Man is burying his generation; on viewing Foch, he cried and said, "They are all going away and leaving me."

When the catafalque was exposed beneath the Arc de Triomphe, children who had been up all night in trains were held shoulder-high to view the bier. In the jam, orphan girls, tied to each other by a rope whose end was around the waist of an anxious nun, were pulled up and down the curb like Alpine climbers. Taxis and Rolls circled in an endless gyrating ring around the Étoile, whole families seated on the hoods. Seven thousand mourners an hour passed the bier. Before dusk, two million were packed for blocks in the side streets and helplessly broke the police barrage, thousands being swept past without seeing anything but their own fright. It was therefore under cover of darkness and before the stated hour that the late Marshal was removed to Notre-Dame, escorted by cavalry riding with lighted torches and demanding entry to the church with muffled trumpet calls.

The biggest, least glamorous, and most touching part of the funeral procession was the detachment of *anciens combattants*. By six o'clock they started forming in the Quai de Montebello —peaceful polite little men, wearing fabulous clusters of medals and derby hats slightly too small. By the time they were called into line, they stretched in a solid mass for half a mile. Over their heads hung a thick pall of cigarette smoke, like fumes from a small battle.

The ceremony in Notre-Dame, to which no woman outside of the Marshal's entourage was admitted, was of a musical splendor and pomp—drums were rolled and trumpets sounded in the choir for the Elevation. All the official costumes of the law courts, silver, gold, and scarlet toques and furs, ushers in silver buckles and chains, churchly vestments not seen since the Dissolution that separated the Catholic Church from the French State fifty years ago, were on view. In the street, in brilliance of coloring the only rivals to the Moorish Spahis and the Coldstream Guards, were the marching Cardinals of Paris and Rouen. It was the first time in half a century that such dignitaries have crossed the city on foot, their shoulders draped with their ermine palatines, their long scarlet trains held up by hatless gentlemen in evening clothes. They were a cynosure for all, and were, perhaps, the only section of the procession recognizable to the eyes and opera glasses of the millions who lined the distant roofs and windows along the line of march.

Since 1918 the war has not been so close as it was during the obsequies of Marshal Foch. Satisfaction was, however, much farther away. It was estimated that three million people saw the procession; but only a fraction could have done it comfortably, well, or even at all. The few tribunes were erected for official families only. Windows in the Rue de Rivoli rented at five thousand francs. A perch on a lamppost cost fifty. Men swarmed in trees, on roofs, and sat on chimney pots. For the most part women saw the Marshal's caisson by turning their backs to it and looking into mirrors held aloft. At his house and at the Cathedral, while thousands waited to pay homage, the lines were closed from twelve to two—in deference to that unflinching French luncheon, a tradition which apparently even death does not alter.

Jacques-Émile Blanche

The Hôtel Charpentier's exhibition of Jacques-Émile Blanche was prettily entitled by the master, "Mes Modèles; Images pour Illustrations de Mémoires, 1881–1929." The smartest artist of his day, who painted in and dined out only at the most fashionable houses, a technician who could paint something like Manet, something like Degas, and even something like himself, Blanche was negligible as a creator, but as a young-man-about-town and a society reporter he was a genius. His true vogue and social comprehension ended with 1914; his period thus coincided with Proust's, when the Champs-Élysées was the scene for the fashionable drive, Dieppe was all the go, and ladies in evening dress wore black feathers in their topknot. The originals of Odette and Swann were among the admirers of Blanche's works.

Those who sat to him presented a gallery no less real for being less literary: "Mrs. Lily Langtry at Dieppe"—"about 1855," the painter piously notes; "Head of Mrs. Cornwallis West"; "Mabel Dodge at the Villa Curonia—Florence, 1911, Epoch of Schéhérazade," he adds, to give Mrs. Dodge's costume its snobbish historicity. "Head of Mme. Letellier—hat by Virot," and so he rattles on, coming a cropper only in an "Imaginary Portrait of Virginia Woolf"—whom his imagination led him to believe looked like Queen Mary—and in a sketch of the famous Marquise de Casa Fuerte—where his signature had been cut off, as the catalogue states, by the jealous and malicious hand of his friend Comte Robert de Montesquiou, supposedly a model for Proust's Baron Charlus.

The *succès de scandale* of the show was, of course, the two portraits, one entitled "Profile" and the other "Apparition," of the Comtesse de Castiglione, beauty and mistress at the court of Napoleon III, which she left the night she discovered her first wrinkle. She lived on for thirty years in her mansion, where daylight was never allowed to enter, hiding herself in shadows and her face behind a black-spotted veil that became her legend. Blanche shows her late in life, an embittered old lady.

For those whose living, or even whose reading, took place in the Paris of before the war, the Blanche show has been an item of pleasure, malice, and psychological profit.

Diaghilev's Ballet

Diaghilev's Ballet has presented its annual trio of novelties and certain standbys at the Théâtre Sarah-Bernhardt. Among the intellectuals who justly acclaimed the ballet two decades ago—during the riots attendant upon the launching of iconoclasts like the *Sacre*—there has been of late, and perhaps equally justly, a tendency to sniff at the troupe. The Ballet is not what it was, but neither are the sniffers. In 1909 both the new art and its audiences were fresh to each other, a happy aesthetic circumstance which could not last forever. It is the passing of time which has weakened the authority of the Ballet—that and the later Stravinsky. For *Reynard*, his last contribution to the Ballet repertory, is not ballet music. This year's best bet, passing over *Le Bal* by Rieti as a pleasant enough piece, was *Le Fils Prodigue* by Prokofiev. The choreography was by Balanchine, and the décors by the famous Rouault resulted in sets of dark nondescript colors. It starred not only Lifar but the witty, graceful, brutal, burlesquing, intellectual legs of the Russian Ballet. Capable of psychology in their muscles as well as in their minds, the dancers, in their geometric contrapuntal routines, facetious pantomimes, deliberate juggling of grave and gay, annually make for a complex, good-natured entertainment mistakenly offered a public which solemnly yearns for what it used to call Modern Art. As a matter of fact, it is getting it.

o o o o o

As usual, critics ask why more new music is not presented. As usual, it may be because the music-makers are so badly paid. For his charming ballet of *La Chatte*, Sauguet, it is said, received five thousand francs from Diaghilev, less than a thousand from the publisher who edited the score, and royalties to the tune of ten per cent, or another seven to eight hundred francs, each time the score was danced in France. About seventy-five francs was paid when it was danced in England, where apparently there is no copyright protection for French musicians. The Russian Ballet is annually credited with losing money on its Paris venture, trying to make up at Monte Carlo and London what the Parisian season takes out of its blood. Diaghilev's expenses are, as his Ballet used to be, imperial; his is the largest private repertory troupe of any sort playing in Europe today. Five thousand francs for Sauguet's *Chatte* is doubtless as much as the master can afford. In this day of rich patrons, composers are still supposed to starve.

Little Review

The interment number of the famous *Little Review* has at last been published here; like any other mythical good American, this Middle-Western radical finally went to heaven in Paris. And not unsuitably. Of the many illustrious and now salable writers whom it was the first in America to print, if not to pay —Sherwood Anderson, Ernest Hemingway, James Joyce, Gertrude Stein, Glenway Wescott, etc.—the greater number today live in France. Picasso, Léger, Picabia, Juan Gris, Miró—all were introduced in the States by the *Little Review*, and all are residents of Paris. In a sense, then, the *Little Review*, though it had never been in Paris before, came to its home to die.

More than in America, it has left in Paris recognizable marks of its influence. *Exiles*, Ford Madox Ford's excellently edited *Transatlantic Review*, and now *transition*, all similar periodicals, at least in their international scope, have found their unique field in France. Of the younger American writers to be translated into French, the better part have been from the *Little Review's* original list.

Perhaps the greatest difference between its native and foreign epitaphs is that here the *Review* is still granted full credit for all its discoveries. This has been particularly apparent in the widespread comment on the recent French translation of Joyce's

Ulysses (published by Adrienne Monnier's admirable Maison des Amis des Livres).

In the light of the memorable police-court reception given the book in New York, it is worthy of note that the leading French literary organs reviewed it as if it were a book and not a misdemeanor. No outcry has been heard except one of astonishment at the labors of the translators, Morel and Larbaud; five years having been consumed. Of all the appreciations, only the stodgy *Revue de Paris* sounded a warning cough. After cerebrally connecting *Ulysses* with the stained-glass windows in the cathedral at Bourges, then with Huysmans, then with Voltaire, it goes on to remark that *Work in Progress,* Joyce's latest manuscript, is "so difficult in style that even the most literate English fail to comprehend it. . . . Let Monsieur Joyce beware lest he become the prey of isolated commentators who fatten on high and heady dishes which even they have not properly digested."

Napoleon's Table

The French have just gained a precedent and an important legal victory in the Franco-American skirmish for French antiques that has been raging in auction rooms here since the war. The terms of the triumph have been announced by the Musée de Malmaison, where all major Napoleonic relics except the ten thousand beds he was supposed to have slept in (one for every village in France) are rightfully made national deposits. The fight centered around the famous Sèvres Marshal's Table, made at Napoleon's command after he became Emperor, and which, via the recent dissolution of Prince de la Moskova's collection, passed to the auction rooms. There Sir Joseph Duveen gobbled it up at four hundred thousand francs for "an American client."

When the client was found to be *"Monsieur Guillaume Hearst, trusteur de journaux américains,"* the national dissatisfaction became acute. Fortunately, the curator of Malmaison at that moment dug up the Law of the Thirty-first of December; "which law," he admitted, "has been for a long time forgotten" —so long that it is not clear on which December 31, usually part of the New Year holidays, the French lawmakers might have been sitting and passing laws about antiques. However, passed it was, with the statute book to prove it, reading that "right of pre-emption is given the State and authority to substitute itself as adjudicator of an object which is part of the historic patrimony of France."

All this provided, of course, that the State could put up the price which M. Hearst could afford for the bit of historic patrimony. The State (or Malmaison) unfortunately couldn't; at which point Mr. Edward Tuck interfered. In order to prevent the rich American Mr. Hearst from having the Marshal's Table, the rich American Mr. Tuck, known and beloved here for his many princely restorations to France of her own property, paid the price. The table, as is fitting, has just been interned in Malmaison. The comedy was without errors.

The table itself, now on view, is in flawless condition and was worth the fight. It took four years (1806–1810) to make, is of porcelain and *biscuit* with bronze, and shows the Emperor in coronation robes, encircled by his thirteen favorite marshals.

The number thirteen was inauspicious. After Elba, Berthier, Prince de Neuchâtel and son of a concierge, leaped from a window to evade his enemies and was killed on the cobblestones below. Duroc, Duc de Friuli, disemboweled on a battlefield, took a day to die, promising to meet his Emperor in eternity. After his party's fall, Marmont, Duc de Raguse, raised merino sheep, which he herded in military formations with sheep corporals and captains. The belligerent fantasy ruined him; he died in poverty. Murat, son of an innkeeper and brother-in-law to the Emperor, was first made King of Naples, then condemned to death and shot. Mortier, Duc de Trévise, receiving a bomb meant for Louis-Philippe, died on the billiard table of a Paris café. Only Ney, whom his Emperor called "the Bravest of the Brave," died nobly, though also in disgrace. To soldiers reading him his list of titles when he was condemned to death, he said, "Why don't you say simply Michel Ney, once a French soldier and soon to be dust?" One of his titles was Prince de la Moskova. It was through Marshal Ney's family, as well as the generosity of Mr. Tuck, that the Marshal's Table is restored to all of France.

Princess Bibesco

Likely to excite the attention of American translators is *Tour d'Égypte,* by the Princess Bibesco, already beloved by American bookworms for her *Catherine-Paris* and *Le Perroquet Vert.*

So far as the French are concerned, Egypt was discovered by Napoleon: as a result of his campaign, sarcophagi first settled in the Louvre, and the Sphinx entered the Empire drawing room as a mantelpiece decoration. Princess Bibesco's discovery of the Delta, however, will have less far-reaching effects. Regarded as the most intelligent woman in France, in this book she unfortunately proves that she is. The volume is her too-logical Q.E.D. By the rectangle of its pages one deduces that the Princess, the desert, the Nile, and a certain amount of literary local color sat up all night together in the Princess's room (probably at Shepheard's Hotel) while the Princess measured off a certain number of right-angled witticisms and drew cerebral conclusions in which nothing, unhappily, was left to her imagination.

Georges Clemenceau (1841–1929)

Georges Clemenceau, twice Premier of France and chief antagonist of Woodrow Wilson during the Paris Peace Conference, was considered the greatest Jacobin and fighter of his time. Known as the Tiger, he fought everybody, including his government, until he was near to his ninetieth year; died poor; and asked to be buried standing upright. The position suited him. Even his enemies never questioned his probity and by his friends it was known he never lay down before events; he even attempted not to lie down for the last event of his life. Forced to bed, finally, he still kept his clothes on.

He was a lifelong member of any opposition and defender of all lost causes. After the fall of the Commune, he fought for the Communists' pardon, he fought for revision in the famous Dreyfus Case, he fought for Zola during his infamous *procès,* he fought for Impressionist art and posed to Manet for his portrait when posing to that painter was still a brave deed. In 1917 he fought the French Defeatists with one of the most terrifying battle cries ever hallooed over Europe: "*Je fais la guerre, je fais la guerre, je fais la guerre.*" He fought for the morale of the tired soldiers by trudging the front line and addressing anyone less than a general as "*mon enfant.*" As the French now know, he made a good war and a bad peace; but so great was his godhead after the armistice that it cost *Le Matin* half its circulation when it prophetically pointed out the fact.

French men of state are rarely ballad writers, ex-saloonkeepers, or reformed ward heelers, as in the States. Clemenceau, by profession a doctor, wrote a book on *The Generation of Atomic Elements,* taught school to Americans somewhere in Connecticut, wrote a novel entitled *Les Plus Forts,* an essay on philosophy called *Au Soir de Ma Pensée,* a one-act play produced as *Le Voile du Bonheur,* and was a member of the Academy.

He was buried without benefit of clergy. All his life he thought coldly and believed hotly. As he said, "The greatest sin of the soul is to lack warmth."

Les Enfants Terribles

Jean Cocteau's *Les Enfants Terribles* is a truly terrible and touching tale of immaturity ripe only in its disorder, its suicides, and its sadness. The book is a *roman à clef,* the brother and sister who serve for its plot being as well known in certain circles in Paris as they are easily identified.°

Cocteau has always been a writer in the tradition of the great medieval mountebanks who worked with the charlatans of the Pont Neuf: as tightrope walker he gathers his crowd, and as soothsayer-dentist he pulls teeth and illusions, he dazzles and delights, and sells moon-powder guaranteed to cure any human ill—and truly cheap at the price. In his latest book, perhaps more than in any since *Thomas l'Imposteur,* he is less interested in prestidigitation than in persons; he is more human and hu-

---

° Jean and Jeanne Bourgoint, a tragic pair. Jean was a lover of Cocteau, who introduced him to drugs. He later entered a seminary and became a Trappist monk. Jeanne contracted gonorrhea on her wedding night and soon after committed suicide.

mane. Youth—a subject utterly unknown, despite its having been successfully endured by all mortals who live to tell the tale —gave him a strange land for *Les Enfants Terribles* perfectly to his own liking, a horizon on which anything may happen (and in his book usually does), a little desert of subtle suffering dotted with stiff events and cactus-like descriptions.

Sergei Diaghilev (1872–1929)

Genius is a talent only for living; those who possess it have little gift for dying. Diaghilev's recent demise has furnished a new and sadder version of *Death in Venice*. His famous Russian Ballet would soon have been twenty-five years old, a remarkable antiquity for a theory and practice so dependent upon youth. Mimes, musicians, and manners by becoming part of his troupe became part of his twentieth-century aesthetic movement —one which in many ways was as influential as the new school of painting, but which unfortunately left nothing but memories as its masterpieces. Memories do not pay. Of its great originals —Mordkin, Bakst, Pavlova, Nijinsky, Stravinsky, among others —Diaghilev was the only one who persisted in following the initial imperial tradition; the others quietly became middle-aged, went mad, grew addicted to perpetual farewell tours, or died. Therefore, the recent coffers of the Ballet that altered stage décors in England, France, and America, and left a new rich heritage of color and form to a generation that originally wished for neither, were often empty. According to report, Diaghilev had only two thousand lire to his name at the beginning of his last illness and hoped by dying quickly to die within his means; but bills to Venetian chemists and hotelkeepers left him a posthumous pauper. It is said he was buried through the generosity of his friend Gabrielle Chanel, the famous and loyal dressmaker.

Wall Street Crash

The Wall Street crash has had its effect here. In the Rue de la Paix the jewelers are reported to be losing fortunes in sudden cancellations of orders, and at the Ritz bar the pretty ladies are having to pay for their cocktails themselves. In the Quartier de l'Europe, little firms that live exclusively on the American trade have not sold one faked Chanel copy in a fortnight. A wholesale *antiquaire* in the Boulevard Raspail has a cellar bulging with guaranteed Louis XIV candlesticks which are not moving. In the Rue La Boëtie a thrifty young Frenchwoman, who as a Christmas gift bought herself a majority of stock in the art gallery where she works, finds that all the forty-nine blue Dufys are still hanging on the wall and that it is not likely her stock will pay a dividend. In real-estate circles certain advertisements have been illuminating: "For Sale, Cheap, Nice Old Château, 1 Hr. frm Paris; Original Boiserie, 6 New Baths; Owner Forced Return New York Wednesday; Must Have IMMEDIATE CASH; Will Sacrifice."

Generally, the French people's sympathy in our disaster has been polite and astonishingly sincere, considering that for the past ten years they have seen us through one of the worst phases of our prosperity—which consisted of thousands of our tourists informing them that we were the richest country in the world, that they should pay their debts, that we had made the world safe for democracy, that we were the most generous people in the world, that they should pay their debts, and that we were the richest country in the world. Only in a few malicious French quarters has it been suggested that now certain small American investors can afford to paste Wall Street stocks on their suitcases or toss them to the crowd, as they pasted and tossed five-franc notes here that marvelous summer when the franc fell to fifty.

1930

Gaby Deslys (1884–1920)

The government is continuing its efforts to find out whether Gaby Deslys was Marie-Élise-Gabrielle Caire of Marseille or Hedwige Navratil of Hatvan in Hungary. If the latter was the case, she was one of three Hedwige Navratils, as it seems there were a couple of others, one of whom has just turned up in the Paris courts. The fight, of course, is for money; Gaby Deslys left a fortune of nine million francs, a quarter of which went automatically to her family, the Caires; a quarter-million unautomatically to the American dancer Harry Pilcer; and the rest to the poor and tubercular of Marseilles. The Navratils now say the Caires were not her family; neither Pilcer nor the poor of Marseilles know what to think, and the government gets nowhere.

Gaby Deslys's star ascended in 1904; she was a gay brunette whose voice, as the French say, was full of "yes." She starred at the Folies-Bergère, at the Olympia, and introduced American dancing here on the arm of Harry Pilcer. She had a pavilion in the Rue Villebois-Mareuil, a private *hôtel* in the Rue de Bornier, and a magnificent London establishment in Kensington, where the bed lay on a dais beneath an arch of black marble supported by marble pillars. She refused to marry the Duc de Crussol, stating that no man was rich enough to buy her liberty. She died imploring the doctors to disfigure her beauty if necessary but to leave her her life.

The Ambassadeurs

The Ambassadeurs is being razed; by the time its old, overhanging chestnut trees are in bloom, nor stick nor stone will be left of the famous old Champs-Élysées *café-concert*. Its site was occupied as early as 1764 by a humble pub of the same name; in

1824, rebuilt, it became more pretentious with the addition of a merry-go-round; in 1840, again in new form, it became almost elegant, owing to the Champs-Élysées being lighted by that newfangled stuff called gas. Then a small stage was added and the Ambassadeurs' popular *café-chantant* was born. The next year the modest boards made way for the charming rococo edifice of our day, which was a center of fashion during the Second Empire and a center of singing from the end of the war of 1870 to the beginning of the war of 1914. During this long epoch the Ambassadeurs' galaxy of songsters included Fagette, whose bolero jacket was embroidered with real diamonds; Yvette Guilbert, noted for her Chat Noir black gloves and Montmartre artists (Toulouse-Lautrec made her posters for her); Mayol, of the Concert still bearing his name; an eccentric named Mistinguett, who sang about *apaches;* and a talented youngster, with a new way of wearing his straw hat, called Maurice Chevalier. After the war, when the Gallic tradition of entertainment weakened and Harlem and jazz were what Paris preferred, Florence Mills and her *Blackbirds* and Cole Porter's first musical show, which included Gershwin at the piano in the first Paris audition of the "Rhapsody in Blue," both had their French premières in the hall where, in his heyday, Offenbach had been enthusiastically hummed.

Four times in less than two hundred years the Ambassadeurs has been razed to the ground only to rise again more grand. Nor will it now fail to continue in its fine phoenix tradition; the new Ambassadeurs, which will open under the chestnut blooms of a year from now, will comprise not one theater, as in times past, but two. The first will consist of seats and stage only, in the modern manner; the second will have the champagne tables and *petite scène* of the good old classic days.

D. H. Lawrence (1885–1930)

The death of D. H. Lawrence cuts short the actively influential position he was beginning to assume in the estimation of France's leading literary lights. Exiled by his malady from the fogs of his native land, he spent the better part of his maturity in Continental towns. He was one of the first of what later became a large colony of Britons in Taormina. He lived for a time in Florence, where his *Aaron's Rod* was considered a portrait gallery of his local friends, Norman Douglas and Reginald Turner among others. He was a brilliant talker but, despite his years of living among foreigners, no exceptional linguist. Ill most of his life, he by degrees developed the erratic psychology of the brilliant invalid to whom, living among natives in out-of-the-way corners, anything was permitted. He had, among other eccentricities, a fancy for removing his clothes and climbing mulberry trees.

At the last he also suffered actively from persecution mania; he thought Jung had stolen his theories of psychoanalysis from a reading of the earlier Lawrence works; he thought his writer friends stole his ideas. Owing to the peculiar quality of his later novels, he was constantly accusing printers everywhere, usually with justice, of stealing and pirating his works. A cheap edition of his much discussed *Lady Chatterley's Lover* had, just before his death, been brought out by him in Paris for the express purpose, so his preface stated, of justifiably allowing him to reap some meager royalties and, less justifiably, of permitting the book, because of its low price, to be within easy reach of every young boy and girl. The last work of Lawrence to be translated into French consisted of excerpts from his Mexican novel, its title, unfortunately, being construed as *Serpent Dépouillé*. Thus as *The Plucked Serpent, The Plumed Serpent* enters, with the author's death, into the lexicon of French letters.

Ballet Décor

The new Galerie de France in the Rue de l'Abbaye has just held an art exposition as full of melancholy as a first-class funeral. By exhuming the *maquettes* for the costumes and décors of the great ballet seasons and galas which were Paris's high point and high pleasure in the springs of the early 1920s, a form of theatrical life is recalled which any mourning critic admits is definitely defunct, but whose mummy, embalmed by memory, is still livelier than anything that has appeared since to take its place.

The list of artists whose sketches make up the show and bring a tear to the eye includes, among others, Bakst, Braque, Chirico, Juan Gris, Jean Victor-Hugo, Per Krogh, Marie Laurencin, Laprade, Fernand Léger, Picasso, Rouault, Steinlen, and Touchagues—masters, for the most part, whose paintings now sell for thousands of francs an inch. The spectacles for which they once made vast curtains and voluminous clothes, and whose premières were as exciting as election nights, included all of everything that was danced in the great Continental days by the Swedish and Russian Ballets, all that was played during the hectic spring nights of the galas at the Cigale, the Atelier, at the Soirées de Paris. From those brief seasons when the greatest artists of Europe were scene-painters for the brightest theatrical flush Paris has known since the operatic ball days of Gavarni, little is left except these sketches in the Galerie de France's show. What remains of the Swedish Ballet sets is in the collection of Rolf de Maré; what is left of the Russian Ballet's fabulous curtains seems unequally divided among the Comte Étienne de Beaumont's salon, public auction rooms, and theatrical storage rooms where the mice eat what is otherwise held for debt. Two of the booths for *Petrouchka*, though of considerable size, have long since been casually lost; Picasso's big bull-ring painting for *Le Tricorne* (the only theatrical décor entirely from his own hand) was recently divided into small pieces and sold for big sums. Of the greatest theatrical push Paris has known for a hundred years, nothing remains in the way of documentation but memory and *maquettes. Sunt lacrimae rerum.*

Yvonne George (1897–1930)

It is given to few people to be posthumous the greater part of their lives. The first erroneous report of Yvonne George's demise, because of which she was mourned by her literary friends in exquisite prose, was not so much a false rumor as a characterization. Yvonne George, in her active days, was *une grande malheureuse.* Her songs, her voice, her long sleeves, her lovely mouth, even her talent were tokens of grief. The brilliant galaxy called *les jeunes* fought for her with the loyalty of old men used to lost causes. Cocteau, Jean Richepin, Simon Gantillon were her allies and wrote her legend in talk over bars, on nocturnal

promenades, at matinal levees of which nothing now remains
but their memory. She was ephemeral. She could magnetize
only small groups; before the great audiences of the Palace, the
Olympia, and the bigger music halls, she failed—usually magnificently. She lacked the lion-tamer's quality which marks big
artists. She was unpopular with the masses, who were uncowed
by such slight perfection as was hers. Her forte was marine
songs; she sang of sailing ships, which her tenderness reduced to
the size of the little barks retired sailors imprison in bottles.

Fancy-Dress Balls

The June season of 1930 will be remembered as the greatest
fancy-dress-ball season of all years; masquerades were given
which in other centuries might have made their way into memoirs but which will now probably only land in light literature.
In Paris, where entertaining has long been an art—and was, as
much as war or wit, one of the civilizing French forces in
Europe—parties have always been taken seriously, even by
those who weren't invited. Those the Duc de Saint-Simon went
to a few hundred years ago filled twelve volumes; while the Pil-
grims were still settling on Plymouth Rock, the Duc was step-
ping it at Marly or Versailles, in châteaux where each room
was specially decorated for the night—one for maskers, one for
musicians, one for actors, and so on—through which the hostess
moved "with a politeness, a gallantry and liberty as if she had
naught to do with it all. One diverted one's-self extremely nor
did one leave till after eight in the morning."

The parties just given in Paris were not so ultra-modern as
Saint-Simon's, nor so elegantly *démodé* as those for which Boni
de Castellane rented the entire Bois de Boulogne to receive his
guests, and Paul Poiret, the other fabulous prewar host, dressed
an actor in seed pearls, served a thousand liters of champagne,
and three hundred hen lobsters, to divert his friends at his great
"Arabian Nights" fete. The 1930 Parisian parties, however, by
being unusually frequent, fantastic, and mostly foreign, were remarkable for representing the true spirit of their time.

One of the largest masquerades was given by Miss Elsa Maxwell and the Honorable Mrs. Reginald Fellowes, to which

everyone was bidden to come dressed like someone everybody else knew—at least by sight; Miss Maxwell, for example, going as M. Briand and Mrs. Reginald Fellowes as a *préposée du vestiaire*. Jean Frank went as the Comtesse Charles de Noailles; Stanislas de La Rochefoucauld as Mme. Marthe Letellier, the famous beauty; and Chanel did a land-office business generally, cutting and fitting gowns for young men about town who appeared as some of the best-known women in Paris.

Probably the most ethereal and beautiful of all was the White Ball, given by Mr. and Mrs. Pecci-Blunt. (Mrs. Pecci-Blunt is the niece of the late Pope Leo XIII.) At the White Ball guests fancy-dressed or not; they merely had to wear something white. The most acclaimed entree was made in fabulous white-plaster masks and wigs concocted by Jean Cocteau and Christian Bérard.

A third party, in exquisite settings, was given by the Caen d'Anvers in his country place at Champ. According to legend this château, which belonged to the Pompadour, fell by loot to the lot of the Revolutionary drummer who beat for the heads to fall from the guillotine. Being popular, he was able to prevent his new property from being pillaged, so it has remained intact, supposedly the only perfectly furnished courtesan's house of the epoch.

A further feature of June was a series of formal balls given in turn by various Rothschilds—the Barons Eugène, Maurice, Robert, and Henri—which might have led to the season's being called Rothschild Week had not Catholic Paris more ironically referred to it as *la Semaine Sainte*.

Another important and exquisite masquerade was given by the artist Drian at his country mill, the subject being Louis XV shepherds and shepherdesses, a dainty group enlivened by the appearance of a lone but witty wolf in black pajamas, as sheep's clothing.

The second party inspired by Miss Elsa Maxwell was that of Señor and Señora Alvaro Guevara, the former Meraud Guinness. It was an As-You-Were-When-the-Autobus-Called party, owing to the fact that the guests, warned that a charabanc would call for them at no specified hour, were to come in whatever attire was theirs when the chauffeur tooted his horn. Cocktails were served in the charabancs to the guests outside waiting for the guests inside to finish being as they were when the chauffeur tooted his horn. Another unusual item about the party was that the moment the assembled guests reached the studio in Rue Notre-Dame-des-Champs, the electric lights blew out.

Among the artfully unfinished costumes was that of one guest who had exactly one side of her face made up, a gentleman clad in shaving soap and a hotel towel, and several ladies in half-fastened skirts. The Rue Notre-Dame-des-Champs, accustomed both to the Café du Dôme and the Grande Chaumière, the great life-class atelier of Montparnasse, is still discussing the charabanc party.

Perhaps one of the most agreeable parties, from the viewpoint of the guests, was that of the Duchesse de Clermont-Tonnerre, since it was given in the old-fashioned manner—primarily to amuse the hostess. It was also unusual in the recent round of Parisian parties in that it was given by a Frenchwoman and featured only good food and good friends. Among the latter were Miss Dolly Wilde in the habiliments of her uncle, Oscar Wilde, and looking both important and earnest; Miss Natalie Barney, the *amazone* of Remy de Gourmont's letters, as a *femme de lettres;* and the Princesse Violette Murat, who led in a Harlem wedding party as mother of the bride.

The most calculatedly dazzling of the soirees was given by the dressmaker Jean Patou, the guests being largely Italian, British, and American, and the decorations silver. To obtain the desired effect, the garden was roofed over, and not only were the walls and low ceiling laid with silver foil but also as much of the trees as was left visible, trunks, branches, even the twigs being wrapped in silver paper; and from the metaled boughs hung silver cages, as tall as a man, harboring overstuffed parrots as large as a child. One of the attractions was the Whispering Baritone, Jack Smith, who swept out after vainly whispering against the noise of illuminated fountains, electric ventilators, and friendly guests seated, as at a night club, at different tables.

The second attraction was three small lion cubs, led in by lion-tamers in flowered shirts and imposing breeches; the cubs were then given as grab-bag prizes to guests who, as the story says, may not have wanted but drew them.

On lions, wolves, shepherdesses, and charabancs the Paris season thus formally closes. Everyone is now supposed to leave town. Of the city's three million inhabitants, several thousand probably will.

Sido

The reception accorded *Sido*, Colette's new book, has been exceptional even for a writer to whom exceptional receptions have become a commonplace. Once again and at greater length than usual she has been hailed for her genius, humanities, and perfect prose by those literary journals which years ago (when hailing any one of these three would have encouraged a young provincial writer) lifted nothing at all in her direction except the finger of scorn. *Sido* follows in the high terrestrial tradition of *La Naissance du Jour* and *Les Vrilles de la Vigne*. It is enemy to all urban novels, has no plot, and yet tells of three lives all that should be known; it is, indeed, merely a fertile furrow plowed through the writer's past and turning up her progenitors, their habits, hats, horses, and souls—the little cosmos they swung among, living and loving on the land.

France is familiar with Mme. Colette's family, fed to them through the years in different books and under different names. Her calm father-who-fed-snails in *Claudine à l'École* becomes, in *Sido*, her fiery father-who-was-a-captain. But it is in the titular tutelary Sido, her mother, that Colette has excelled to such an extent that she should never dare use the face or figure again, this time finally exhausted by too much perfection. For Sido is the dominant, earthy individual, half Hera, who "senses the changes in the weather by her antennae"; who, like a weather-vane, calls her two neighbors mere East or West; who, the mother of many, blushes at seeing a bride of four days: in short, a personage on whom "every vegetal presence acted as an anti-dote and who had an odd way of lifting roses by their chins to look them full in the face."

French literature is peculiarly devoid of nature—indeed, there is hardly a tree in the whole lot of it; and to the French, despite their instinct to appreciate him, Hardy reads rather like pages from a seed catalogue. In their fine letters Colette is the first dendrophile they have possessed, the first writer to give them news of nature; she has the strangeness of a traveler who tells of an unknown land.

The Well of Loneliness (Drama of)

The frost is not on the pumpkin and the fodder (because of the wet weather) is still far from the shock, yet even at this early date it may be that the real harvest of the winter theatrical season has already been gleaned. For the première of the stage version of Miss Radclyffe Hall's *The Well of Loneliness* has been given in American at the Théâtre de La Potinière, and it seems unlikely that anything faintly equaling it can break ground before spring.

The first night was something of a riot, owing to the pacific timidity of the ushers in making large ladies sit in the right seats and the belligerent broad-mindedness of the large ladies toward everything except the ushers. Also, to top three acts of *tableaux vivants*, containing eleven scenes, Miss Wilette Kershaw made a curtain speech in which she begged humanity, "already used to earthquakes and murderers," to try to put up with a minor calamity like the play's and the book's Lesbian protagonist, Stephen Gordon. However, she made up in costume what she lacked in psychology: dressing gown by Sulka, riding breeches by Hoare, boots by Bunting, crop by Briggs, briquet by Dunhill, and British accent—as the program did not bother to state—by Broadway.

For several seasons Miss Kershaw has been kindly supplying her compatriots here with what she advertised as banned plays (principally *Maya*), with the Radclyffe Hall opus repeatedly dangled as "coming soon." Miss Radclyffe Hall's press statement that she knew nothing about the adaptation of her novel, and as soon as she did would go to law, made the public fear that her —well, loneliness was greater than had been supposed.

Morisot-Manet

By what amounted to an unnecessary and droll bit of bribery, the Louvre has just become the richer by two Impressionist gems of the first water. It is to be supposed that the museum would gratefully have welcomed Berthe Morisot's canvas "Le Berceau," on no matter what terms her daughter offered it; but when her daughter, adding that she was also Manet's niece, said she would throw in Manet's marvelous "Dame aux Éventails" to boot, if the directors would only deign to accept her mother's masterpiece, the Louvre probably could hardly believe its ears. The "Dame aux Éventails" is particularly precious to Paris since it is a portrait of a local lady of the Impressionist eighties, one Nina de Villard, recalled by George Moore in a chapter of his young-manly confessions, and a great patroness of rude young blades, such as Batignolles painters, Irish idlers, and others, by whom she finally, poor thing, became immortal.

Josephine Baker

If you can get away for a day or so, it might be a good plan to fly to Paris and spend the evening at Josephine Baker's new Casino show. You would have plenty to think about on the return trip, for the revue contains something of everything, including Pierre Meyer, and practically no feathers and furs. It is, as much as the Folies' show, one of the best in years, is as full of staircases as a Freudian dream, has excellent imported British dancing choruses of both sexes, a complete Russian ballet, trained pigeons, a live cheetah, roller-skaters, the prettiest Venetian set of the century, a marvelous first-act finale, acres of fine costumes, the four best cancan dancers in captivity, a thriller in which Miss Baker is rescued from a typhoon by a gorilla, and an aerial ballet of heavy Italian ladies caroming about on wires. The show even contains long glimpses of the beautiful Baker—longer, certainly, than when she appeared as a headliner at the Folies five years ago, but all too brief compared with the hard-working tradition of the Casino set by her venerable predecessor, Mistinguett.

Perhaps, however, enough is seen of Miss Baker in the present instance, for she has, alas, almost become a little lady. Her caramel-colored body, which overnight became a legend in Europe, is still magnificent, but it has become thinned, trained, almost civilized. Her voice, especially in the vo-deo-do's, is still a magic flute that hasn't yet heard of Mozart—though even that, one fears, will come with time. There is a rumor that she wants to sing refined ballads; one is surprised that she doesn't want to play Othello. On that lovely animal visage lies now a sad look, not of captivity, but of dawning intelligence.

At the Casino, beautifully costumed, staged, chorused, in a fair way to becoming what is called an artiste, she is far from that unknown chorus girl, selected by Miguel Covarrubias, who a few summers ago made her Paris debut carried in upside down, *à poil*, and doing the split. She is far from the banana-belt costume that made her the idol of Berlin, Barcelona, Budapest—but she is not far from being the Casino's dream girl. Mistinguett can now, though we hope she won't, take things easy during her late sixties. For in Miss Baker the French revue has apparently finally found its new star.

Barbette

Barbette, who performs his high wire and trapeze stunts dressed in female attire, has opened at the Cirque Médrano. In honor of this pretty young Texan (whose real name, we understand, is Mr. Vander Clyde) there assembled at the ringside a *tout Paris* audience such as formerly gave color to the Cigale and *chic* to the Diaghilev Ballet. For his triumphal entry in his first scene (and certainly on the first white carpet and to the first *Schéhérazade* music that the Médrano had ever known) he wore, besides his diaphanous white skirts, fifty pounds of white ostrich plumes. Before and after his fabulous *chute d'ange* fall, which against the blue background of the Médrano took on the mythical quality of a new Phaethon deserting the sky, his dressing room was filled with what Lone Stars would term the *crème de la crème*. It only remained for Barbette to call forth from a leading literary journal the comparison, "He is, apparently, like Wagner, of whom it was said, 'He was only himself when dressed as a woman.'"

Well, remember the Alamo.

1931

Marshal Joffre (1852–1931)

Of the great military leaders of the world war, Marshal Joffre was one of the first to be born and the last to die. He had out-lived saving the Marne, outlived being disgraced, outlived Foch, who was made generalissimo over his head; he had outlived his old enemy Clemenceau. Though his more appreciative oppo-nent, von Kluck, said that had France been a monarchy, it must have made Joffre Duc de la Marne, France almost failed to in-vite him to take part in the grand Champs-Élysées Victory Pa-rade at the end of the war. To the embarrassed envoy from Cle-menceau who bore the tardy invitation and protests that, what with one thing and another, the committee had been so busy, etc., the old Martian made the only ironic comment of his ca-reer: "No apologies, dear sir; there are moments when one can't think of everybody!"

Joffre's father was of Spanish ancestry (the name was origi-nally Goffre). Joffre himself was one of eleven poor children, as a boy spoke Catalan, and in consequence as a man spoke French with a strong border accent. When still a stripling he was commissioned second lieutenant in time to take part in the defense of Paris in the War of 1870; in the late nineties he re-ceived his lieutenant-colonel's stripes for planting the French flag in Timbuktu. He was elected a member of the Académie Française in 1918 and, although he made no speeches, always turned up on dictionary days when military terms were to be defined.

Like many Catalans, Joffre was taciturn, unimaginative, a good feeder (very fond of his native goose liver), and originally an avowed Freemason and nonchurchman. On a Good Friday during the war his commissariat served him a lean, pious meal. "I'm a good republican," the old Marshal roared, *"et je mange gras, t'entends?"* He got his goose liver, a special supply of which followed him all over France.

By his request he was buried with full benefit of clergy. For now it appears that of recent years he had entered the Episcopal fold. His wife being a divorcee, their marriage had only been civil, but at the end of their long life together he had it blessed and died in the Church's arms. It is stated that faith first came to him after the Armistice. "After all, there must be a God," he said solemnly, "for we have triumphed."

The Strange Death of President Harding

Those Americans in Paris who last year failed to borrow a copy of *The Strange Death of President Harding*° may now peruse it, stranger than ever, as *La Mort Étrange du Président Harding* in *Les Annales*, a fortnightly ordinarily given over to politics and aesthetics, among which the Means recital comes as a great novelty. Nor does the novelty stop there; refined by the nobility of the French phrase, the Department of Justice investigator's nuggety style takes on the gleam of glib gold, and the conversations between M. Means and la Première Dame du Pays rise to the passionate purity of the Comédie-Française. "At any other epoch," declaims Mme. Harding, darkly referring to Mlle. Britton ("that demoniacal seductress"), "I could have purchased a *lettre de cachet*. That would have been the best solution." "And certain it is," reflects Means in one of his unexpectedly historical asides, "that had America possessed a Bastille ready pitilessly to make mortals disappear, Nan would have had a place." However, it is in speaking of her spouse that Mme. Harding puts over some of the best lines: "From the day that I entered the Maison Blanche, this thing has weighed upon my bosom like the rock of Sisyphus. I must be freed. The prophetic words come constantly to my mind: of us two the President will

° By Gaston B. Means "from his diaries, as told to May Dixon Thacker." It purported to be the inside story of the corrupt Harding administration (1921–1923). Means, a convicted perjurer, published these revelations after he had served his prison term. The book contained hints that Mrs. Harding had poisoned her husband, presumably because of his affair with Nan Britton. Miss Britton, also contributing her historical footnote, wrote a book called *The President's Daughter*, in which she claimed Harding as the father of her illegitimate child.

die first! This verdict is ineluctable. I am a Child of Destiny, and forget not, Monsieur Gaston Means, that from this day, this moment, I commence to accomplish my destiny." "God in heaven," mutters Means, apparently frightened into piety and Romanticism at the same time, "what devilish history does this combination reserve for us?"

Chanel in Hollywood

As a further ripple in the wave of *bon marché* that is sweeping through Paris, it was authoritatively announced by Mlle. Chanel that she is going to Hollywood to work for Mr. Goldwyn. This is the first time a *couturière* of such importance, or indeed any, has left the native heath. Considering what universal style-setting means to Paris for the maintenance of its financial and artistic pulse, the departure of Chanel for California must be more important than that of Van Dyck for the English Court of Charles I. But in a hundred years, the results will probably photograph less well.

Georges Simenon

The *Nouvelle Revue Française*, which ordinarily expends its strength publishing rhymes by Paul Valéry, essays by André Gide, and similar intellectual fare, has taken an option on crime. The popular detective story, originally nurtured here by Gaboriau, Gaston Leroux, and Maurice Leblanc, has suddenly developed a new local vogue and a new writer: M. Georges Sim, who at the age of twenty-eight has already written two hundred and eighty yarns. He is of Breton Dutch stock, is handsome, can write an excellent book in four days (one was started in a glass cage, for publicity's sake), lives on a yacht in canals, and has used sixteen pseudonyms, of which Simenon (the signature of the latest dozen of his books) will probably become permanent. To turn out mystery stories as novel as *Monsieur Gallet Décédé, Le Chien Jaune*, and *Le Charretier de la Providence* once a year is rare; to turn them out at the rate of four a month is rarer.

Simenon's detective is stout and named Maigret; the crimes he solves are published monthly, are the talk of the town, and sell for six francs. The stories are distinguished by a talent for suspense, begin better than they end, and contain in each case a crime curiously suitable to the geographic setting: Antwerp for *Le Pendu de Saint-Pholien*, and the Brittany town and inhabitants of Concarneau for *Le Chien Jaune*, so realistically undisguised that Simenon will probably be sued. And after his *Crime en Hollande*, it is unlikely that he can ever steam back to the Netherlands again.

However, according to his admirers, he never goes any place twice anyway. He always travels (always on his boat, and always on canals), hates heat and wants to go to Tahiti, and spends half a million francs of his royalties a year doing what his year's characters do: hiring a liveried chauffeur because his villain does, losing two hundred thousand francs at Monte Carlo because his hero must. For he says, "I have no imagination; I take everything from life" (and from the exploits of certain of his acquaintances, who apparently include some of the liveliest crooks in France). "I get up at half-past five; go on deck; start typing at six, with either a bottle of brandy or white wine at my side; and write a chapter an hour until noon, when I go on land and lie down in the grass, exhausted. My ambition is to arrive little by little in the class of a Jack London, or—who knows?—even of a Conrad." Monsieur Simenon is mistaken; he is already in a class by himself.

Crime (*a la* Cayenne)

Within the past year or so France has enjoyed peculiarly picturesque homicides and trials. Yet the stories of Mestorino, the murderous jeweler; of Barataud, the charming man from Limoges; of Rigaudin, unfortunate inert occupant of a trunk, all seem innocuous in comparison with that of the handful of French Guiana Negroes now on trial in Nantes. In the criminal court there the police have recently assembled a group of men and women (fourteen, on trial for the deaths of eight) accused of crimes that for dark politics, passions, witchcraft, and brutality would be hard to equal.

The deaths occurred in 1928 in Cayenne, a town near the penitentiary on Devil's Island, and were involved with the mysterious demise of Papa Galmot, a white man from Périgord who had become the Negroes' god. Apparently he was a tiny creature carried about the streets in the arms of his blacks, at least when he was not in jail for the frauds which twice prevented his enjoying his election to the French Senate. His death, supposed to have been by poisoning (the only means of making gods die), led not only to Blaise Cendrars' admirable novel *Rhum* but also to massacre and pillage, and eventually to the trial of his black devotees, now up for lapidation and other forms of murder unpracticed since the days of the Christian martyrs. Those who were stoned to death were doctors, counselors, witches, and bizarre colonial-government figures who seem like Tories in comparison with the pagan figures of the accused.

Indeed the prisoners' very names have enchanted the citizens of France. Buckaroos with gentle voices (and criminal records) are called Mith, Parnasse, Pilgram, Avril, Mars, even Time. The woman who is said to have aided them in casting stones is a Mlle. Radical, possessor of four children and three professions, only one of which, prostitution, could be acknowledged. The giant Iquy, a deaf fisherman, was Galmot's mameluke. An octogenarian named Moustapha is accused of having beaten men to death with his umbrella on the big day. When at home, he lives in an inn called The Thirty Knife Cuts. None of the prisoners speaks French grammatically, all refuse to have interpreters, all mix their genders, lie magnificently, are affectionate, polite, and, as a means of showing their admiration, call all the lawyers and the judge "Papa."

Dying, some of them, from tuberculosis contracted in the cold prison where they have waited two years for trial, the accused, attired in evening clothes, green mittens, and varnished boots, probably await either the guillotine or Devil's Island. The giant Iquy wears a sweater embroidered with his motto: "Life Is Lovely." If the evidence is long, the prisoners remove their boots. Those beheaded would remain in France. Those sentenced to hard labor for life would merely, ironically enough, go back home to Guiana. One can only regret that Conrad died too early to have written of their hearts of darkness.

Alice in Wonderland

What might be regarded as a new and disturbing note of insanity has invaded the Mad Hatter's tea party via Parisian printing circles. The Black Sun Press has emitted what it announces as *"une édition de haut luxe de 'Alice in Wonderland' par Lewis Carroll, illustrée de six lithographies en couleurs par Marie Laurencin."* The text, one is relieved to note, is still in English; only the drawings are in French. The fine type is hand-set Doric, the paper soft enough for a sybarite to lie on. Unfortunately, however, the Rabbit wears a little pink Marie Laurencin hat and looks like a French poodle; in revenge, Alice, though she wears no hat, looks like Marie Laurencin. Also, the Red Queen, to add to the freshness of the scene, looks enough like Marie Laurencin to encourage even the Dormouse to scream, "Off with her head!" The Mock Turtle never shows, so he doesn't get a pink hat.

As a result, the *haut luxe par Lewis Laurencin* is being absorbed like hotcakes. The unique sixteen-thousand-franc volume, the twenty at one thousand francs apiece, have all gone, perhaps down the Rabbit Hole. Owing to their success, the other two editions, originally announced at three hundred and five hundred francs a copy, are even more originally being offered at the Press itself for five hundred and seven hundred francs respectively. Well, as Alice once remarked, "Curiouser and curiouser."

1932

Ravel (Music by)

For years it has been known that, out in the fastness of his country cottage in Montfort-l'Amaury, Ravel was writing a pair of piano concertos. One, being only for the left hand, was definitely associated with the one-armed Austrian pianist, Wittgenstein. The other, Ravel said as late as three years ago, was "completely terminated—all except the themes" and would be associated with Mlle. Marguerite Long, an obedient and powerful French pianist popular in ministerial circles; a Chevalier of the Legion of Honor; and the like. The themes, Mlle. Long, and Ravel, as conductor, were all finally brought together for the first time at the recent Ravel gala at the Pleyel. Every seat in the house was taken, a tribute the French rarely pay except to German sopranos, and the concerto was worth waiting all these years to hear. Professedly written, as its author states, in the brilliant manner proper to a *divertimento*, its *allegro*, *adagio*, and *presto* presented rhythmic, melodious modern music as personally pure as it will be publicly popular. Its timely appearance as a Durand-published, silver-backed score was the signal for more noisy page-turning than was necessary at a concert already fashionably fussy.

Since so much has lately been said, principally by Ravel, as to the correct tempo for his too famous "Boléro," considerable interest attended his directing of that piece as a final act of a long evening. May we state that those who thought a bolero was a short, bright jacket worn for fancy dress had better make other plans? According to Ravel, a bolero is apparently a long, black crepe cape with a train the length of a hall carpet, worn exclusively when walking to funerals.

Aristide Briand (1862–1932)

The death of Aristide Briand, rated as an advocate of pacifism, was truly timely. He loved peace and politics; in Europe at the moment there is no spiritual peace, and as for politics, Briand was politically embalmed when he lost the presidency, months ago. His death, therefore, was almost an anachronism. Tardieu, who hated him, was selected to preach his funeral sermon, and his body, in a dress suit, was fated to lie, as a form of diplomacy, before the Minister of Foreign Affairs in the Quai d'Orsay. Briand was never trusted, always admired, rarely loved. The day after his death, at high noon—the most fashionable hour for fulfilling such social functions—the mourners assembled to sign the book in his apartment were a scant dozen. For men less brilliant, signers have recently assembled in hundreds.

Briand was born in the port of Nantes seventy years ago, supposedly a son of a noble of the Vendée and a fishergirl. He was short of stature, devoted to pacifism, women, politics, and brilliant speech. He was silver-tongued but natively salty in his discourse; when he lifted his arm in gesture in the Chamber, he looked like an untidy Neptune. A trident should have sprung from his cuff. For his noon *apéritif*, he lately frequented the new gin palace in the old Hôtel Élysée-Bellevue on the Rond-Point, where he appeared always alone, always hatted, a crusty old cynic with spots on his clothes and pockets full of folded newspapers.

President Doumer (1857–1932)

The assassination of President Doumer threw the country not only into real dismay (murder, except for a serious motive like money, being almost unknown in France) but into exceptionally pleasant and protracted Pentecostal promenades as well. By his being interred among the Immortals of the Panthéon on a Thursday, the Pentecost weekend (France's great spring bank holiday) stretched from the first tolling of the funereal bells in

Notre-Dame to the last honk of incoming motors on the following Monday night, or twice as long as it should have. Paul Doumer was a poor man from the provinces who had worked hard
all his life; by his death, he gave Parisians the longest vacation
they had enjoyed in years. The eulogies that surrounded his demise were equally long-drawn-out. The President of the Republic has little to do but live; in being violently deprived of that
exercise of office lay Doumer's greatest political contribution
(coming, as his death did, between elections) and the press
made the most of it.

Taste varied as to his cry when he was shot down, the more
popular papers preferring his despairing "Oh, là là!," the graver
dailies favoring "Is it possible?" What few reported were his
dying words: "But what kind of chauffeur was it?" Having been
told by his aides not that he had been shot but that he had been
struck by a taxi, the President spent the last conscious moments
of his life wondering how an automobile got into the charity
book sale at the Maison Rothschild, where his assassination occurred.

In France, being a barefooted boy is usually preparation for
becoming not President but a barefooted man. M. Doumer altered his fate through education, through leaving home early,
through honesty, luck, and longevity. His father was an Auvergnat ditch-digger. As the grandest innkeeper of the nearby city of
Albi delicately put it, "I knew President Doumergue; he had a
château near here. But I never came in contact with President
Doumer; he was of humble birth." In Doumer's home town of
Aurillac, where I chanced to be on the day of his death, the excitement was intense at the weekly fair (important local mart for
chestnuts, tripe, wooden shoes, umbrellas, and a peppered, gar-
licked cheese). The oxen were left to chew their cuds beneath
the flowering chestnuts on the square by the Church of Our-
Lady-of-the-Snows while their masters, in smocks and gaiters,
swarmed into the cafés for white wine, indignation, politics, and
some fisticuffs, all carried on in Languedocian, their peculiar
language. For, as one speechifier translated into French for our
benefit, "Doumer was the only President of the Republic Aurillac ever made. Most of us never saw or heard tell of him until
he was elected. And, my faith! now that he's assassinated, we'll
never hear tell of or see him again."

The 1931 presidential election killed two elderly Frenchmen: Briand because he lost and Doumer because he won.

Mlle. Hamlet

Hamlet is a ladies' man in France. The greatest Princes of Denmark have been Mmes. Sarah Bernhardt, Suzanne Desprès, and, of our generation, Marguerite Jamois. At its recent trial reading before the cast of the Comédie-Française, the script was voted a worthy literary curiosity by Shakespeare, "who was a contemporary of Louis XIV, the Danish prince not having lived till the reign of Louis XVI"; which made the play even more curious than usual in France. As a matter of fact, if the Comédie ever went to listen to anything except one another, within the past two seasons they might have heard Messrs. Ruggieri, Pitoëff, or Moissi as Hamlet (providing they understood Italian, Russian, and German), or even the 1603–1930 First Text revival in French by Baty, at the Montparnasse, when, for the first time in any age, the Ghost was part of the mural decoration. The state theater's present resuscitation is the Divine Sarah's '99 prose version, made for her by the poet Marcel Schwob and his friend Eugène Morand (for which the program gives Paul Morand, at that time a lad of about ten, the half-credit line).

One can only suppose that *Hamlet* is still useless to Parisians and that M. Yonnel's interpretation of the role is perfect, since the Prince was criticized by *abonnés* (accustomed to the gaiety of *Le Cid*) as being a neurasthenic young Nordic of melancholy mind, addicted to wearing black and to garrulousness. Oh, wormwood, wormwood!

"Gyp" (1850–1932)

Gabrielle-Marie-Antoinette de Riquetti, Comtesse de Martel de Janville—or "Gyp," as she signed her hundred novels and was known to the millions in France—is dead. Descendant of Mirabeau, pugnacious aristocrat, transplanted Bretonne, anti-Semite whose wicked wit helped skin Dreyfus alive, *romancier* old enough to have twice come back as a best seller in her life (once in '90 and again before the war), she died more quietly than she had ever lived in all her eighty-two years, expiring in style and without pain in her private *hôtel* in Neuilly, where she received, bedridden but still brilliant to the last. "Gyp" saw and made history, detailing the fall of the polite Third Empire and the rise of the impolite modern generation with its uncorseted *jeunes filles* and its divorcing duchesses. No popular French writer ever covered so much time or took so little trouble about it, since she wrote as easily as she remembered. She was a trenchant conversationalist, no prude, despised the tepid mind, hated fakes, fatuousness, and, on the whole, the Third Republic, under which she died. She was said to have chosen the nom de plume "Gyp" because it sounded like the crack of a whip. Much of what she wrote will be immediately discarded. Some of it will be permanent, a calendar of customs to be consulted in the future like the more racy works of Restif de la Bretonne, or the less unjust pages of Saint-Simon.

"The Widow"

The execution of Gorguloff, assassin of the late President Doumer, had a bad press. Fewer people turned out for it at dawn than the special reinforcements of police expected. Perhaps because the criminal was unpopular, the whole process of capital punishment was suddenly criticized here as old-fashioned, though not for the humanitarian reasons you might think. It was criticized because the executioner's cart is horse-drawn and lantern-lit, in an age when even the paperhanger has his automobile; because the guillotine hasn't been improved since its invention, except by the substitution of a gadget instead of a pulley to make the blade fall.

The guillotine itself is still popularly called The Widow, because she makes so many; it still has to be assembled by hand and spirit level by the headsman's valets just before dawn; is still the private property of the Executioner of High Works, as the *bourreau* is called; is still tested, before the prisoner appears, by a bundle of straw; is still kept in a suburban barn when not in use. In France, the assassin is never told the day of his death till he is waked with the phrase "Have courage," a cigarette (Gorguloff was no smoker), and rum (Gorguloff drank a double helping and asked for what a condemned man may ironically have: a double portion of that long bread which is the Frenchman's staff of life). The prisoner is still saluted by drawn sabers, as a final honor, when he is led before the assembled Garde; if his family reclaims him for burial, it must be done without pomp and the headstone may bear no name. The headsman is still called Monsieur de Paris; is permitted to address his victims as "thou," as one speaking to a lover or child; but does not always wear the scarlet flower in his buttonhole which is his sanguinary privilege. (In old days, it was tucked behind one ear.)

As a matter of fact, the present Monsieur de Paris wears, not a blossom, but a derby hat; is in private life a M. Deibler; is middle-aged, taciturn, and married; limps; and is morbidly jealous of his position as fourth generation in a Breton family of what amounts to hereditary high executioner, which post he, lacking a son, has fought to have passed on to his daughter's husband. (The job pays three thousand francs a head.) Upon recent rumor of his retirement, there were four aspirants. Though Deibler is still officially Monsieur de Paris, his nephew's hand let fall the blade that punished Gorguloff. It is to be supposed that the sinecure is now secure.

Gabrielle Chanel

It is not undescriptive that, owing to an odd cæsura in her signature, Gabrielle Chanel's name, as she signs it, reads "Gabri elleChanel." In her long, dramatic career as a dressmaker, she has never been more *elleChanel,* or herself, than in the curious exhibition of diamonds just opened in the interests of charity (and diamond merchants) in her sumptuous private *hôtel* in the Faubourg St.-Honoré. With that aggravating instinct to strike when everyone else thinks the iron is cold that has, up till now, made her success, she has, at the height of the depression, returned to precious stones "as having the greatest value in the smallest volume"; just as, during the boom, she launched glass gewgaws "because they were devoid of arrogance in an epoch of too easy *luxe.*" As a result, what is regarded by underwriters as fifty million francs' worth of borrowed brilliants, and by the pairs of private policemen at every drawing-room door as a terrible responsibility, judging by their miens, has just been put on display among the Coromandel screens and rose-quartz chandeliers which have made Chanel's home notable, if not for its simplicity.

Mlle. Chanel's mountings for the jewels are in design dominantly and delicately astronomical. Magnificent lopsided stars for earrings; as a necklace, a superb comet whose nape-encircling tail is all that attaches it to a lady's throat; bracelets that are flexible rays; crescents for hats and hair; and, as a unique set piece mounted in yellow gold, a splendid sun of yellow diamonds from a unique collection of matched stones unmatched in the world.

As a hint to matrons who may have a gill of old-fashioned diamonds lying loose in their drawers at home, all the Chanel-mounted stones are of the prewar brilliant (as against the more recent, destructive table) cut. Also, in the interests of further economy, all of the more elaborate pieces come to pieces: the tiaras turn into bracelets, the ear-drops into brooches, the stars into garters. Indeed, at Chanel's it's rather a Left-Over Diamonds Week.

It is perhaps of interest to add that two days after the Chanel Paris diamond show opened, De Beers stock was reported to have jumped some twenty points on the London exchange.

1933

Duchesse d'Uzès (1847–1933)

The last great lady of old France, the Dowager Duchesse d'Uzès, is dead at the age of eighty-six in her castle at Dampierre. As she died, her latest great-grandchild was being born in another wing of the historic house. Of the last three powerful dowagers, she was the dominant one, since the other two, though known for their poetry and hunting, were also known by their titles as Duchesse de Rohan and Duchesse de Chartres; the Duchesse d'Uzès was known simply as The Duchesse, or The Amazon. She was a lieutenant of the Louveterie, an old office of wolf-hunting that demanded the ownership of a pack of hounds, of which she kept twelve hundred; she rode to the hunt the week before her death; was the first woman in France to receive her automobile driving license; believed in charity, God, and gracious manners as part of her aristocratic responsibility; and in her hunting regalia, which included the conventional cocked hat and a more personal gentleman's winged collar, looked rather like an eighteenth-century county judge. She was born a Mortemart, the wittiest fine family in France, though she had no wit but, rather, great good sense in speech.

Like most great ladies today, the Duchesse saw her fortune reduced. It was no secret that while many believed in General Boulanger's reckless failure in the eighties, she was the only one who paid for it. Indeed, she paid for everything, even for being an old-fashioned lady who found herself alive in modern times; as she had been trained to do as a girl, she rose for Communion in her private chapel every day at seven-thirty, and then sat up with the young folks till midnight, that being the present style. She gave time to her friends, money to the poor, and sat her horse like a field marshal riding sidesaddle. She will be unduplicated, she will be missed and mourned.

The Autobiography of Alice B. Toklas

A Paris-written book of extreme interest to both sides of the Atlantic, and, indeed, to one side of the Pacific, since both the ladies hail from California, will shortly be published in New York under the sly inscription *The Autobiography of Alice B. Toklas*. As some young foreign painters like Picasso, Juan Gris, and Matisse, and later some struggling expatriate writers, like Joyce and Hemingway, discovered years ago, Miss Alice B. Toklas is the friend who lives on the Rue de Fleurus with Gertrude Stein. And certainly any autobiography of the one must necessarily be a biography of, if not even by, the other, plus a complete memoir of that exciting period when Cubism was being invented in paint and a new manner of writing being patented in words, an epoch when not everyone had too much to eat but everyone had lots to say, when everything we now breathe was already in the air and only a few had the nose for news to smell it—and with most of the odors of discovery right under the Toklas-Stein roof.

Considerable mystery and some secrecy still surround the book here—but not much, really. Among the few privileged to see it in MS., it has already provoked quarrels as to its merit, the quarrels being about which of its hundreds of merits is the most meritorious: the Picasso part, or the analyses of Hemingway, the long, marvelous description of the cranky old picture merchant Vollard, the piece about William James in Harvard, or about Johns Hopkins. . . . However, on one point, the public will be glad to know, all the privileged agree, and that is that the book is written simply—not in the manner of *The Making of Americans*, but, rather, completely in Miss St— that is to say, Miss Toklas's first, or easiest, literary manner.

Bernard Faÿ is busy making the admirable French translation and giving the hoax away.

Sarah Bernhardt (1844–1923)

The tenth anniversary of Sarah Bernhardt's death has just taken place. Ten years ago, her funeral was such a sight for flowers, followers, and fanaticism as hadn't been seen here since Victor Hugo's obsequies, and wasn't to be seen again till Anatole France was laid to rest with equally handsome blossoms but some less fragrant political pamphlets. For days after what seemed Bernhardt's last public performance, mourners stood in line in the cemetery to get a view of where she lay dead, just as they had made the box-office queue to see her alive on the stage. Today, in the French estimation, she still seems lifelike and, despite her absence from it, one of the most popular figures of the French theater. Maurice Rostand has just written nineteen stanzas of six lines each, rhymed, in her honor, which were read as eagerly as a first-night critique. Drian has just finished a new portrait of her for which she posthumously sat in his memory. Her face in all its roles and ages has suddenly peopled the press: Sarah at her debut, the ugly, skinny failure whose name was really Rosine; Sarah in '87, with fine rolling eyes, as Tosca, and already a favorite; Sarah in '90, kneeling as Jeanne d'Arc, and in '93, fainting as Phèdre; in 1900 as l'Aiglon, her great breeched and booted success; Sarah Somewhere in the United States on Independence Day in 1917, her tragic visage tilted back as Bleeding France on a bandstand packed with American banners and bald heads. And suddenly, a few years later, Sarah Infirm—a one-legged, insoluble mystery on a litter, muffled beneath wigs, false teeth, furs, veils, leopard skins, and make-up. She made a museum of all the false limbs manufacturers sent her on approval, and planned to buy a park to try them out in, but forgot. She kept a lion in a cage in her house until he smelled too bad, then filled his cage with little birds which smelled only something less. At her last dinner parties, she was brought in after her guests, was propped up at the end of her table like a painted mummy, alternately simulating fright, shyness, and loss of memory, though forgetting nothing, seeing all —an amazing old actress and female, still rich in wit, revenge, surprise, chatter, contempt of and hunger for the human comedy.

Dressed in chinchilla and cock's plumes, she was the witness, years ago, at the marriage of Yvonne Printemps and Sacha Guitry. Today, Guitry probably spoke for all of France when he said, "That anyone compares Sarah Bernhardt to other actresses, that they discuss or blame her, is extremely odious to me."

[*The first time I saw Mme. Sarah was on one of her American Midwest vaudeville tours, where her partner on the program was a plump white tenor whose contribution consisted of singing, "I'm mammy's little coal black rose." She seemed to be excessive, too French and too false to most of our then-youthful eyes and ears. But years later, at the Paris theater that bore her name, she could not be gainsaid as a magnificent if mutilated theatrical relic. The last thing we all saw her in was L'Aiglon, in which with great dignity she rose on one remaining limb from her chair and, holding herself firm with one hand, swung her arm into the theatrical air to salute France as Rostand's young leader who never led or ruled. She always had a bleating voice. Paris never heard the like of it again until the country fell under the rule of Marshal Pétain. Whatever Pétain said in his public speeches to listening France had the tremolo of Bernhardt's vocalization, though of course he never said as she so often did in her most melodramatic scenes, "Je t'aime! Je t'aime!" J. F.*]

Ravel's Concerto

At the Triton Concert, the big, brilliant event was Ravel's Piano Concerto for the Left Hand, written for and played by the Viennese pianist Wittgenstein, mutilated in the war. Wittgenstein's courage was almost as fine as his *Klavier* work and naturally lifted the performance beyond the realms of music into that of noisy emotionalism. The piece itself, played without intermission, is, Ravel notes, based upon one development, or, rather, upon two chained together; takes some of its influence from jazz; is more difficult and orchestral than the concerto of last year; and is played with a full, rather than a reduced, band. Owing to the obvious technical difficulties and the stubborn fullness of harmony Ravel has injected into this work, one may now expect to see two-handed pianists playing as a bright trick what Wittgenstein plays as a tragedy.

Comtesse de Noailles (1876–1933)

Another fatality of a famous female. The greatest poetess France has ever possessed—and she was really Rumanian—has just expired in the celebrated person of the Comtesse de Noailles, *née* Anna de Brancovan. The funeral floral offerings could not all be contained even in the vast Madeleine but overflowed onto the porch and steps, where they lay like scattered pages of iris, rose, and anemone assembled from her occasional pastoral verse. In life, she was an aristocratic lady with small features and large eyes, who posed prettily with a parasol. But in inspiration, she wrote unclothed by anything except those draperies of anguish, passion, grace, and great human conclusions which dress the rare players of the really golden lyre. Of her school of verse, she was excelled only by Paul Valéry; her passionate friends were the great writer Barrès, and one great mathematician, Painlevé. She loved Greek temples and her son, traveled, read the classics, painted flower pictures, suffered from the war as though she had been wounded in it, and of late so lived in lonely retirement that it was said she died of languor. Her malady, which she never admitted, was apparently carcinomatous. Incredulous about her increasing illness, her noble relatives and friends, it is said, failed to call; but her faithful maid peopled her reclusion with imaginary visitors by utilizing old visiting cards of other days, which she presented at the bedside with sympathetic messages. The Comtesse de Noailles died after having said clearly, "I have so loved France and the French."

Anti-Semitism

The Nazi anti-Semitic campaign is not only a matter of shocking rumor here but also one of troubling proof, Europe being so small. Brussels is packed with refugees; at Verviers, near Belgium's German frontier, the customs officers are up all night, forced to a halfhearted chase and search of poor pedestrians, with packs on their backs and no visas on their passports, trying to sneak through the fields and over the border by dawn. As has been its gesture through history, Switzerland has greeted the persecuted with open arms—pretty nearly open, anyhow. The city of Zurich, already troubled with unemployment, forbids the new Jews to seek work, which is no hardship, since Zurich, along with Paris, has received the Kurfürstendamm limousine trade. The Hôtel George V here has as a result blossomed like Aaron's rod and is known as the *Generalquartier* or Parisian German G.H.Q. Certainly the Ufa studio has moved into it in a block. Fritz Lang's latest film, *Das Testament des Doktor Mabuse*, has been forbidden distribution in Germany because it has been claimed that his backing was Jewish. Pabst's ill-fated new *Don Quichotte* was also supposedly angeled by the same source, which is now considered almost the only thing, besides its fine panchromatic photography, in its favor. With the best cinematic talents and organizations of Berlin disrupted, from now on there will apparently be no more of those excellent modern films coming out of Germany, except maybe some featuring Friedrich der Grosse with a little up-to-date swastika mustache.

Mae West

There are two period-furniture hits in Paris: the Louvre's glassy and fine-legged "Décor de la Vie de 1870 à 1900," and Mae West in what is called here *Lady Lou*. Miss West has elicited praise from Paris that would give her a liberal education if she traced it all down. By *boulevardiers,* she has been compared to Réjane in *Zaza;* by *littérateurs,* she has been discovered as the perfect illustration, if a little late, of the early works of de Maupassant; by musicians, to be "the voice of Madame Angot," who was a mouthful of a mouthpiece for the upstart Directoire; and by playwrights, to have "the dialoguing genius of the Commedia dell'Arte." She is furthermore described in the movie sheets as being variably of Jewish, Russian, or Finnish origin, with one vote cast in favor of her being blond Negro because of her "robust and grave singing which recalls the plantations of cotton along the Missipi on which the Show boats ply" (*sic*).

As to what she has written, beyond what the Parisians have written about her, Miss West would be even more mystified. Not only, according to them, has she, in her literary labors, been "actress, writer, impresario, fatal beauty, and even worse," but she has, it seems, "after having left a troupe of 'burlesk,'" become author "of a novel called *Constant Sinner*, of pieces called *Sex, Drag, The Wicked Age, Pleasure Man*, and finally her great success from which sprang her scenario for *Lady Lou—Lil Diamond*."

Lil Diamond, eh? They done her wrong.

Cécile Sorel

The retirement of Cécile Sorel as *doyenne*—or oldest living leading lady—from the Comédie-Française provoked a magnificent night of simulated mourning at the Maison de Molière. Subscribers had been promised a sight of her young husband, the Comte de Ségur (whose family is so famous that its name serves as a telephone exchange, an eponymous marital convenience, since the couple will live in its encompassing district). Her advertised program included an appearance by Marlene Dietrich, Mary Garden in bits of *Mélisande*, Tilly Losch in bits of ex-Cochran revues, and something of *Camille*—with Chaliapin and Serge Lifar in the cast—which Sorel acted with what has for a quarter of a century been called "acute sensibilities." It is difficult now to give Sorel her true rating as a theatrical artist. Certainly, no matter how high she lifted her arms to heaven and the gallery gods, she never touched the hem of Bernhardt's garments. Sorel's greatest role was Du Barry, since she played it more as a tribute to the taste of modern France than to that of Louis XV. Boxes for her last performance, popularly supposed to be a benefit, were reported at a thousand francs. Sorel retires with a rich future and a poor past.

Les Ballets 1933

The French are still fond of dancing. As proof, the opening of the newly organized *Les Ballets 1933* at the Champs-Élysées was the most brilliant first night of *tout Paris* since the *ouverture* of Comte Étienne de Beaumont's *Soirées de Paris* in '24, which was the most brilliant première since Diaghilev's *Sacre* in the spring of '13. Which was probably the most brilliant debut since Fanny Elssler's at the Opéra in 1834, which was probably the most brilliant first night since the court ladies of Louis XIV applauded themselves as ballet-girls in Lulli's *Triumph of Love*, by special request. For four hundred years Parisians have been regally addicted to ballet, and if the 1933 group lacked Bourbon appreciation, it enjoyed Ritz royalty, much more tastily dressed. London's season this summer is reported a formal landscape of white ties and whiter tiaras, with champagne flowing like a tiny Thames. Owing to the heat, beer was what flowed like a Seine for the Champs-Élysées launching, between acts floating a cargo of gregarious gorgeous gowns, of pretty women pruned and painted, of feathers, furs, and furbelows as exotic as merchandise for a zoo escaped from a ship's hatches—and as rarely seen in full display in the foyer of a Paris public house.

Les Ballets 1933 was presented by Edward James, new optimistic British art patron, at a cost of a million francs. The program consisted of six Balanchine ballets, only half of which, or around five hundred thousand francs' worth, the public appeared to enjoy. The three granted admiration were *Fastes* and *Les Songes*, with music by Sauguet and Milhaud and lively lovely décors by Derain, and *Les Valses de Beethoven*, mounted in a sweet ballroom set by Emilio Terry. The other trio—like dishes on a table d'hôte of which you could select one though you weren't expected to like all three—consisted of *Mozartiana*, with a fecund décor of statues erected to the state of mind of the painter, Christian Bérard, and Mlle. Toumanova, dancing like a diva, with motions more musical than miming; *Errante*, to tunes of Schubert, before a precise paradisaical picture of clouds, aspirations, and the four winds of Tchelitchev; and lastly, *Les Sept Péchés Capitaux*, décor by Neher and music by Kurt Weill—a concoction for which no one seemed to have an appetite but yours truly.

Certainly *The Seven Deadly Sins* turned out to be less a ballet than an immorality play, with Lotte Lenya (Weill's wife) singing the plot in German for Tilly Losch (James's wife) to dance to, which she did, unfortunately, in the language of Wigman rather than Taglioni. The two ladies, by cynical symbolism, were supposed to represent the Good or Material-minded Side and the Bad or Spiritual-souled Version of the same girl, named Anna. They were supported in their mixed mutual endeavors by a male Teutonic quartet which sang that its Vaterland was in Louisiana, plus a masculine *corps de ballet* in straw boaters and tights, jumping through seven paper doors all of which, so far as Bad Anna was concerned, could have been marked "Gentlemen," since 'twas they who led to her downfall each time, but which were more ecclesiastically marked "Sloth," "Greed," etc., instead. Herr Weill, who is always reported an intellectual Communist and who, with his wife, was on this trip to Paris a house guest of the Vicomte de Noailles and *his* wife, took his bow and his boos for the première while standing in the door marked "*Luxure.*"

Marlene Dietrich

Marlene Dietrich's Paris visit, which began with the Prefect of Police asking her to leave town in trousers, is ending with her being asked everywhere in skirts. She is the sweet pepper that brings crowds to the modest Hungarian restaurant on the Rue de Surène where she customarily dines; she is the bitters at fashionable cocktail parties only when she fails to appear. She was the belle of the Baron de Rothschild's ball—or would have been had she consented to dance with any husband but her own. At Cécile Sorel's farewell to the Comédie-Française, when the Comte de Ségur made his debut as an actor, she was more observed as her old self in a box than he was on the stage as a new Hannibal. At Richard Tauber's chic *auf Wiedersehen* concert, her silent silhouette was the most effective part of the program. She speaks excellent French, deports herself modestly, and lives with husband, mother, and child at the Trianon-Palace Hôtel at Versailles, where the *gendarmerie*, perhaps recollective of the past, don't care what a local lady wears and where she goes in slacks. On days when she comes to Paris, she wears everything but: collar, tie, boy's jacket from the young-girls' department of Lucien Lelong, man's hat from the matrons' *rayon* at Rose Descat.

Fräulein Dietrich is the first foreign female personality Paris society has fallen in love with in years. She is also apparently the first male impersonator to be under a government cloud since Christina of Sweden, or about three centuries ago.

The Murder in Le Mans

When, in February of this year, the Papin sisters, cook and housemaid, killed Mme. and Mlle. Lancelin in the respectable provincial town of Le Mans, a half-dozen hours from Paris, it was not a murder but a revolution. It was only a minor revolution—minor enough to be fought in a front hall by four females, two on a side. The rebels won with horrible handiness. The lamentable Lancelin forces were literally scattered over a distance of ten bloody feet, or from the upper landing halfway down the stairs. The physical were the most chilling details, the conquered the only dull elements in a fiery, fantastic struggle that should have remained inside Christine Papin's head and which, when it touched earth, unfortunately broke into paranoiac poetry and one of the most graceless murders in French annals.

On the day he was to be made a widower, M. Lancelin, retired lawyer, spent his afternoon at his respectable provincial club; at 6:45 he reported to his brother-in-law, M. Renard, a practicing lawyer at whose table they were to dine at seven *en famille*, that, having gone by the Lancelin home in the Rue La Bruyère to pick up his wife and daughter, Geneviève, he had found the doors bolted and the windows dark—except for the maids' room in the attic, where, until he started knocking, there was a feeble glow. It had appeared again only as he was leaving.

Two lawyers this time set off for the Lancelin dwelling, to observe again the mansard gleam fade, again creep back to life as the men retreated. Alarmed (for at the least a good dinner was drying up), the gentlemen procured a brace of policemen and a brigadier, who, by forcing Lancelin's window, invited Lancelin to walk into his parlor, where he discovered his electric lights did not work. Two of the police crept upstairs with one flashlight and the brother-in-law. Close to the second floor the trio humanely warned the husband not to follow.

On the third step from the landing, all alone, staring uniquely at the ceiling, lay an eye. On the landing itself the Lancelin ladies lay, at odd angles and with heads like blood puddings. Be-

neath their provincial petticoats their modest limbs had been
knife-notched the way a fancy French baker notches his finer
long loaves. Their fingernails had been uprooted; one of Geneviève's teeth was pegged in her own scalp. A second single orb
—the mother's, this time, for both generations seemed to have
been treated with ferocious nonpartisanship—rested shortsight-
edly gazing at nothing in the corner of the hall. Blood had soft-
ened the carpet till it was like an elastic red moss.

The youngest and third policeman (his name was M. Truth)
was sent creeping toward the attic. Beneath the door a crack of
light flickered. When he crashed the door, the light proved to be
a candle, set on a plate so as not to drip, for the Papins were
well-trained servants. The girls were in one bed in two blue kimonos. They had taken off their dresses, which were stained.
They had cleaned their hands and faces. They had, the police
later discovered, also cleaned the carving knife, hammer, and
pewter pitcher which they had been using and put them neatly
back where they belonged—though the pitcher was by now too
battered to look tidy. Christine, the elder (Léa, the younger,
was never after to speak intelligibly except once at the trial),
did not confess; she merely made their mutual statement: they
had done it. Truth took what was left of the candle—the short-
circuiting electric iron had blown out the fuse again that afternoon and was at the bottom of everything, Christine kept saying, though the sensible Truth paid no attention—and lighted
the girls downstairs, over the corpses, and out to the police station. They were still in their blue kimonos and in the February
air their hair was wild, though ordinarily they were the tidiest
pair of domestics in Le Mans.

Through a typographical error the early French press reports
printed the girls' name not as Papin, which means nothing, but
as Lapin, which means rabbit. It was no libel.

Waiting trial in the prison, Christine, who was twenty-eight
years of age and the cathartic of the two, had extraordinary holy
visions and unholy reactions. Léa, who was twenty-two and
looked enough like her sister to be a too-long-delayed twin, had
nothing, since the girls were kept separate and Léa thus had no
dosage for her feeble brain.

Their trial at the local courthouse six months later was a national event, regulated by guards with bayonets, ladies with lor-

gnettes, and envoys from the Parisian press. As commentators
Paris-Soir sent a pair of novelists, the Tharaud brothers, Jean
and Jérôme, who, when they stoop to journalism, write of themselves as "I" and nearly even won the Goncourt Prize under this
singular consolidation. Special scribes were posthasted by
Détective, hebdomadal penny dreadful prosperously owned by
the *Nouvelle Revue Française,* or France's *Atlantic Monthly.*
L'Œuvre, as daily house organ for the Radical-Socialist party
(supposedly friendly to the working classes till they unfortunately shot a few of them in the Concorde riot), sent Bérard, or
their best brain.

The diametric pleas of prosecution and defense facing these
historians were clear: either (1) the Papins were normal girls
who had murdered without a reason, murdering without reason
apparently being a proof of normalcy in Le Mans, or else (2) the
Rabbit sisters were as mad as March Hares, and so didn't have
to have a reason. Though they claimed to have one just like
anybody else, if the jury would only listen: their reason was that
unreliable electric iron, or a mediocre cause for a revolution.
. . . The iron had blown out on Wednesday, been repaired
Thursday, blown again Friday, taking the houselights with it at
five. By six the Lancelin ladies, in from their walk, had been
done to death in the dark—for the dead do not scold.

While alive, Madame had once forced Léa to her housemaid
knees to retrieve a morsel of paper overlooked on the parlor rug.
Or, as the Tharauds ponderously wrote in their recapitulation of
the crime, "God knows the Madame Lancelins exist on earth."
This one, however, had been rare in that she corroborated Léa's
dusting by donning a pair of white gloves; she commentated on
Christine's omelettes by formal notes delivered to the kitchen by
Geneviève—both habits adding to the Papins' persecution complex, or their least interesting facet. Madame also gave the girls
enough to eat and "even allowed them to have heat in their
attic bedroom," though Christine did not know if Madame was
kind, since in six years' service she had never spoken to them,
and if people don't talk, how can you tell? As for the motive for
their crime, it was again the Tharauds who, all on the girls' side,
thus loyally made it clear as mud: "As good servants the girls
had been highly contraried" when the iron blew once. Twice "it

was still as jewels of servants who don't like to lose their time that they became irritated. Perhaps if the sisters had been less scrupulous as domestics the horror which followed would never have taken place. And I wish to say," added Jean and Jérôme, without logic and in unison, "that many people still belong to early periods of society."

Among others, the jury did. They were twelve good men and true, or quite incompetent to appreciate the Papin sisters. Also, the trial lasted only twenty-six hours, or not long enough to go into the girls' mental rating, though the next forty or fifty years of their lives depended on it. The prosecution summoned three local insane-asylum experts who had seen the girls twice for a half-hour and swore on the stand that the *prisonnières* were "of unstained heredity"—i.e., their father having been a dipsomaniac who violated their elder sister, since become a nun; their mother having been an hysteric "crazy for money"; a cousin having died in a madhouse, and an uncle having hanged himself "because his life was without joy." In other words, heredity O.K., legal responsibility one hundred per cent.

Owing to the girls' weak, if distinguished, defense—high-priced French lawyers work cheaply for criminals if bloody enough, the publicity being a fortune in itself—their equally distinguished psychiatrist's refutation carried no weight. Their lawyer was Pierre Chautemps, cousin to that Camille Chautemps who, as Prime Minister, so weakly defended the French Republic in the 1933 Boulevard Saint-Germain riots; their expert was the brilliant Parisian professor Logre, whose "colossal doubt on their sanity" failed to count since under cross examination he had to admit he had never seen the girls before even for five minutes; just knew all about them by sitting back in his Paris study, ruminating. He did, too, but the jury sniffed at the stuck-up city man.

Thus, they also missed Logre's illuminating and delicate allusion to the girls as a "psychological couple," though they had understood the insane-asylum chief's broader reference to Sappho. Of paramount interest to twelve good men and true, the girls' incest was really one of the slighter details of their dubious domesticity. On the jury's ears Christine's prison visions also fell flat.

[*Indeed it was not until six months after she was sentenced to be beheaded that these hallucinations were appreciated for their literary value in a scholarly essay entitled "Motifs du Crime Paranoïaque: ou Le Crime des Soeurs Papins" by Dr. Jacques Lacan, in a notable Surrealist number of the intelligentsia quarterly Minotaure. J. F.*]

In court, however, Christine's poetic visions were passed over as a willful concoction of taradiddles that took in no one—except the defense, of course. Yet they had, in the limited data of lyrical paranoia and modern psychiatry, constituted an exceptional performance. Certain of the insane enjoy strange compensations; having lost sight of reality they see singular substitutes devoid of banal sequence, and before the rare spectacle of effect without cause are pushed to profound questions the rest of us are too sensible to bother with. "Where was I before I was in the belly of my mother?" Christine first inquired, and the fit was on. She next wished to know where the Lancelin ladies might now be, for, though dead, could they not have come back in other bodies? For a cook she showed, as the Tharauds said, "a bizarre interest in metempsychoses," further illuminated by her melancholy reflection, "Sometimes I think in former lives that I was my sister's husband." Then while the prison dormitory shuddered, Christine claimed to see that unholy bride hanging hanged to an apple tree, with her limbs and the tree's limbs broken. At the sad sight crazed Christine leaped in the air to the top of a ten-foot barred window where she maintained herself with muscular ease. It was then that Léa, whom she had not seen since their incarceration six months before, was called in as a sedative. And to her Christine cried with strange exultation, "Say yes, say yes," which nobody understands to this day. By what chance did this Sarthe peasant fall like the Irish Joyce in the last line of *Ulysses* on the two richest words in any tongue —those of human affirmation, *Yes, yes. . . ?*

Thus ended the lyrical phase of Christine's seizure, which then became, maybe, political. At any rate she hunger-struck for three days like someone with a cause, went into the silence, wept and prayed like a leader betrayed, traced holy signs with her tongue on the prison walls, tried to take Léa's guilt on her shoulders, and, when this failed, at least succeeded in freeing her own of her strait jacket.

"Wasn't all of that just make-believe?" the prison officials later asked her. (All except escaping from the strait jacket, of course, or a reality that had never occurred in French penal history before.) "If monsieur thinks so," said Christine politely. Both the girls were very polite in prison and addressed their keepers in the formal third person, as if the guards were company who had just stepped in to the Lancelins' parlor for tea.

During the entire court proceeding, report on visions, vices, and all, from 1:30 after lunch of one day to 3:30 before breakfast of the next, Christine sat on the accused bench with eyes closed. She looked like someone asleep or a medium in a trance, except that she rose when addressed and blindly said nearly nothing. The judge, a kind man with ferocious mustaches, was, in his interrogation, finally forced to examine his own conscience, since he could not get Christine to talk about hers.

"When you were reprimanded in your kitchen, you never answered back but you rattled your stove-lids fiercely; I ask myself if this was not sinful pride. . . . Yet you rightly think work is no disgrace. No, you also have no class hatred," he said with relief to find that he and she were neither Bolsheviks. "Nor were you influenced by literature, apparently, since only books of piety were found in your room."

(Not that printed piety had taught the girls any Christian mercy once they started to kill. The demi-blinding of the Lancelins is the only criminal case on record where eyeballs were removed from the living head without practice of any instrument except the human finger. The duplicating of the tortures was also curiously cruel; Christine took Madame in charge, the dull Léa followed suit by tending to Mademoiselle; whatever the older sister did to the older woman, the younger sister repeated on fresher flesh in an orgy of obedience.)

As the trial proceeded, the spectators could have thought the court was judging one Papin cadaver seen double, so much the sisters looked alike and dead. Their sanity expert had called them Siamese souls. The Papins' was the pain of being two where some mysterious unity had been originally intended; between them was a schism which the dominant, devilish Christine had tried to resolve into one self-reflection, without ever having heard of Narcissus or thinking that the pallid Léa might thus be lost to view. For, if Christine's eyes were closed to the judge, Léa's were as empty in gaze as if she were invisible and incapable of sight. Her one comment on trial for her life was that, with the paring knife, she had "made little carvings" in poor spinster Geneviève's thighs. For there, as her Christine had said, lay the secret of life. . . .

When the jury came in with their verdict Christine was waiting for them, still somnambulant, her hands clasped not as in prayer but as if pointing down into the earth. In the chill pre-dawn both sisters' coat collars were turned up as if they had just come in from some domestic errand run in the rain. With their first effort at concentration on Léa, whom all day the jury had tried to ignore, the foreman gave her ten years' confinement and twenty of municipal exile. Christine was sentenced to have her head cut off in the public square of Le Mans which, since females are no longer guillotined, meant life—a courtesy she, at the moment, was ignorant of.

When Christine heard her sentence of decapitation, in true belief she fell to her knees. At last she had heard the voice of God.

Crime

Things are looking up for convicts in France. At any rate, they're taken wherever they're going, if it is only to hard labor for life, in cell-equipped autobuses now, instead of in the old "salad-basket" cars which figured like extra cabooses on freight trains, and allowed prisoners to languish in freight yards days or nights, or even both, if there was much besides jailbirds to unload. The new penitentiary buses have just carried some two hundred "lifers" to La Rochelle, where they embarked for the island prison of St.-Martin-de-Ré, next to the *bagne* near Cayenne the worst that can happen to them, and usually first step toward it. These sail-offs of convicts attract observers from all over France, in addition, that is, to the mothers and wives, who stand and watch and cry. The stars of this year's embarkation were the prisoner Dr. Laget, "freshly shaven, attired in tortoise-shell glasses, golf suit and cap of pearl gray, and yellow polka-dot tie"; a strangler named Morveau, whose accomplice was a motorcycle acrobat named The Death-Defier, since dead of tuberculosis; and young Davin, a rich moron who murdered an American playboy pal for fun and pocket money. Clearly, French criminals do not operate in gangs. Three of Kid Dropper's old mob could stop one of these new cell-buses with three hands tied behind them. As Davin *mère* said, "My son is a lonely irresponsible." Yet convicts escape from the Devil's Island *bagne* not singly but in groups of ten or fifteen, rather like tropical walking clubs. Dr. Bougrat, one of the most popular poisoners of Marseilles, recently fled from his cell to Caracas, where he now enjoys a flourishing general practice, though nose and throat were his original specialty. It took the cooperation of twenty men to effect his escape. Apparently, French criminals learn the value of trade solidarity only when it is a little late.

Daguerre (1789–1851)

For the centenary of Joseph Niepce (1765–1833), French army officer who discovered the process of the photographic *chambre noire*, Thérèse Bonney has shown at the Colle Gallery some of her twenty thousand daguerreotypes by Louis Daguerre, panorama-painter and partner of Niepce. Mlle. Bonney's tintypes are rare, are really silvertypes, or sometimes typed on copper, and once on oilcloth (it was not a good plan). She has rare examples of landscapes, Daguerre's earliest form, and of his first portraits in the 1840s, when portraiture became possible by taking a snapshot in one minute instead of the original eight hours, though it often looked the same around the eyes.

Ambrose Vollard

For initiates in modern French art, the most interesting exhibition ever shipped will shortly open in New York, featuring the private collection of old Vollard, crossest, craftiest merchant of Paris. In 1894, he met Mary Cassatt through Degas; through Pissarro he met Cézanne, and gave him his first show, of a hundred and ninety-five canvases, in '95. He then met everyone, including Renoir and Rousseau, and quarreled with most. He occasionally starved. In 1907, he discovered Derain and gave him ten thousand gold francs for the output of two months in London. He sold Mrs. Havemeyer the picture that was the beginning of her collection and his fortune. He inhabits a house of twenty-three rooms here, all but two of which are stuffed with canvases, most of which have never been shown. The things to look for among them are the rare red, green, and monochrome Cézannes, almost unknown; one of his master paintings, "The Bathers," recently acquired by the Barnes Foundation; and the exceptionally fine Renoirs. Many Paris art-lovers would give anything to see this show. Anything they could, which at the moment is not the price of a transatlantic ticket.

Sorel at the Casino

So much has been going on in Paris that you wouldn't believe it, even if we merely claimed to have witnessed only half of it. However, some of the things we did see with our own eyes, such as Cécile Sorel starring in the new Casino nude-Negress-ostrich-plume revue, will sound as incredible as the fact that we had sat, delighted, in the balcony and bad air from nine sharp to twelve-five flat. Apparently, what the nude-girl-show game here needed to brighten it up was a few clothes and a (retired) sixty-year-old Comédie-Française star reciting Molière couplets, plus "Shuffle Off to Buffalo," featuring Second Empire bustles, chignons, and a polka. Anyhow, *Vive Paris!* has founded a new revue tradition by slipping really *mondaine* Mainbocher-like gowns on the chorus girls and having its décor beautifully designed by worldly artists. The big moment in the show comes when Sorel makes her entry in silver, imitating Mistinguett as she descends, step by step, a gold staircase that supposedly represents Les Cent Pas at Versailles, which as a matter of history are stony and straight rather than curved and gilt, as her decorator, Drian, seems more happily to recall.

Sacha Guitry, in writing Sorel's dialogue, gave her her quotable opening line, delivered at the bottom of the stairs, which, literally translated, is "Did I come down good?" Well, yes; good and hard, if one recalls that for two generations Sorel has been the great de Musset-Molière interpretress in the greatest classical repertory theater in Europe.

Sorel's husband, the Comte de Ségur, figured in her Casino

Molière character sketch somewhere. Perhaps he was playing the Misanthrope.

Chrysanthemums

At the annual Chrysanthemum Show, the American Viola Rodgers was awarded a gold medal. Coincidentally, it has just come to light that the old spinster granddaughter of Captain Blancard, who brought the first blossoms back from Japan in 1789, lives on a pittance of two thousand francs a year in the town of Limay.

François Mauriac

So far, the literary event of the winter has been not a book but the making of an author into an Immortal. The reception by the Académie Française of the novelist François Mauriac, in silver-embroidered green dress suit, cocked hat, and gold sword, which in France are the final proofs that a man writes well, was the real best seller of the fortnight. The sword cost thirty thousand francs, of which half was paid by Mauriac's admirers in his southern home town. He passed beneath the cupola to the roll of drums and between the elbows of his sponsors, Paul Valéry and Henri Bordeaux, also in green capes, admirals' bonnets, and swords. The Gardes Républicains (his other attendants) waited in the handsome court outside. Owing to the Académie's considering Mauriac a young fellow (he is not quite fifty), for the first time schoolboy gadgets were permitted, such as indirect lighting on the statue of Bossuet, a microphone, and two loudspeakers for Mauriac's speech, though you could have heard a pin drop when in his strange veiled voice—he has throat trouble —he read his address on Brieux, that morbid-minded social reformer, whose empty chair he inherited. This tradition which makes the incoming Academician lecture in praise of his predecessor must peculiarly have troubled Mauriac, a man tormented by talent and conscience.

On this day of triumph, had he been surrounded by his mental rather than by his earthly family, he would have been in cruel company—a regular *Vipers' Nest,* as one (and why not all?) of his novels was aptly entitled. However, those who saw him become an Immortal were his fleshly kin—a lawyer, a doctor, a priest, the widow of a professor, the daughter of a government paymaster, and his own elegant adolescent sons. The Mauriacs are important people around Bordeaux, rich and ultra-Catholic.

He was also surrounded by an absolute crush of literary and political lights, leaders from all the professions, snobs, ladies of quality, and clergy. The Académie ceremonies, with their handsome period costumes, always attract dowagers, and fashionable father confessors. They also attract the rabble on the quais outside; the Gentlemen in Green Suits are considered as entertaining as a Mummers' parade.

Mauriac's first four novels were regarded as failures. His fifth, *Le Baiser aux Lépreux*, placed him top. He knew and was influenced by Anatole France when too young to know better, was discovered when still a poet by Bourget, who recommended him to Barrès. Mauriac is now forty-eight, thin as a fashion plate, sallow-skinned, and armed with an enormous, well-bred hooked nose. In his flashy Academician's uniform, he looked like an intelligent, unheard-of southern king.

War Talk

Among upper-class Parisians, there is constant talk of, fear of, war. Daily, the journals print warnings. They print pages from Pestalozzi, official schoolbook-printer of Munich, whose First Reader illustrates the Nazi ABC's with a portrait of Horst Wessel and the words "Student; leader; poet; shot; dead; hurrah for our Führer," which is *that* day's lesson; another warning reproduces a vocabulary attendant upon the pictured Treaty of Versailles; and these are big, hard words, too. *Sehr hart*—on the French ear and pride.

1934

Stavisky (1886?–1934)

The Stavisky scandal has for a fortnight kept France in an unpleasant uproar. Because of the public's violence, the Chautemps government has not dared even to fall; its Minister of Colonies has resigned in what they called good odor and everyone else named a stench; two deputies are in jail in Bayonne; Prefect of Police Chiappe, though doubtless innocent, may lose his official head to the Socialists; Herriot's Radicals are covered with mud, with side splashes for every other party, and parliamentarianism in general; a military *coup d'état* was rumored; and there was an ugly evening of rioting in the Boulevards Saint-Germain and Raspail, in which skulls and street lights were broken, shock troops guarded the Chamber, and the Concorde bridgehead was barricaded against the mob, led by Royalist agitators, as usual. Not since the Panama Canal scandal has there been such astonishment at corruption among governing bodies.

Most French financial frauds have a funny side, if only because of the wit of the swindler. Alexandre Stavisky was a solemn fellow who got up promptly at nine to start swindling, whose table jokes fell flat before his ministerial guests, and who, though forced for business reasons to have mistresses, loved only his wife. The scheme which finally killed him, his political guests' reputations, and the uninvited public's peace of mind, was his emission of hundreds of millions of francs' worth of false bonds on the city of Bayonne's municipal pawnshop, which were bought up by life-insurance companies, counseled by the Minister of Colonies, who was counseled by the Minister of Commerce, who was counseled by the Mayor of Bayonne, who was counseled by the little manager of the hockshop, who was counseled by Stavisky. Since the little manager was the only person involved who made nothing out of the fifteen-million-dollar scandal, he was the first to be clapped in jail, which should teach him. Since the only others arrested have been the deputies (one the Mayor of Bayonne), and a couple of scapegoat publicists of Paris—though the Seine magistracy, the Sûreté Générale, ministers past and present, and an acre of other politicians are clearly involved—this should teach the public.

Part of the public's shock when the Stavisky scandal broke came from the fact that no one had ever heard of him before—except the judges, lawyers, political mandarins, and detectives who had been stretching the jailbird's provisional liberty for the last six years. Though at the last he was close to being a little Kreuger in his secrecy, boldness, earthly immunity, and celestial stock-pyramidings, he began his humble career in 1906 by failing as a café singer. In succession, during the next nine years, he failed at managing a night club, illicit gambling dens, a nude revue, a tinned-soup company, an electric-icebox company, a shyster brokerage desk, and drug-running. His first high-finance success did not come till 1925, when he raised a check on the nightclub owner Joe Zelli from two thousand to sixty thousand francs, was arrested, and released. Encouraged, in 1926 he was arrested, as M. Stavisky, for embezzling five million francs' worth of bonds, and in 1927 was released, under the name of M. Alexandre, to continue his next six years' thieving under protection of the Sûreté's rare immunity card and two passports, one in each name. Last month, they even gave him a third, to kill himself under—if they didn't do it for him; it bore the financier's photo, but the name and measurements of his masseur, Niemen, once middleweight boxing champion of Europe. In Stavisky's heyday, his wife won the Prix d'Élégance at Cannes, and his horses, Grand Cyrus and Généralissime, under false stable colors, won at Longchamp, when he didn't make them lose to rook the pari-mutuel.

All of Stavisky's recent schemes were marked by *folie de grandeur* and a patent inability to come off. To expand the credit of the hockshop at Orléans to float bonds, he put in pawn what he called the late German Empress's crown emeralds, or fifteen million francs' worth of spinach-colored glass. His Hungarian agrarian-bonds scheme got him into immediate trouble with the International Settlement Bank at Basel. His last idea, for an International Public Works Corporation, founded on some clause in the Treaty of Versailles, was so idiotic that it even attracted the official patronage of the French ambassador to the Vatican.

Of twenty-two Paris papers relating the story of his police-tracked end in Chamonix, fourteen referred to Stavisky's suicide as "suicide." His is a corpse the police will never manage to bury because they supposedly shot him to keep him quiet.

It is difficult to know what Stavisky was like, since his former friends now don't remember him. As recently as the conferences at Stresa and Vichy, he was noticed at the dinner tables of ministers by everyone, except, apparently, the ministers. As a fellow lodger, the novelist Colette knew him by sight at the Hotel Claridge, and says so. "He excelled at having no face; at counting, when he chose, only as a silhouette. But he never lost a chance to show his good figure, his persistent and cultivated youthfulness. He was a falsely young man; his delicate complexion, perhaps also his fragile mental equilibrium, demanded constant care. He was at an age which in women is called the menopause—marked with neurasthenia, capricious weaknesses, doubts. Ten years ago, he could have faced the law courts. But in 1934 he was, behind that extraordinary façade, a finished man."

His fortune was also finished. Those who helped him get it got it—all. He was able to leave nothing to his wife but a tender letter in which he begged her to rear their little boy and girl "in the sentiments of honor and probity, and when they reach the ungrateful age of fifteen to watch over their associations." The touching and domestic love between this Russian-born swindler and his French ex-mannequin spouse seems the single true story in the whole incredible affair.

The only message Mme. Stavisky received from her husband after his flight was a pot of white hyacinths.

The only message she has received from the thousands of men who battened on him was a tailor's bill.

"Bloody Tuesday"

Nobody knows how many people were on the Place de la Concorde the night of February 6; maybe forty thousand, maybe sixty, with hundreds of thousands more on the Left Bank, be-

hind the Madeleine, down the Rue de Rivoli, up at the
Étoile, over on the Place des Ternes, struggling to join them.
For no matter what the sectarianism of the French is now,
or a future bloc of other European nations may make of that
evening, its initial importance lay in its unheralded unity, its
passionate, complete popularity. For several years, every class
in France has been banditized by state taxes, state politicians,
state-protected swindlers; on that one night every class in Paris
turned out to protest—from men in Republican derby hats
down to chaps in Communist caps, from middle-aged, medaled
war veterans down to Royalist adolescents who had never bat-
tled for anything except, in dreams, for an exiled king. Against
horses' hooves, gunshot, and police clubs, this unpartisan mass
fought in surprise, struggled with mutual courage, and was
struck down without party distinction.

However, by morning, when the papers came out, the
strugglers—those who weren't unconscious in hospitals or
morgues—knew better. Or worse. For headlines in the Communist *L'Humanité* informed them that the fight the night before
had been against Fascism and that the Working Men of Paris
Had Answered. *L'Action Française,* Royalist gazette accused of
Fascism, said that the noble riot had been against Communists,
Socialists, Radicals, Republicans, Jews, and Freemasons. *La
République* (Left-Wing Young Radical) said that the Republicans Had Quelled the Uprising. Léon Blum's Socialist *Populaire*
said that dictatorship had been attempted by War Veterans and
the Right; Léon Bailby's Conservative-Nationalist *Le Jour* later
said that War Veterans had defeated dictatorship attempted by
the Left. *L'Œuvre,* which, as Radical-Socialist party sheet for
Chautemps, Daladier, and others recently spat out of power,
which had to expectorate on as many as possible in return, said
that the sixth had been An Evening of Fascist and Communist
Riots in Which Royalist Camelots, Blue-Shirt Young Patriots,
Fiery Cross Veterans, and Bolsheviks Had Vainly Attempted to
Take the Palais-Bourbon by Assault. Well, so they had, along
with thousands of other men, who couldn't be called anything
specially except Honest Citizens moved to a Sense of Outrage at
Last. Only *Le Matin,* sole among twenty-seven dailies, simply
had significantly called the sixth "A Day of Civil War."

The *Revue des Deux Mondes'* comments on the riots of February 6, 7, and 8, 1834, just one hundred years ago to the dot, are not unlike those of last week. The Revolution of 1848, which also began in a February, and also started, as on last Tuesday, as a just manifestation against corrupt politicians—though it ended dissimilarly, let us hope, in the killing of twenty thousand people—was also almost partisaned out of its original force by odd French factions in favor of lots of things beside the point, including Poland. If the French still insist on going out of their own back yard, one can only trust that their wandering interest today falls not on that constant Corridor but on Austria and the Saar, two European spots as important to Paris for their events as its own Place de la Concorde.

Five simple, stupid steps led up to February 6. In their inept ness, they could serve as easy lessons on how to make a revolution. (1) Premier Chautemps's refusal to retire after the Stavisky scandal had involved his Radical-Socialist party (especially after the Oustric, Sacazan, Aéropostale, and Hanau scandals had involved nearly everybody else's party). Chautemps resigned only after the Boulevard Saint-Germain riots, and the clear evidence of insults and paving bricks that the public was tired of hushed swindles, lost savings, what were called party loyalties, and, worse, what were called Corpse Cabinets, consisting of men revived from a previous dead regime. (2) To pacify this public, Daladier was called as Premier, he being another member of the Radical-Socialist party, by this time the last party Parisians wanted to see, hear, or smell. After promising to investigate the scandal and put in new, lively men, Daladier hushed up the scandal and set in the customary Cabinet cadavers. However (3), for a change, and in order to gain Socialist support, he dismissed the Prefect of Police just at a moment when the city most needed a prefect; and (4) ousted the venerable director of the Comédie-Française theater, who had been giving Shakespeare's mob-inciting (and box-office-filling) *Coriolanus*, replacing him with a Sûreté Générale police officer. On top of this, with tension and by now ridicule in the city air (5), Daladier appointed as Minister of the Interior, or chief in charge of the patrolling of Paris, a personal friend from the provinces who so little understood Parisians that he ordered them shot at on the Place de la Concorde.

The rest is data, details. Examples: War veterans protesting to government that Gardes Mobiles, before firing on crowd, failed to sound regulation three trumpet calls, which makes resulting deaths illegal; also signal fact that their and all paraders' permits had been okayed, thus making troop charge on them irregular. Two riot widows have brought complaint against X for willful murder of their husbands. Official number of dead, twenty, obviously too small; unofficial number, around seventy, also too small except for miracle, considering that over two thousand machine-gun shots were fired into twenty thousand people. French cost of living, compared to French wages, higher by thirty per cent than any other on earth. Taxi strike plus riots coming during spring fashion shows estimated to have lost big houses one million francs each. By breakfast after February six riot, Paris cleaner than New York any day, and by noon immaculate and mended. Prime Minister Herriot was nearly undressed on street by the mob; one deputy taken from bus, detrousered; one horse guard ditto, being paddled bloody by his own sabre; three horse guards still missing after riot, supposedly having been thrown in Seine. Socialist leader Blum's Quai Bourbon house lighted at night and soldier-guarded to make Royalists think he's living there, which is not true. Wednesday night some *apache* looters racketeered motorists one hundred francs each to let cars cross Rue de Rivoli without being somersaulted. Sixteen theaters dark, only Bourdet's new *Temps Difficiles* selling out, since it describes *haute bourgeoisie* as either rotted by money-love or else not worth their salt to France as a class. It is a terrible and timely play, historically no *Barber of Seville*, one hopes, but still a temporary substitute.

Stavisky

CONTINUED

To keep up with the Stavisky scandal—i.e., the French government—anyone would have to read the newspapers three hours a day, which is what everybody does. It is curious to be living in a land where the government is busy not governing but sucking pencils over the scenario of a super-production, thirty-million-dollar gangster film on which it will not get a penny back—if it can help it. Daily, the concocted plot arrives at a peak of ingenuity, complication, villainy, and breathless surprise which simply cannot be beat—until the next day's new twists beat it all hollow. The most unlikely people have lately been involved: Lucienne Boyer, smart night-club queen, who was asked to tell the judge how she happened for two years to have lived with M. and Mme. Romagnino, M. having been Stavisky's right bower (if not fatal ace of spades). Mistinguett was asked to explain to her public how she happened to be photographed at a Montmartre supper table with a bunch of posies and Jo-Jo-the-Gray-Haired-Boy, sometimes called Jo-Jo-the-Terror, Stavisky's crazed muscleman (whom she had innocently taken for a provincial notary public). Even Galmot, a fantastic *rhum* Deputy for French Guiana, where the blacks worshiped him as king, is now supposed to have been murdered there in 1928 on the orders of his pal Stavisky, whom—one good turn deserves another—he had sold out to the police in 1926. Galmot's death had been till today a mystery to everyone except the Sûreté, who know everything until it no longer pays. It also seems, according to the recently shown movies made by cameramen called to Chamonix in preparation for Stavisky's "suicide," not only that the crook didn't shoot himself in two impossible spots, but that he wasn't even potted by the police. He was killed by a friend. After all, what are friends for? . . . Everywhere one turns here, past, present, future, theater, police, weekly magazines, casinos, bordels, parliament, government-backed bonds, senators, magistracy, one sees the triumph of the criminal mind

And of the detective-story writer. The series of Stavisky Scandal investigation articles by Georges Simenon—France's Dashiell Hammett, hired along with Sir Basil Thompson, late of Scotland Yard, by the evening journal *Paris-Soir* to solve the remaining mysteries—have been magnificent for writing, sense, and bravery. Simenon's articles on Stavisky's aide Jo-Jo, handsome, strange brute, "caring," so he admitted, "neither for women nor men, but only for radical books," led the latter to surrender to the embarrassed police, who didn't want him, since they knew where he was and that he knows too much. Stranger still were Jo-Jo's corrections of Simenon's report on Jo-Jo's interview in his hideout hotel near Prunier's Traktir Restaurant, corrections solemnly printed in *Paris-Soir* next night, and including such items as the muscleman's having said he said he would knock six of Simenon's teeth out, not crack his head in, as had been printed. Or "Let's not exaggerate," as Jo-Jo editorially suggested. Since then, Simenon has, by printing initials, names of streets, hangouts, color of car, beard, or girl friend's eyes, repeatedly identified dozens of important Stavisky clues and key individuals without either losing his molars or the police making any new underworld arrests. In the midst of the latest Stavisky government investigations, some senator or other proposed some law or other about the price of wheat, on which the French farmer's next summer's crop, and city folks' next winter's bread, depend. But nobody paid any attention.

Sanctuaire

The first of William Faulkner's works to be translated into French has just made its appearance here in the selection of *Sanctuary,* and among the critics the sound and the fury of praise have only been less loud than the confusion. No English-language work since ˆand except James Joyce's *Ulysses* has ever caused such an uproarious volume of comment in literary France. "*Sanctuaire,*" remarks Malraux, recent Goncourt prizeman in the preface, "is the intrusion of Greek tragedy into the detective story." "*Sanctuaire,*" comments the columnist Maxence in *Gringoire,* "will aid in the forming in the Latin mind of a new picture of America. Veritably, between the Faulkner heroes and we French there is some kind of fraternity which up to now we have never found in American novels."

"The principal personage in *Sanctuaire* is a young girl, beautiful as one of our European sisters," continues Maxence earnestly. "What is interesting about her is not her legs but her eyes, not her white arms but her soul. I don't know if one can fully measure the consequence of the entry of such a person into the American novel. Temple Drake is certainly no Racine heroine, but she exists. That she is kidnaped in—how typically American—an automobile, that she falls into the hands of gangsters, becomes the mistress of a sad and cowardly bad man—these turns of fate seem to us, perhaps, too predictable, too conventional. That she is thrown by her feeble lover into a house of prostitution and that this gives rise to the most banal and boring police chase is also unimportant. The greatness of *Sanctuaire* lies not in what happens in it but in its somber, ardent poesy. Faulkner's craftsmanship," he adds more sternly, "is forced and unbearably facile. His analysis, sometimes, is pitifully insufficient. But his characters, especially Temple, are admirably drawn. They carry their horrible destinies like a cross bruising their shoulders. Living as we now are, in a tragic epoch, one may suppose that the French public will by instinct turn toward this most profound and original work." *Sanctuaire* is already selling in its eighth edition.

Mme. Marie Curie (1867–1934)

The death of Mme. Curie here was an international death. A native of Poland, a worker in France, with radium donated by America, she was a terrifying example of strict scientific fidelity to each of those lands, to all civilized lands. During the early years of her marriage, "I did the housework," she said, "for we had to pay for our scientific research out of our own pockets. We worked in an abandoned shed. It was only a wooden shack with a skylight roof which didn't always keep the rain out." In winter, the poor Curies worked in their overcoats to keep warm; they were then, as always, very much in love with each other and with chemistry.

Today, in America, radium is characteristically supposed to have been found by Mme. Curie, and in France, naturally, the discovery is accredited to Monsieur. Probably both discovered it together, since they were never apart until he was killed in 1906 on a Paris street by a truck. Certainly the husband's first work was with crystals. And no Curie at all, but a friend of theirs, Henri Becquerel, discovered uranium rays. Still, it was Mme. Curie, intrigued and alone, who devised a method of measuring this radioactivity, as she named it; her proving that it contained essential atomic properties instituted a new method of chemical research, altered the conceptions of the nineteenth century, and for the twentieth gave the base for all modern theories concerning matter and energy. Eventually her husband deserted crystals to work with her on the discovery of polonium (which they named after her native land; Madame, *née* Sklodowska, was always a patriotic Pole); then she or he or they discovered radium. Madame thereupon determined the atomic weight of radium and obtained radium in metallic form. For this she was crowned with the Nobel Chemistry Prize. She was the only woman ever permitted to hold the post of university professor in France.

She called fame a burden, was busy, sensible, shy, had no time for polite palaver, was a good mother to her two girls. The younger, Éve, is beautiful and a professional pianist. The older daughter, Irène, carried on her mother's tradition by also marrying a scientist, Fred Joliot; they are the most promising laboratory couple here today, and have already made extremely important discoveries concerning the neutron.

When the Curies were first wed, Madame put her wedding money into a tandem bicycle; later they got around, financially, to two bicycles. Early snapshots show her young, fetching, in short skirt, mutton-leg sleeves, and an incredible hat, flat as a laboratory saucepan. Later in life, her husband said, "No matter what it does to one, even if it makes of one a body without a soul, one must go on with one's work."

Mme. Curie had long since been in that zealous condition before she finally died.

Pleyel

The greatest piano name in French history has just passed from sight with the rechristening of the Salle Pleyel as the Salle Rameau. The name Pleyel has been associated with the best music-making of France for the past hundred and fifty years, or considerably longer than it should really have been, since the last of the name to function professionally was active in Napoleon's heyday. The founder of the clan was an Ignace Pleyel, who was a friend of Mozart and one of twenty-four children born to a poor schoolteacher and a noble lady who was no snob. After the Revolution, he composed, and played on the organ at Strasbourg Cathedral, an opus devised to include offstage cannons as percussion instruments, fainted when they went off on time, and went to Paris to found his fortune manufacturing pianos and managing the greatest concerts of his time. His son Camille carried on the business with a Mr. Wolff as partner. On Camille's death Wolff took over the piano and concert affairs, but acted like a Pleyel, since he invented the harmonic pedal, the transposing keyboard, and the baby grand, which Gounod honored by nicknaming it the toad, or *crapaud*. The Pleyel *crapaud* was such a hit that a special Wolff factory had to be built to meet the fad. On Wolff's death, his son-in-law, Lyon, now an old gentleman, kept up the family tradition by inventing the chromatic harp and lute, the double piano, and various acoustic theories. Old Lyon's son, Robert, invented nothing for the Pleyels except, one hears, the habit of giving the pianos away free to his friends. With the new Pleyel concert program heads reading SALLE RAMEAU and the Wolffs and Lyons being replaced by an even more incognito board of business directors, the great musical name of Pleyel now becomes for France nothing but a distant echo.

Frederick Delius (1862–1934)

Frederick Delius, the English composer, was recently discovered dead at Grez-sur-Loing, a river hamlet not far from Paris and close to where Strindberg and R. L. Stevenson once lived. Delius was seventy-two years old, had lived in seclusion for thirty-six, was paralyzed and blind. His optical malady came from shock suffered at having to flee his home before the Germans at the Battle of the Marne. At the age of seven, Delius played *Götterdammerung* from memory after hearing it once. His father was a Yorkshire magnate; in trying not to be a magnate but a musician, the son did many odd jobs in his youth, including raising oranges in Florida. For fifty years, England said nothing about his music. During those years, the musician said about England that it had "a predilection for mediocrity. Emotion is not liked by the English. It is not good form." In 1929, his admirer Sir Thomas Beecham made a last attempt to conduct Delius into popularity. Delius became a fad, there were Delius Festivals, Oxford made him a Doctor, his home town made him a freeman.

Delius was too old and faraway to do much about his English

triumphs. Sightless, motionless, he just listened to them in Grez-sur-Loing on the radio.

Goldwyn's *Nana*

An important international legal decision is about to be handed down here, since the Zola children, all middle-aged, have gone to court against Samuel Goldwyn for what he and Anna Sten did to their dear father's novel *Nana*. As a film, *Nana* aroused almost more literary discussion here for being what the book wasn't than the book once aroused for being what it was. The French Authors' League even said the picture "seemed part of a plan to weaken France's prestige, literary and moral," which was the first anyone knew that *Nana* had anything to do with either. After all, the literary style of Zola is still considered gross, and *Nana's* publisher had to hurry to England to escape not prestige but prison. While Hollywood is thanked for having flatteringly atmosphered the film in the manner of Manet (owing to its ignorance of the fact that the inartistic Zola thought Greuze the greatest French painter), to real Parisians the movie Parisians suggested that they hailed not from the capital of France "but from some baroque land, maybe a kind of Patagonia." The critics also complained that the story had not been followed closely enough, especially, thank heaven, in the vulgarer details. Madame Leblond-Zola complained to her lawyer that the story hadn't been followed at all and thanked heaven for nothing, not even for the fat sum Goldwyn had paid her. Unfortunately for her, she has just made public her contract with him, which states that "the buyer will have the right, in employing the book, to make any changes, additions, or modifications he thinks proper, and to eliminate any part he sees fit, without harming the general plan of the book." Or as *Comœdia* sharply inquires, "What are the Zolas complaining about?" With such a contract, *Nana* could have been filmed as a Second Republic gold-diggers' musical comedy with cancan chorines.

From the Yussupoff ° and the Zola cases, Hollywood has

° Princess Irina Yussupoff was awarded twenty-five thousand pounds (one hundred and twenty-five thousand dollars) and costs from M-G-M by a British court, which upheld her claim that she had been libeled in their film *Rasputin and the Empress*.

learned with surprise that history is not necessarily dead, especially if there are any living relatives.

Mme. Lydia Stahl

Until Lydia Stahl was arrested last December, her French friends regarded her as an exceptionally bookish, art-loving private individual. The French secret police saw her as an unusually erudite, cultivated international spy whom they'd had their eye on since 1920 but could not trap till thirteen years later. Even then she was so persistently brainy that the final roundup took three months, of which the last three days and nights were spent without sleep by detectives who knew she was their mental superior and so were nervous. At the moment when they arrested her, she was studiously occupied with a Chinese translation—of Japan's war plans.

Mme. Stahl was born in Kozlov in 1885, married a landed baron in the Crimea, divorced him in Constantinople, took her degree of master of arts at Columbia and her doctor of law at the Sorbonne, was a polyglot who spoke English, French, German, Russian, some Finnish, and a few of the Little Russian dialects, and had prepared a thesis on Confucian culture from original sources. In art she was particularly interested in contemporary sculpture. Of her marriage was born a son who died and to whom she was tragically devoted. After her arrest it was found that her largest trunk, as she told the police, contained the little boy's toys. As she didn't tell the police, it also contained photographs from the French Ministry of Marine's secret dossier on its coast defenses. In general, her spy work sounded like a dull postgraduate course in political economy—since she specialized in French land and sea armament figures and, above all, in French economic policy.

However, her profession had its moments of gaiety. After she was taken to jail, detectives found she had pasted French fortification plans on her Paris flat's parlor ceiling and then pasted flowered wallpaper over them. When she was trying not to be put in jail, she threw off her detective shadowers by shopping in the Trois Quartiers department store; she would hurry in the Boulevard de la Madeleine side door, lose one detective among the umbrellas, shake off another in the leather goods by the main entrance, and slip out through the lipstick and perfume counters by the side door into the Rue Duphot. As part of her lighter spy work, she also had a lover, Professor Louis Martin, code expert for the French Ministry of the Marine. He decoded in twenty languages, was a tall, white-faced, red-haired, middle-aged scholar whose chief complaint, during the seventeen months he was in jail before being tried for espionage and acquitted on a technicality, was that the French jail contained no dictionary in Sanskrit.

Professor Martin for five years lived in a modest Left Bank Paris hotel. [*Where I myself lived at the time. We were on speaking terms only insofar as we said, "Bon jour," to each other when we met on the narrow staircase. J. F.*] For a man who was a spy, or even for a man who was not, the professor's clothes were extraordinary: he affected a Wild-West sombrero and vivid mustard-colored suits which made him noticeable to the whole neighborhood, including the corner policeman. Though he supposedly spoke eight living languages, in all those five years he seldom said a word to anyone in the hotel. Also, after five years of living in the same third-floor back room, when he moved out—to go live nearer Mme. Stahl—he didn't leave so much as a scrap of paper behind him. The hotel-keeper's wife thought such tidiness, for a man, remarkable. The police thought it remarkable, too. However, in his new rooms they later found the scraps of paper they were looking for: missing documents from the Ministry of the Marine, marked SECRET—CONFIDENTIAL

Lydia Stahl's debacle as a really fine spy came from two factors affecting all business today—overexpansion and competition. Though working for the Russian government, she was sold out to the French government by a Finnish counterspy working for the German government. At the time of Mme. Stahl's arrest, she had nine spies in her employ—two French, including one suburban schoolmistress; two Rumanians, man and wife; two Poles, also married; one Serb, and two married Americans, Mr. and Mrs. Robert Gordon Switz. Their mixed professions were mostly all high, the list including—besides the schoolteacher and the professor—a sculptor, doctor, dentist, a biological chemist, a journalist, a factory foreman, one hardware merchant, one boilermaker, and one aviator, or The Aviator, as the American Switz was known to the spies by code.

This was a big business group for one woman to run, and costly; when rounded up, 99,200 francs, or close to seven thousand dollars, in cash was found on their persons. As the judge said, no French schoolteacher, with her miserable pay, could have ten one-thousand-franc notes sewed in her petticoat and also have a clear conscience. Besides her bad conscience, the schoolteacher had a short-wave wireless for receiving messages, and a wireless-telegraphy set.

Aviator Switz was Mme. Stahl's pay-off man for the band—in more than one sense, unfortunately. He and his wife turned state's evidence when arrested, and according to an old French law benefiting spies who betray other spies, were automatically acquitted at the group trial. The French schoolteacher and the Rumanian wife, who both had babies while awaiting trial, took their babies to court and even took their babies to prison with them. Each got three years. The intelligent Mme. Stahl, who got a longer sentence, remained intelligent to the end. As for the Switzes and the rest, she said she'd never heard of them. The only one she knew was Professor Martin. For he, like herself, was a scholar.

Mata Hari (1876–1917)

The recent arrest and conviction for spying of the Russian Mme. Lydia Stahl has brought back memories of Mata Hari, the Dutch-Javanese dancer, whose real name, Gertrud Margarete Zelle, sounded less terpsichorean than deadly domestic. The most famous of all modern *espionnes*, she was finally captured and shot in Paris during the last World War.

Mata Hari was an unmental woman of mixed north and south blood, half Dutch, half Javanese. Both bloods dominated, giving her the benefit of neither. She was laborious and reliable-minded; she had flesh and coloring which looked exotic. She was not beautiful but had regular features that made up well on the stage. Though undercover a secret agent, she made her public entry into Paris as a professional dancer. In her dances she displayed her lean, lithe, muscular limbs and her excellent simple body, which lacked corporeal exaggerations and was no more exciting nude than dressed. This was the body which was later to be shot. Though she has enjoyed, especially since her death, the reputation of being *une grande amoureuse,* her real love was the German government, and as a woman and a spy she was faithful to it. When she finally faced the French firing squad, she courageously cried, "*Vive l'Allemagne!*" as her last words.

Ten years before the last great war, she was already an important matinal spectacle in Paris when she rode each morning in the Bois de Boulogne. Her androgynous physique looked its best on a horse, which she was careful should always be a dappled gray. She affected a fascinating and old-fashioned equestrian getup—the top hat with flying veil, the voluminous draped skirt, the tight-fitted coat designed for the Empress Eugénie forty years before. Her street clothes, if more up to date, were pleasantly eccentric rather than chic; her coats had always an Amazonian touch; she inclined, perhaps because of her unsuspected profession, slightly to the military in her tailoring.

As a dancer in select salons, she was in considerable demand among daring international hostesses. She danced for the great Emma Calvé in her apartment in the then much discussed new glassmaker Lalique's building in the Cours la Reine. Certainly one of Mata Hari's most astonishing performances was held in the Neuilly garden of an American lady over a long period noted for her intellectual energy and sardonic social indifference. While duchesses gaped, the spy-dancer made her entry, nearly nude, on a rented, turquoise-blue caparisoned circus horse. (She had wanted to make her entry on a rented circus elephant, which the American had thought would be difficult to manage, since there were tea and cookies to follow.) At another and more intimate feminine fete, she engaged herself—at a high price, for she never forgot she was a mercenary—to dance entirely nude before ladies only. In the midst of her number, which was a Javanese warrior's dance, done with weapons, she rightly suspected, because of the large shoes, that one of the assembled ladies was a lady's husband, disguised. She nearly ran him through with her spear, right in the parlor. She was always courageous.

Though she had lived at first in the modest Hôtel Balzac in the Étoile quarter, as time and prosperity went on, she moved to the Hôtel Crillon. It had two doors, always useful to a spy—one onto the Place de la Concorde and not too far from the French Ministry of War, and one onto the Rue Boissy d'Anglas, not too far from the President of France's palace. In her Crillon days, Mata Hari moved up in the world, was much noted at theaters on first nights and in cafés on the right afternoons, and made the acquaintance of the snobbish, elegant, limited Robert de Montesquiou, who was later to be known to the world as Charlus in Marcel Proust's remarkable and relevatory novels on Parisian prewar life. The men who knew her best, though, were the ones who knew her least. These were the unfortunate young French lieutenants who, before and especially after the war broke out, she made so shameless a set for as to make their confidence and confidences seem strange even to this day. What she wanted from them was endless news of troops; what they wanted from her was a brief story of love. The exchange was, considering the dramatic circumstances, probably equable.

Mata Hari has come down in Parisian history as a great courtesan. She was not. By tradition, a prewar great courtesan was a venal, public, pretty woman of enormous social influence who was customarily kept by a kind of cartel—three millionaires, or two dukes—or by one royalty, and who, if she knew her business (which she usually did), had no private life or love. Mata Hari was a prewar demicastor, a precise professional rating lost in the vulgar organic confusions of today. A demicastor was a venal public woman, not necessarily over-pretty, and of so little social influence as to be permitted all the private life and love she desired. Mata Hari desired only one of both—spying for and being devoted to the German military command.

When she was arrested, the evidence of her brilliantly successful competence as a spy was so great that none of her astonished social friends could properly protest. Anyhow, such protests were not frequent during the war in French courts martial. Mata Hari was sentenced to be shot by a firing squad of French soldiers in the Paris suburb of Vincennes. Legend states that she dressed for her last moment in a fine mink coat—over her nude dancer's flesh. According to the American lady ° in whose Left

° Natalie Barney.

Bank private garden she had once danced semi-nude, this is in-
correct. She died wearing a neat Amazonian tailored suit, specially made for the occasion, and a pair of new white gloves.

The young French noble who, as officer of the day, was faced
with the dreadful duty, afterward said that she stood so still that
she made him tremble when, his saber lifted in honor to one
about to die, he gave the command, "Fire!"

Charles Boyer

Charles Boyer has gone to Hollywood to become, with luck,
the latest imported American movie star. Boyer is The Young
Man of Paris; an actor so talented that he evades the grand old
tradition only by being naturalistic; has been coupled with both
Henri Bernstein and the Guitrys, or normally the best that
French stage writing and playing offer; is the only French male
movie star whose box office here has registered his sex appeal;
and has what the French admiringly call *le regard de Vénus,*
which we call a little cross-eyed.

1935

Gounod's *Faust*

In September 1858 a Paris musician named Gounod hummed to the cast of the Théâtre Lyrique snatches of his new *Faust*, which, since he was mad about Goethe, he had, as he said, "had on his stomach since youth." That *Faust* is about to have its triumphal two-thousandth representation at the Opéra, with new scenery, dresses, and tights, Yvonne Gall, and Georges Thill. The piece was first given on March 19, 1859; Gounod was forty-one; a Mme. Ugalde rehearsed Marguerite but thought her silly, so was replaced at the last minute by Mme. Carvalho, wife of the Lyrique's director. *Faust's* press criticisms were bad—except for that of Berlioz, then music critic for the *Journal des Débats*; his *Damnation of Faust* having been given years before, he could afford to be generous, and was. Meyerbeer said the Gounod work lacked melody; other critics said it had too much. Because its press was bad, its attendance was good; Parisians went to *Faust* to hear for themselves how awful it was. Attendance developed its success. By 1887 it was an established hit, with Gounod conducting its five-hundredth performance.

Today it is given thirty times a year at the Paris Opéra alone; de Choudens, the publishing house which originally bought the rights for ten thousand francs, never repented of its bargain. The most celebrated Marguerites in France, after Mme. Carvalho, have been Christine Nilsson (1869), Rose Caron (1886), the diva the French call La Melba (1890), Eames, Calvé, and, in the twentieth century, Geraldine Farrar and Mary Garden. Of recent years Gounod's old-fashioned, ugly house on the Rue Gounod in Saint-Cloud (fine telescopic view over Paris) has been for rent, furnished, to any renters who were willing to pay for the fact that *Mireille* was composed there and thus were able to consider that the astonishing Victorian furniture came free.

Shakespeare and Company

Miss Sylvia Beach, who is Shakespeare and Company, the most famous American bookshop and young authors' fireside in Europe, is shortly to sell in manuscript important modern writings which she, along with the world's other booksellers, has been selling only in print. As first publisher of James Joyce's complete *Ulysses*, Miss Beach has unique Joyceiana, comprising collector's items that no one else on earth has, not even Mr. Joyce. To bibliophiles, the sale's finest item will be her first edition of *Ulysses*, 1922, blue-morocco binding, printed on white Dutch paper, the second volume off the press in the rare edition of two hundred, and containing a poem Joyce wrote her, his inscription, and, bound in the back, his original plan of the book. Item two will be *Ulysses* proofs and various typescript versions not included in the final book, plus marginal notes and pen corrections. Item three will be a manuscript version of *Portrait of the Artist as a Young Man*—about six hundred pages, being what was left after Joyce threw it in the fire in despair at publishers' refusals. This MS is written in ink on white copybook paper, unlined, with very wide margins. Further rarities will be a partial MS of *Dubliners*, "A Painful Case" and "Grace" complete, "The Dead" incomplete. Also the MS of *Chamber Music* from which Joyce read the poems to Yeats, the MS of *Pomes Penyeach*, and the MS of a lecture in Italian on Defoe given by Joyce at the Universita del Popolo, Trieste, in 1913. Also pamphlets published by Joyce, including that by Skeffington, murdered in the Irish revolution, and Joyce's own *Day of Rabblement*, both in original pink covers; as well as (a great rarity, since most pious people destroyed it) a blasphemous broadside Joyce wrote and left at leading Dublin citizens' doorsteps on quitting the town. For autograph-hunters, the hundred and fifty signatures, some with letters attached, to the "Protest Against the Pirating of *Ulysses*" is an unusually complete selection of modern literary lights from A to Y, there being no Z; just from Aldington to Maeterlinck to Wells to Yeats. Non-Joyceian items in the sale will include two original drawings by Blake, a first edition of *Lady Chatterley's Lover*, a MS of Walt Whitman, etc. Miss Beach's sale will be the first first-water Joyceiana marketing since the Quinn sale. It will probably take place in her Rue de l'Odéon Shakespeare shop.

[*Sylvia had told me at this time, with sadness, with grief, that her bookshop and personal finances were at a low ebb and she would have to sell some of her treasures. She asked if I had any American friends who were collectors and might be interested. Because her coming sale was important if melancholy international news, I suggested that I ought to announce it in the Paris Letter in* The New Yorker, *optimistically assuring her it would surely attract the eye of some useful bibliophiles. To my humiliation no Americans who later attended her sale and made purchases seemed to have been brought there by my Paris Letter announcement, a mortification intensified when Sylvia insisted upon giving me, for my effort at least, a numbered uncut first edition of* Ulysses *on vergé d'Arches paper, which carried with it an original page of the manuscript, which Joyce had overwritten with his typical extra entangling sentences, dealing with the so-called Circe incident. This concerned the music-hall actress Fay Arthur and the "non political concupiscence" caused by "Fay Arthur's revelation of white articles of underclothing while she [Fay Arthur] was in the articles."*

It was not until after the second war, in 1950, when Paris was still chill and expensive, that I decided to sell my Ulysses, *which she had given me, for her benefit, without informing her until it was a fait accompli. A Boston bibliophile friend of mine, in France for a visit, had happened to say he wished to give a fine modern book to the Morgan Library, one not already included in its collection, his gift to be made in memory of Miss Belle da Costa Greene, a friend of his during her post as the library's first director. What would I suggest as a suitable book? I said that if the library contained no* Ulysses *I myself could furnish one with a rather special history, which I related to him, which I would cede to him at the going market price for such a rarity, adding optimistically (once more!) that it would probably be around five hundred dollars—I hoped. It turned out that the current price at this time was exactly one hundred dollars. This still seems to me shockingly little for a first edition of a book which had in 1922 created such a stir that even pirated copies sold for far more. My only satisfaction was that Sylvia ac-*

*cepted the sum, perhaps because it was so niggardly, without
demur and was actually delighted that her volume, and in a
way mine, would now belong forever to a great and glorious
third party, the Pierpont Morgan Library. In consequence the
1950 Report to the Fellows of the Library announced the acquisition of "a first edition of one of the most famous contemporary
novels, James Joyce's Ulysses. This volume is a presentation
copy from the publisher, Miss Sylvia Beach, and is in mint condition in its original printed wrappers. Accompanying it is an
early draft of the manuscript, a portion of the controversial
Circe episode." The card catalogue on the acquisition further
noted that it was accompanied by Miss Beach's engraved calling
card, pasted on the book's front lining, and bearing her auto-
graphed inscription, "For Janet Flanner with Sylvia Beach's love
and gratitude."*

*She always gave more than she received. Publishing Ulysses
was her greatest act of generosity. J. F.]* °

André Citroën (1878–1935)

The recent bankruptcy and death of André Citroën, France's
greatest automobile manufacturer, ends a curiously un-French
career. Before the war, he was a salesman in a motor house,
which promptly failed; during the war, he was the organizer of
the arsenal at Roannes; after the war, he was the father of the
little five-horsepower car that gave him international fame and
over a billion francs annually. He sent great photographic expe-
ditions into both Asia and Africa, as publicity wrote his name in
electricity on the top of the Tour Eiffel, built beautiful model
factories with playgrounds and nurseries, gambled a million
francs a throw at gaming tables, believed in mass production in
the American manner, and so died without a franc. Before his
death, his furniture had been sold, along with his wife's pearls
and the villa at Deauville. In the last of his frequent bankrupt-
cies, the anxious government itself took charge. It was his boast
that he never paid his taxes; it was a fact that by his uncontrol-

° From a memorial volume, *Sylvia Beach* (1887–1962) published 1963 in
Paris by The Mercure de France and containing reminiscences by various of
her friends.

lable visions and bluff he ruined his stockholders, bankrupted his creditors, and threw thirty thousand skilled workmen onto the street. He had unlimited energy, was a megalomaniac and a great jollier. He loved making banquet speeches. Once he gave one at London in English, a language he did not speak; he had had his remarks translated and had memorized them. Nobody understood a word. His French speeches he invariably learned by heart and never followed. One time when he was about to read a speech that was to be broadcast all over France (after he had promised to follow its text), he said, "Oh, let's tell funny stories instead," and was immediately taken off the air. When he crossed the Spanish border on a motor trip, he was stopped by a customs officer, who asked, "Name?" "Citroën," he replied. "I didn't ask the car's name but yours," said the officer. "Oh," said the manufacturer, "I'm a Citroën, but it's a Hispano." It was. He was a likable, sly little man with charm and the ability to wrap people and banks around his finger. His errors lay in believing that Paris was Detroit and in stating with satisfaction on his deathbed, "After I'm gone, the House of Citroën will fall." It had fallen long before. It was, indeed, doomed to fall from its inception. For France is not the U.S.A.

Josephine Baker

The answer to Cécile Sorel's having gone into the nude Casino revue is that Josephine Baker, once of banana garb and the Folies-Bergère, has gone into Offenbach and bustles at the Marigny. *La Créole* is not Offenbach's best work, but it is Miss Baker's, up to date, and might have been written for her, so appropriate are the light, innocent melodies—composed in 1875, a quarter-century before she was born in St. Louis—to her high, airy voice, half child's, half thrush's. The role was created fifty-nine years ago by the famous Anna Judic, who, according to photos in the possession of F. Boutet de Monvel, administrator of the Théâtre des Variétés, played the Creole as a white; critics of the period stated, however, that she blacked up with licorice for the part; her son, on the other hand, affirms that his father "was too well read not to know that a Creole was of white blood, born 'neath tropic skies," which is no clear clue at all as to what hue the female of the family appeared under. Today Miss Baker's superb brown thighs, especially when prancing in *Restauration* lace pantalets, seem without argument what Offenbach must have had in mind.

The Swindling *Présidente*

In a country where, in business, the female sex is not given half a chance, the achievement of a Frenchwoman by the name of Marthe Hanau was remarkable. Mme. Hanau was the most inventive, brainiest, most convincing confidence woman modern France ever produced. Indeed her swindling during France's unrestrainedly dishonest 1920s was topped only by one performer, and he was the prince of his profession. Serge Alexandre Stavisky outdid her by stealing nearly ten billion francs and causing the February 6 riots of 1934, in which fourteen people were shot dead by soldiers in the Place de la Concorde. Mme. Hanau merely caused seven citizens to quietly do themselves to death at home when they discovered her schemes had taken their last sous. As she was a spicy, eccentric Paris personality, her death in prison was a loss to the *chroniqueurs*. Her life also represented a loss—one hundred and fifty-five million francs— to her investors.

Marthe Hanau was born Parisian, commercial-minded, and respectable. Her mother, a patient, penny-pinching Jewess, was owner of a small Montmartre baby-clothes shop called La Layette pour Fr. 8.45. Though the profit was slight—one of everything an infant needed for $1.69 took close figuring even in those days—she was able to give a dot of three hundred thousand francs to her daughter Marthe when, in 1908, at the age of twenty-four, she married Lazare Bloch, a handsome, callow suitor whose family had done nicely in the jute business. By the time he and his wife arrived in the Correctional Courts twenty years later, they were divorced but still inseparable. She had taken back her maiden name; he had lost his patrimony and her dot, had been through bankruptcy, and was working for his ex-wife as a jolly, cigar-smoking customer's man in her so-called investment house. Bloch described himself to the judge as "the kind of fellow who could sell peanuts to the Pope." Police rec-

ords showed that the only thing he ever sold was a bottled refreshment called the Tube du Soldat, described on the label as
"*Café et Rhum,*" an unholy fraud palmed off on soldiers during
the war. Because he omitted the word "imitation," in relation to
the word "rhum," Bloch was arrested for misrepresentation of
merchandise.

By the time Mme. Hanau came to court, she had for three
years been one of the most talked-of figures in Paris. The financial pages of certain newspapers had given columns to her me-
teoric rise, the front pages of all newspapers had given double
space to the facts of her sudden fall. During her apogee, millions
of French had read about her and thousands had, unhappily,
written to her, enclosing checks. Comparatively few people had
seen her till she appeared, aged forty-six, in the prisoner's dock.
She was an unusually short, round woman, with vulgar, virile
gestures, a taurian head, small even features, full rouged lips,
sharp almond-shaped eyes, and a fulminating vocabulary and
voice, both indicative of the crass energy on which she had built
her career.

She had started her career, after her divorce, by selling per-
fumes and soap. The war was just over then and helping make
women attractive once more had seemed a good, peaceful business. It was not, however, sufficiently exciting or devious for
Marthe. She had learned through her ex-husband's mishandling
of their little fortunes how money could be lost on stocks; she
was curious to know how it could be gained. She was an exceptionally intelligent woman, as the prosecution later stated; so intelligent indeed that, as the judge agreed, only when she was in
prison would the stupid be safe. She had been educated to be a
schoolteacher and had taken a first prize in mathematics; her
brain had a native preoccupation with, and a fabulous memory
for, figures. In the postwar air of France, Marthe Hanau had
sensed the gathering of the monetary clouds which were to represent the true atmosphere of the 1920s. She suspected that
credit, not cash, and that speculation, not investment, would be
the crazy climate the world would have to weather, and she
made herself ready.

It took time. It wasn't till 1925 that she managed to open a
one-room curb brokerage shop in one of the narrow streets behind the Opéra-Comique. There she also started publishing her

famous *Gazette du Franc*, at first a tipster's sheet. In three years
it had become powerful enough to worry the French government and upset millions of gullible investors. For in casting
about for a new method of arousing the postwar French financial appetite, Hanau had hit on an ideal excitant—a mixture of
publicity and patriotism. The average provincial xenophobic
Frenchman swallowed it like a tonic. To appeal to him, she advertised herself as a new broker loyally supporting the French
franc and French investments in opposition to the well-estab-
lished brokers then universally boosting the English pound and
American Can.

She furthermore managed to be the one European of her time
who made a good thing out of the League of Nations and the
Treaty of Locarno, both then in high international favor owing
to the signing of the Kellogg Pact. Hanau honored Mr. Kellogg's
work by getting out a special Kellogg Pact *Gazette* number. It
was skillfully compiled by a new editor, Pierre Audibert, a
high-class journalist who was a League fanatic and former political protégé of Minister Herriot. Through his Herriot and Ge-
neva connections, Audibert obtained signed photographs and
letters from some of the leading political and public figures of
France and Europe: Briand, Barthou, Paul-Boncour, Primo de
Rivera, Cardinal Dubois of Paris, and Poincaré. These photos
were published in the flamboyant Kellogg Pact *Gazette*. There
was even a picture of Mussolini, dedicated to "*Il mio amico,
Bloch*," which was a result of an interview Hanau's ex-husband
had had with Il Duce when they discussed some bland Franco-
Italo-Hanau farm-mortgage scheme. Because of a political tie-up
with the Minister of Education, the Kellogg number was franked
to all ambassadors in Europe and, what was worse, to every
schoolteacher in France. Though the diplomats doubtless realized that Briand, Barthou, *et al.*, in donating their photographs,
were merely getting advertising for themselves and their political policies, the schoolteachers thought the leaders were en-
dorsing Hanau and were, in fact, okaying her investments along
with Locarno and peace among men. For, besides Poincaré's
face, the *Gazette* also included announcements of Hanau's proj-
ects—her Consortium Français, Société des Valeurs, Ile-de-
France real estate, Midi golf courses on abandoned farms—all
offered with the pledge, believe it or not, that they would not

be permitted to pay dividends of more than forty per cent. To the little French speculator, investing with Hanau seemed like investing with the League, *la belle France,* and heaven on earth, with, for once, a fat reward for his virtue. Investors' money began pouring in from all over the Republic.

Then followed Hanau's greatest period. By 1928 she had installed herself in impressive quarters at Nos. 124-6 Rue de Provence, with four hundred and fifty local employees, one hundred and seventy-five agents operating all throughout France, and a job for her ex-husband which gave him, among other things, seventy-five hundred francs weekly for cigar money. She paid herself one hundred and fifty thousand francs a month. Marthe Hanau had become *la présidente* of the Compagnie Générale Financière et Foncière, which advertised itself as "a center of brokerage operations and administration of capital." Madame Présidente, as she was called, was the busiest woman in France, advising her sixty thousand investors, supporting the franc, raiding the Stock Exchange, running seven new syndicates in oil, textiles, etc., and managing a business called Interpresse, which published two daily customers' sheets, one of prophecy before the Bourse opened for the day, one of explanation after it closed. She was also busy paying her bank depositors eight per cent and telling the public that any bank which paid less was a robber. She worked from ten to fifteen hours a day.

Her special power as a promoter apparently came from the facts that she half believed in what she was selling and that, being French, she regarded cupidity as a national virtue. This last gave strength to her gift for advertising. Since she was contentious and well informed, her shrewd attacks in the *Gazette* on big business and its privileged profits made her seem a champion to the small bourgeois, squeezed between the depreciated franc and the new postwar industrialism. Her relations with her readers and investors became half avuncular, half demagogic. Being a dominant personality, she was obeyed as if she were a man; being a woman, she was loved as if she were a friend. Along with their checks, provincial investors sent presents of homemade *pâtés,* garden flowers, and knitted scarves. Her customers were principally the clergy, widows, retired military fogies, schoolteachers, and small-town shopkeepers.

Hanau's psychological chemistries were violent and personal.

She hired people just as she wrote her market prophecies—on hunches. Her staff adored her. Competence and experience were of no interest to her and probably she sensed that such qualities would have cramped her broad style. She saw herself as a woman of destiny. She had a tremendous gift of gab. Her conversation, whether with a customer in her office or with her Bourse touts at a Montmartre café table, was a swift alto combination of swearwords, salty repartee, unbalanced invention, and unvarnished common sense.

She loved hard-luck stories; she gave thousand-franc notes to down-and-outs and costly gifts to her pals. As she said, "I give an automobile away the way I give a box of candy." She gave three handsome motors to herself: a Hispano, a Voisin, and a Panhard. Because she was too busy to fuss with fine clothes, she wore outsize schoolgirl black dresses with schoolboyish white collars and cuffs. However, she found time to purchase 2,000,048 francs' worth of diamonds and pearls and some sable coats as a sort of distraction. She always kept a minimum of a half-million francs in her checking account; during one market crisis, she carried one million in cash in her pocketbook. Though her ex-husband, Bloch, had moved up enough in the world to buy Chez les Zoaques, Sacha Guitry's Normandy estate, Mme. Présidente's official residence remained a simple suburban villa in the outskirts of Paris. There she lived with a lady's maid so devoted that she later helped her lady escape from prison. For her occasional flings at gay night life, Hanau also had a little town flat in the Rue de Varize, decorated with racy mythological scenes. With her favorite friend, Mme. Joseph Pollack, exotic-looking offspring of a respectable Parisian jeweler, Marthe sometimes rushed overnight in the Hispano to Monte Carlo for a weekend of gambling. Money was the only thing Hanau could work at or even play with.

As the winter of 1928 opened, the French Radical-Socialist government began being alarmed. Its leaders had rashly lent their faces and sentiments to Hanau's house-organ, *Gazette,* and were under suspicion of having done far worse; smaller party figures had accepted tips, subscriptions, or cigars from the ubiquitous Bloch. Savings banks reported enormous withdrawals; it was rumored that six hundred billion francs had been turned over to *la présidente* for speculation. The French government was in financial difficulties, as usual. It was feared the Banque de France was going to have to offer another measly three per cent national loan, and as long as Hanau and her promised forty per cent were on hand, who would buy?

On December 3, 1928, a special cabinet meeting was held to decide what to do with the woman. It was done the next day. A year after Premier Poincaré had given Hanau his photograph in the interests of world peace, he made war on her by having her arrested. She was locked in Saint-Lazare Prison, accused of swindling, abuse of confidence, and infraction of corporation laws. Bloch was lodged in La Santé Prison as her accomplice, along with editor Audibert and an elderly Count de Courville, Hanau's business manager, who had been hired because he had a title and knew nothing about business.

Though they were to discuss her in detail in the courts for the next twenty-seven months, it took the state's financial experts only an hour in the Hanau offices the next morning to see that she was a crook. Her underwriters in her promotion schemes were dummies, usually her ex-husband, operating under a series of fictitious names. Her investment syndicates the experts described as cisterns from which she dipped old investors' capital to ladle out as dividends to new speculators. Her eight per cent bank had neither ledgers nor bonded cashiers, having operated through pretty girl secretaries who fluttered around with loose-leaf notations, with the totals on file only in *la présidente's* head. As the government's spite and legal machinery, now both powerfully directed against her, proceeded, Hanau was declared bankrupt. She protested that her assets "almost equaled her liabilities," and though this was no ideal of solvency, it was nothing to go bankrupt about in the then money-wild France. The sum of her *escroqueries* was figured at 155,971,000 francs. Her bankruptcy was based on a little estimated deficit of twenty-eight million francs.

To Americans, it seems that French trials consist of two trials, with something being decided at the second one. This is because at the preliminary hearing, called an "instruction," prosecution, defense, experts, eyewitnesses, and the accused offer to an official called the instruction judge all the information they are later going to use at the actual trial, and which is all that they may use. So great was the mass of evidence and confusion at the "instruction" of Mme. Hanau that the sessions, which began early in 1929, lasted sixteen months, and her trial was one of the most melodramatic, quarrelsome, befuddled, and hilarious ever known in Gaul.

Its least humorous aspect was that, during its first fortnight, the Hanau suicides began all over France. A swindled shopkeeper of Toulouse hanged himself in lodgings far from home, hoping that the neighbors would thus "be unable to gossip about my death." A lacemaker of Calais drowned himself after depositing on the riverbank his best overcoat and his new umbrella, all he had to leave his family after his Hanau investments. A miller of Chambéry shot his spinster sister and himself to evade facing starvation. "Madame," the instruction judge told Hanau, "you have made cadavers." The judge also said that the late perfumer Coty's newspaper, *L'Ami du Peuple,* ought to help reimburse Hanau's victims because the paper's attacks on her in November of 1928 (as part of Coty's political policy against Poincaré) had forced into the courts and the public eye a scandal which might, for the sake of her creditors' pockets, have been more advantageously and quietly settled in the Tribunal of Commerce. This made the Royalist *Action Française* angry, as it claimed it had been the first to attack Hanau—and start ruining her creditors —in October. In the meantime, Hanau attacked *Le Journal,* claiming it had demanded a million in blackmail to cease attacks it had made on her in December; thereupon *Le Journal* attacked the Communist *Humanité,* asking two hundred thousand francs' damage for *L'Humanité's* libelous printing of Hanau's charges that the *Journal* had attempted blackmail.

Then Hanau began suing everyone who appeared in court. She sued her instruction judge because some eighty documents had mysteriously disappeared from her desk owing to his forgetting to have her offices sealed and guarded after her bankruptcy. She sued a police lieutenant because he seized papers in the offices of her *Gazette* without a warrant. She sued the French government's financial experts (one had begun his career as a piano tuner) for making an error of 11,642,269.42 francs in totaling up her accounts. This the experts resented, since, as they proved next day in court, they had made only an error of 10,924,708.28 francs. Sometimes she was kinder to the experts; twice in court when they failed correctly to add up, with pencil and paper, some of her fabulous accounts, she wearily gave them the right answer out of her head. Mme. Présidente also sued X, unknown, for having stolen some of her documents from the public prosecutor's files, where they were supposedly under lock and key. No one sued anyone for mailing the key back to the French Minister of Justice with a malicious message which said, "Ask the prosecutor's chief clerk about this!" and implied that the clerk had been bribed by a higher-up to destroy incriminating evidence.

By this time, the public, at first shocked at Hanau, was horrified by its government, whose corruption, complicity, inefficiency, or at best guilelessness in *l'affaire* Hanau any voter could see with his eyes closed. As Hanau truthfully informed the instruction judge, Quai d'Orsay officials had been guests at a fine dinner she gave at the Ritz the year before, and the Mayors of Marseilles and Strasbourg had attended her business rallies in their towns. All over the country, deputies, prefects, and smaller fry sweated as their names figured publicly in her tale. To prevent her gabbing more than was legally necessary, Hanau and her accomplices had been denied the freedom on bail which other big French crooks have always enjoyed. In their efforts to get released from jail, Audibert, the editor, claimed that he was suffering from angina pectoris, and the aristocratic business manager, De Courville, unused to unheated cells, developed pneumonia. The court became half hospital, half Punch-and-Judy show.

Hanau, scorning masculine maladies, went on a protest hunger strike for her liberty in March, 1930. On the twenty-third day of her strike, she was too weak to be brought before the judge, so she was carried instead to the prison ward of the Hôpital Cochin for forcible feeding. There, despite her feebleness, she bit through half an inch of rubber feeding tube and smashed two stoneware prison cups before the doctors succeeded in nourishing her. On the twenty-fifth night of her strike, she escaped from the hospital's prison ward. After asking for a hypodermic of camphor to give her strength, Hanau later squeezed through a window and slid down one of her own fine linen sheets, which had been tied to the radiator by her devoted maid, Marie Snoeck, come to pay a late call. Attired only in her chemise, stockings, bedroom slippers, and a handsome sable coat, Mme. Présidente hailed a taxi and drove to the Boulevard Malesherbes post office, where she mailed a letter (threatening suit, naturally) to the Minister of Justice. As she later wise-cracked, she'd had a notion to deliver it to him by hand. She then took a second taxi, which she dismissed because the driver took two wrong turnings and she had no intention of being rooked. She walked to a *bistro* and phoned her lawyer that, owing to "the indignity of forceful feeding," she was leaving the Cochin; she then taxied to the Saint-Lazare Prison gate. "It's I, Madame Hanau," she said to the startled guard. "I've come home."

The story of her fugitive wanderings was received by Paris citizens with delight and by the officials with incredulity till the third taxi driver volunteered to the police that a hatless lady had hailed him in the Rue de Lancry, just as she'd said, had asked him to go to 107 Faubourg Saint-Denis, which is a polite way of saying to Saint-Lazare Prison, and had given him a fairly good tip, too.

On the twenty-seventh day of her hunger strike, Paris was less delighted, for Hanau was close to death. Weak as she was, though, she wasn't too far gone to make a deal. She wrote the judge that she would start eating "as a favor and so as not to impede justice." The next day, after sixteen months' incarceration before she had even been tried, Mme. Présidente was let out on bail of eight hundred thousand francs. Half of this sum was raised as a gift by thousands of her still devoted and credulous customers. By now, Hanau's public role had changed from champion to martyr.

Because her red-corpuscle count was dangerously low, by doctor's orders her trial was delayed until October 1930. For its opening in the Eleventh Correctional Court, two hundred cubic meters of documents relative to her case had been assembled. The act of accusation took nearly three hours to read, and was followed, as the court stenographer recorded, by the judge's opening statement: "Now we'll all take a twenty-minute rest [Hilarity]." Hanau had twenty notebooks of refutation in her satchel, Vittel water for refreshment, and cough drops, which she sucked whenever she had shouted herself hoarse. Not only by her noise but also by her brain, memory, and brilliant strategy, the prisoner dominated the court. During her five months' trial, she never ceased putting up a magnificent, futile fight. "You're a terrible client for your lawyer, Madame," the judge admiringly said. "You leave him nothing to add in your defense." Her speeches truly covered everything. From behind the screen of her malpractice emerged her own purer vision of what she called democratized banking; banking in which the depositor was a business associate; in which corporations were to be cooperatives; systems in which bank employees shared, as hers had, in the bank's investments and in which banks were open in the evening—hers was the only one in France which ever was —in order to discourage French workmen from hoarding their wages in their socks. French banking methods and manners date from the time of Louis-Philippe; to the conservative court, Hanau's ideas seemed futuristic rather than modern, though there are liberal financiers today who still admire her ideas as much as they deplore her amorality.

On March 28, 1931, her battle came to its end; she was pronounced guilty, sentenced to prison for two years, given a fine of three thousand francs and costs of nearly half a million. Of her three male accomplices, who she had gallantly insisted were no more responsible than office boys, only one was convicted: Bloch, her ex-husband, got eighteen months. Audibert was acquitted and, at the joyful shock, died that night of a heart attack. Count de Courville had established his innocence by claiming he'd lost half a million of his own savings in the Hanau crash. (Next day his wife sued him for separation; the half million had been hers.)

In April, Hanau successfully appealed her sentence. The remarkable woman left prison, walked into a new office, and started business again. This time it was a brokerage house with the strangest customers' sheet ever published. This was called *Le Secret des Dieux*. The gods were the great international money figures, their secret was whether they would move the stock market up or down. Two thousand investors immediately paid Hanau two-thousand-franc subscriptions each for this odd information, with its mixture of mythology, House of Morgan, Olympus, Sirius, and Sir Henri Deterding. It was suspected that, for their own ends, little gods gave her the remarkably inside dope she used in her attacks on the larger deities. Certainly she prophesied Loewenstein's crash and suicide a week before he threw himself from his private airplane into the English Channel. Three days before Ivar Kreuger shot himself, she warned that he and his affairs were coming to a violent end. She surprised her subscribers by describing the cooperative arrangement between Standard Oil and Royal Dutch; she even surprised Royal Dutch by hammering its stock down a few points on the Bourse. This time, Hanau was out not so much for money as for blood.

In her *folie de grandeur,* she developed a persecution complex; realizing it was impossible to avenge herself on the entire Radical-Socialist party, she concentrated her attacks on big business, which had helped put her away. Unfortunately for her, the talents she brought into play were less destructive than constructive. She could ruin no great gods, but she couldn't help giving a lot of little mortals excellent stock-market advice. Though a crook, she was also a brilliant broker, with a sensitivity for the movement of stocks like a robin's for the movement of worms underground. In one year, from the list of stock selections which her *Secret des Dieux* chose to recommend, French industrials like Schneider-Creusot, Bordeaux Gas, etc., twenty rose handsomely, four were fair, two variable, and only one was bad—a record no Paris house of the year equaled for astuteness and good luck. Her other good luck consisted in going short when customers sent in money to buy stock for them: she usually won, because almost invariably she was able later to get the stock at a lower price than her clients thought she had paid for it. Even though she presently broke her hip in a motor accident, and during *Le Secret*'s two most active years could barely walk, she was still too lively to please the Stock Exchange.

In July 1934, the Paris Court of Appeals finally got round to Mme. Hanau's April 1931 appeal of her sentence. It is dangerous to appeal in France unless you are sure of your ground, for your sentence can be augmented. Mme. Présidente had been too sure of her ground. Her sentence was augmented by a year "because her first sentence," the court said, "had been very moderate, she was disagreeably aggressive, her present destructive publicity [against the gods] was the contrary of the high financial policies she pretended to practice, and she had only paid her creditors a minimum of what she had promised." (She had paid them forty per cent on the franc, a maximum as French crooks go.)

When she moved out of the law court that day for the last time, Mme. Hanau walked with a heavy limp and cane. She was pale, she had aged. The Stavisky swindle, which had broken since she first stood before the bench, had overthrown the double-faced Radical-Socialist party, had caused men to be shot in the streets of Paris. In that courtroom scene, Mme. Présidente now seemed pallid and out of date, like one of her faded, worthless *Gazette* stocks. But she still had the courage to continue to be disagreeably aggressive, since she was fighting for what turned out to be her life. She immediately filed an appeal against the added year she had been given, and lost again. Judgment was delivered on February 22, 1935, at five o'clock in the afternoon. Though it usually takes three days in Paris to file the necessary formalities for incarceration, Mme. Hanau was given exceptionally good service. She was arrested three hours later, at eight sharp, in her office, where she was doggedly working alone. This time she had no million in cash in her handbag; only a revolver, which was taken from her. Five months later, on Friday, July 19, the Prison de Fresnes was forced to announce that Mme. Hanau had died of veronal, which, owing to her jailers' negligence, she had procured and taken the Monday before. In life she had been overhasty. Her suicide took a long time.

No one knows what decided Mme. Hanau to die that week rather than any other, unless it was Montaigne, Marcus Aurelius, and Epictetus. Copies of their works, with the bolder, more fatally philosophical passages underlined by her in red, were found in her cell. She had never been a reader. The belated shock of meeting in books superior and unearthly male minds, so unlike those she had known in the world of politics and high finance, may well have sufficed to unbalance her. But she was ready for the stoics, as her letter of farewell to her lawyer showed. "The only modern efficacious engine," she wrote, "is money. In a corrupted world, the only means of conquering is money, half wrecked though it is and yet still alive. . . . I'm sick of money—money has crushed me. The thought of earning money fills me with horror and perhaps impotence. . . . Today I know absolute peace, the peace of renunciation, the physical peace I knew on the twenty-seventh day of my hunger strike. And so adieu. . . . I desire that mercenary hands should burn my body and the ashes be cast to the four winds."

In life, French law had been Mme. Présidente's enemy. In death, it did her no favors. It being illegal in France for those dead by violence to be cremated, Marthe Hanau was buried in Montparnasse Cemetery. She was followed to her grave that day by her ex-husband, her ex-lady's maid, and a half-dozen ex-investors. They still believed in her.

Jean Cocteau

Jean Cocteau's *Portraits-Souvenir*, just published, is a *demi-chef-d'œuvre*. The first half, dealing with the young scenes seen with the eyes of childhood, "which accepts nothing but poetic intensity," is Cocteau at his best; the latter half, where he is driven to recalling as an adult, is laborious. But for him to have written those first chapters, with their grace, passion, precision, their airy verbal strength and acrobatic genius for daring surprise, is for him to have signed his strange silhouette once more on the very atmosphere of his city and times. His material is rare—recollections of a rich little Parisian boy, living in the family *hôtel particulier* in Rue La Bruyère, where his grandfather had a solid silver bathtub "with the sonority of a gong and full of shoes and books, and where he collected Greek busts, drawings by Ingres, pictures by Delacroix, Florentine medals, autographs of ministers, masks of Antinoüs, vases from Cyprus, and Stradivarius violins." For his grandfather loved music and rejoiced in a private quartet which came and played with him. The first violin was the great Sarasate, who, with his red gloves, "his huge moustaches, gray mane, and frogged coat, looked like a lion dressed up as a lion-tamer." Sivori, second in the band, was a dwarf who refused to sit on Beethoven's scores when placed on his chair at the dinner table. Grébert, the cellist, playing furiously without ever stopping, used to rise and bow elaborately whenever Cocteau's grandmother passed through the salon. Etcetera, etcetera—charming etceteras. Cocteau's mother dressing for the opera—one of the most evocative stylized portraits French filial writing has produced; the first performances of *Around the World in Eighty Days;* the old Nouveau Cirque, with its odor of ammonia and its clowns; the fashionable prewar skating at the Palais de Glace; the costumes of the *grandes co-cottes*, so complicated with corsets, gussets, petticoats, bustles, pads, plumes, garters, gems that "the idea of undressing one of these ladies was a costly enterprise that had to be figured out well in advance, like moving day"—these and other phrases and pictures, such as young Colette, then "like a fox terrier in skirts," make Cocteau's book an hour's delight.

Chambrun-Laval

In marrying Comte René de Chambrun, Mlle. José Laval, Premier Pierre Laval's daughter, married into Roosevelts, Longworths, and Murats, which is pyramidal for the granddaughter of a jolly Auvergnat innkeeper. It was reported, and denied, that Laval gave his daughter a dot of sixteen million francs, which is a dot with a dash. As both the young folk are rich, it's a love match. At the wedding, Laval wore his famous white wash tie, a fetish since his arrival in Paris as a poor provincial schoolteacher with exactly one tie, which was white, and washable so he could look clean. He is now prime minister extraordinary of his country, nearly its dictator, certainly one of its rich men (he started his fortune with money left him by an aunt who was Anatole France's secretary), and his only daughter has married a noble young lord. It sounds like a fairy story in these grim days.

Napoleon-Louis Bonaparte

Summer being the silly season, it's the time to talk about the Republic of France's newest Imperial Pretender—Napoleon-Louis Bonaparte, turned twenty-one, an age to start pretending, last January 23 while in exile at Brussels, and only now delivered of his first public Parisian statement. The great Napoleon Bonaparte was this youth's great-great-uncle; the young aspirer is descended through Jerome (King of Westphalia) Bonaparte's marriage with Catharine of Württemberg, through their son Napoleon-Joseph's marriage with Clothilde of Savoy, and through *their* son Victor-Napoleon's marriage with Clementine of Belgium. The boy is nearly six feet tall, so he can't resemble his little great-great-uncle much except in the face, which has the curious, small-featured handsomeness that marked the original cameo-cut Corsican. As the young Bonaparte, even in exile, is treated to the dignity of the third person in speech and the pronoun in capital letters in writing, and in either case to the title of *Votre Altesse Impériale*, which in gender is feminine, part of the recent interview consisted of the interviewer's asking, "And Your Imperial Highness, does She like sports?" and Her Imperial Highness, the Prince, answering that She did, since they "give energy, without which no action is possible." Some of the things he said were brighter: "I think the material needs of the masses must be satisfied; people who are suffering physically and forced to stifle their needs are an easy prey to those who promise to fulfill their dreams, even though the promises are without sensible foundation. And what's more, the materialism which the young people of the nineteenth and first part of the twentieth century have been swallowing" ("gargling" is what Her Imperial Highness really said, which is pretty slangy) "no longer satisfies the aspirations of today's young minds. Faith in general, and in particular religious faith, is springing up again." Though the interview didn't mention it, there is a Bonapartist party in France which even has faith in the Pretender. The party is headed by General Koechlin, an old Alsatian aristocrat, and its adherents are Murats, de Massas, and other Bonaparte-created nobles. As the party has no money, and so no public backing, the movement is pretty well confined to the *salons*, though occasionally it publishes a paper. The party claims that the boy is brilliant; certainly he was brightly educated in Switzerland. He knows a lot about France, which he is forbidden to enter and through which he has traveled thoroughly on a passport probably made out in the name of one of his Bonaparte-created titles.

At present he lives in his Brussels palace, surrounded by touching souvenirs of his family's former apotheosis: the Legion of Honor collar that Napoleon wore on his green coat at the Battle of Austerlitz; the embroidered Directoire tailcoat he wore after the 18 Brumaire; a white baby dress of the infant King of Rome; the Emperor's Freemason regalia; the double-breasted gray coat he wore at St. Helena when he was sick, aging, and very fat, as the coat's girth shows; and, finally, the original Antommarchi death mask, made about five minutes after life left the great fighter and island exile who had once had Europe at his feet. In profile, his great-great-nephew in Brussels looks like that death mask.

Paul Signac (1863–1935)

Paul Signac, aesthetic, intellectual, *salonnier*, top-hatted Impressionist, and friend of George Moore, is dead.

Since the death of his teacher, Monet, Signac was the last leaf left on the Impressionist tree that temporarily cast in the shade the Luxembourg Museum, which first refused Impressionist pictures as gifts, only to pay fortunes for them later on. On meeting Seurat, inventor of Pointillism, Signac deserted Impressionism to become a Pointillist, and for the rest of his life painted everything in patches. His subject matter lacked Seurat's curious circus complexes and his more workaday water scenes eventually achieved monotony along with fame, but his aquarelles, with their pointed, brilliant-colored touch, were, and still are, justly popular. Rivers being the rage among painters of Signac's generation, he painted the length of the Seine up to the Atlantic and the Rhône all the way down to the Mediterranean, and when he ran out of rivers did the lagoons of Venice, one of his loveliest series. He made a cult of the novels of Stendhal and wrote a booklet on Beyle's life and works. For years he was president of the famous Salon des Indépendants, where as a young radical he had shown his first works. Last season, he resigned, brokenhearted, on discovering that today's young radicals thought him an old fogy. Certainly Signac was seventy-two, but he was also a confirmed Communist. In addition, he was the official painter of bourgeois France's navy.

Gambling

The chain letter has just gripped France. The results are astonishing. Journals are full of mathematics, protests, and praise, of photographs of girls who are getting married on their nine-teen-hundred-franc chain-letter winnings, and of old gentlemen who complain they can't get buried on theirs, since they were paid in stamps. Already a legal complaint has been lodged against Monsieur X, who is France's John Doe, and who in this case is apparently anybody who signs his true name and address to any chain letter he sends out. The banks are angry, since money which should be sensibly deposited is careening around the country by post in sums of one franc fifty centimes, usually in the form of three ten-sou stamps.

France being a Catholic country, the French chain letter contains no superstitious or religious hocus-pocus to frighten off good church members; the French chain-gang scheme is bluntly called *le Club de Prospérité,* and neither Heaven nor good luck are mentioned by it. Article 405 of the Penal Code, under which the sender of a chain letter can probably be prosecuted, doesn't refer to Heaven either, though it does mention five years in prison for those who try to "persuade others of the existence of false enterprises, of imaginary powers or credits; who attempt to give birth to the hope or fear of success, or an accident or any other kind of chimerical event."

It is not likely that the courts of justice will be forced to inflict prison terms on the chain writers. After all, France is a small country, with a population of forty-two million. After the fifteenth mailing of a chain letter that started with five French folk, 305, 575,780 letter-writers would be corresponding, which would involve three-fifths of the population of Europe. France isn't speaking to half the population of Europe, let alone writing letters to them.

Lucienne Bréval (1869–1935)

Lucienne Bréval, one of the oldest perfect Wagnerians, has just died here. She created the role of Brünnhilde in *Die Wal-küre* in Paris when the 1890s, or second, series of Wagnerian battles were at their height and it meant a riot to sing anything old, let alone anything new, by the madman from Bayreuth. (At the first, or 1860s, Wagner battles, members of the smart Paris Jockey Club, all in evening clothes, blew solid-silver whistles in protest at the première of *Tannhäuser*.) By the beginning of our century, however, Bréval was peacefully hailed as France's greatest Wagnerian dramatic soprano. (She was Switzerland's by birth, but had become naturalized.) She formed a tradition, still followed at the Opéra today, with her initial performances in *Lohengrin, Parsifal,* and *Götterdämmerung;* she created the leading role in *L'Étranger,* by Vincent d'Indy, and *Pénélope* by Fauré; and in general for forty years she set operatic precedents more by her superb dramatic acting than by her voice. Even after she retired to the obscurity of a sanitarium in Neuilly, the severity of her judgments could make Wagnerian debutantes at the Opéra tremble—could and did, for she never hesitated to speak her mind. In a way, she spoke it even after her death, since she left a list of the people whom she wished to have attend her funeral. All musical Paris had expected to go, but only a few were invited. Bréval also left orders that the Paris Opéra orchestra, "in full and with its best director, as if for a grand ceremony," should play the Andante from Beethoven's Symphony in A, the Fire Music from *Die Walküre,* and the Funeral March from *Götterdämmerung.* She ordered that there should be no singing.

Mistinguett

Before going into the new nude revue at the Casino de Paris, Mistinguett will spend her first three winter months in an operetta at the Théâtre de la Porte Saint-Martin called *La Bonne Aubaine.* This deals with a tough-little-fresh-flowershop girl who wins the million-franc lottery ticket and is never the same ever after, especially since all the time she has been Mistinguett, who hasn't seen a flower not made of ostrich feathers, rhinestones, or bird-of-paradise plumes for the last thirty years.

Paul Poiret

Paul Poiret's book, *Art et Phynance* [sic], is finally out, and is what no one expected from that racy, artistic, disillusioned *mondain* mind. It is merely a touching, awkward story of how he was fleeced out of his despotic dressmaking business by democratic banks, and lawyers whose names, in the retelling, he changes slightly to escape libel, but whose faces he describes perfectly, so they may not escape unfavorable posterity. It is a pathetic volume, a typical report of the aesthetic nineteenth-century individual gobbled up by the twentieth-century corporation plan.

Poiret was once a sartorial genius of Paris, and its most hospitable, if sharp-tongued, *bon vivant.* Born and bred in the heart of its *bourgeoisie,* traditionally educated in one of the capital's old Catholic *lycées,* Poiret nevertheless escaped with his personality. He became, for many years he remained, one of the city's great *couturiers.*

But he never regarded dressmaking as a closed calling. His energy always led him far and wide and even astray. In the thirty years after he started his aesthetic and financial career by selling fancy umbrellas in a small shop, he developed into an obstinate amateur of every other glittering profession that caught his eye. Close to fifty, he was busy at the writing of one-act plays. In 1926 he made his public debut as a painter somewhat, though perhaps not enough, in the manner of Cézanne. That same year, with Mme. Colette, in her work *La Vagabonde,* he made his bow as a boulevard actor after having barnstormed the Midi with a strolling troupe. The year of the Exposition des Arts Décoratifs, he opened a restaurant barge on the banks of the Seine. He designed a modernistic merry-go-round. Instead of horses he substituted a figure of himself, and caricatures of his friends, *midinettes,* wine merchants, and familiar street types. On their wooden backs the populace of Paris mounted for a ride.

He was among the first *couturiers* to become perfumer and decorator besides. As creator of Martine and Rosine, named in honor of his two daughters for whom these departments were to furnish wedding dots, he scented half the vedettes of Paris with his heavy oils, introduced black carpets, designed salons for Spinelly, and created for Isadora Duncan a room without windows. One year he sold his collection of modern paintings, only to found his vast collection of modern books, each volume bound in a silk he had designed himself, each text illustrated according to his orders with aquarelles overlying the printed word. Pos-

sessed of infinite patience and impatience, nothing was too oner-
ous if pleasing to his talented ego and eye.

Just after the last war ended, he opened a private theater in
his magnificent gardens near the Champs-Élysées. Here in the
open air, but under an artificial, inflatable rubber sky, romantic
pieces were played. Here Yvette Guilbert, enchanting relict
from the old Butte nights, wore her 1890 black gloves and sang.
Big Berthas and Gothas had just ceased splitting the twentieth-
century air. But with the intermittent thoroughness characteristic of him, Poiret piped his theater with prebellum gaslights to
heighten his momentary delusion. He was always magnificently
out of step. A man who has left his mark on the taste of his decade, his decade never satisfied him. He always tried to estab-
lish himself in other centuries as if for him time and history
were optional.

The true explanation of Poiret's curious career, character, and
more permanent fads apparently lay in his belief that, in a previous reincarnation, he was an early Oriental (probably a
prince). As if to surround himself with suitable companions, he
persistently dressed his clientele, whether from Chicago or Berlin, in the beads, gilt, and scarlets of the gorgeous East.

Even his private life when he was rich had the pasha touch.
His dinner parties are still recited in Paris like legends. The famous fetes of Boni de Castellane, while he was still a gilded
youth enjoying the Gould gold, were no more blinding than
Poiret's. At one of Poiret's dazzling costume balls, "La Mille
et Deuxième Nuit," three hundred guests stayed to see the
dawn come up in his garden in the Faubourg Saint-Honoré.
Black slaves served dishes at tables seventy-five feet long. Paler
female slaves lay feigning sleep on an immense golden staircase
erected beneath the trees. In one salon lay Mme. Poiret, dressed
in aigrettes. De Max, the actor, in another, recited poems, his
costume shivering with the shaking of thousands of pearls.
Among electric blossoms, live parrots were chained to the
bushes; their companions were monkeys and cockatoos. Rug
merchants, beggars, and sweetmeat sellers, hired to whine,
strolled among the crowd. Thousands of shrimps were consumed, three hundred each of lobsters, melons, goose livers; and
nine hundred liters of champagne. To contrast with the delicacy
of this scene and to show that the color of the East is really red,

behind the table laden with dead lambs stood a butcher. Surveying this small empire, Poiret sat on a throne.

It is not for nothing that the door of his private room in his *maison de couture* for years bore this sign for the benefit of his half-hundred employees:

STOP AND THINK
ASK YOURSELF THREE TIMES
IF YOU SHOULD DISTURB HIM

The constellation and zodiac painted on the foyer ceiling of his later establishment on the Rond-Point indicated the position of the stars at the moment of his birth. He believed in what he called his destiny.

Before the war of 1914, when he visited the Germanic states to view their new *Münchner-Wiener Werkstädter Kunst* and lecture them on his own aesthetic theories, he took with him as illustration and *réclame* his most beautiful mannequins, which scandalized the burghers. In his American lecture tour in 1927 Poiret was purely Occidental. He journeyed to New York alone, save for his manager. The object of his lecture tour was to beg American women to stop dressing like men or even like other American women, a too democratic tendency at which he found our matrons excelled.

As a spectacular public man of Paris, Poiret was known by all and disliked by many. A man of his energy has strength enough for feuds. In his relations with his employees he was effective, usually invisible, often tyrannical. His business was conducted along strict lines of temperament. (In France fortunes are made by what we would call mismanagement.) "Who designed that gown?" he once asked at one of his crowded formal openings as one of his own mannequins paraded in one of his own establishment's dresses which up to this moment he had never seen before. "Mademoiselle X did it, eh?" as he was given the name of one of his assistant designers. "Well, sack her. And what is the price of that frock over there?" pointing to another novel item that caught his eye. "Three thousand? Mark it at fifteen hundred francs. And you'll probably have trouble," though this may be legend, "giving it away for nothing."

In the early days of his great fame, and behind guarded doors when the fit of inspiration came on him, Poiret did all his own

designing. Fewer of the French *couturiers* than are supposed
personally design the clothes which make them famous. Several
cannot cut out a baby's bib. One of the greatest, a woman, cannot even sew on a button. But in his big days Poiret dominated
what he did by doing it himself. The theory of dressmaking is
that styles should change. Fortunes are made in changing them.
Parisiennes, whose fluctuating modes fashionable women all
over the globe are supposed to follow, have in consequence appeared with the gores, waistlines, ruffles, or whatnot annually
placed in a different spot, each successful shift bringing fortune
to the originator. To all these mutations Poiret remained on the
whole indifferent. Year in, year out, his clientele looked like
Asiatic princesses or Tartar priests in scarlet, black, tassels, and
magnificent gold. (For his purposes the entire East was Poiret's
oyster.) A Poiret dress could be identified as far as it could be
seen, like the brilliant uniform of a prewar hussar.

With the grand obstinacy of a dictator and an artist Poiret as
egotistically designed dresses he liked as if he were the one who
had to wear them. He risked his fortune. With postwar styles
(which means profits) tending toward untheatrical, masculine
simplicity, he stuck to his bizarre, female Oriental last like a
coachmaker who after the invention of automobiles continues to
fabricate magnificent ornate six-horse barouches. Because of this
obstinacy and courage he was one of the few modern *couturiers*
who actually perpetuated his name. In the art of the ultramod-
ern in dress and decoration, Poiret created a genre Poiret, as
definite to the connoisseur as the costumes that give the date of
any period drawing or print. It was no mean historical feat.

As an artist Poiret was not alone in his family. His sister Ni-
cole Groult was a second dressmaker in the group; Mme. Germaine Poiret, afterward a poetess, was the third. Mme. Boivin,
another sister, was one of the first important and influential
modern jewel setters. For several generations, the Poirets were
known as rich, liberal-minded Parisian *commerçants* noted for
their tolerance, their taste in the arts, and their broad emanci-
pated ideas.

Though married to a rich wife and father to a large family,
Poiret was always a public, not a private, man. Ever since his
first easy professional success, following rapidly after his ap-
prenticeship served with Doucet and Worth, he lived in the the-

aters, boulevards, and restaurants of his generation, where his eccentricities made him famous. He attended first nights in capes and flannel evening clothes. Every garment he wore was made to his order, even his hats. For years in summer he affected white. Bearded, dark-skinned, a man with virile eyes and small, handsome feet, he trod the Parisian summer avenues in the immaculate tussor of a visiting lion-hunter.

He was always a great trencherman, an exacting gourmet, an indefatigable eater, and a man of appetites. With his morning post his secretary used to bring in a pitcher of fresh and exotic fruit juices. In his pockets Poiret always carried boxes of comfits and chocolates which he nibbled all day.

In his high period M. Poiret was esteemed a rich man. His life was a series of expensive hobbies. He was reputed to have run through several fortunes like a small boy running through flower beds. Near the close of the 1920s Poiret, to whom earning money always seemed a tedious pursuit, found his affairs too involved for his scant patience. He sold out to a syndicate, later was interested in a smaller dressmaking concern which operated under its telephone number only as its business title. Then he retired completely.

Today penniless, positionless, living on the dole, in his garret chamber he has posted "A List of Former Friends Who Have Not Aided Paul Poiret." The list is quite long.°

Stavisky

CONTINUED

Alexandre Stavisky, the Slav swindler who twenty-two months ago posthumously twice broke up the government of France, has had a bullet through his head for nearly two years, but his case has finally come to trial. Everybody still alive is on tiptoe, especially his twenty friends, including two deputies and one general, most of whom have been languishing in jail since early 1934 waiting for their big day in court. At the first sitting in the Paris Assises de Justice, there weren't chairs enough for all the accused, the two hundred and seventy witnesses, the thirty-six

° Poiret died in poverty in Paris in May, 1944.

defense lawyers and their gowned clerks, the eighteen jurors (six in reserve, in case half of the first dozen crack up, which would otherwise mean a retrial), the ten plaintiffs and their solicitors, the six judges on the bench, two assessors, two consulting attorneys-general, and one overworked court scribe. Seats for the prisoners were handed out as at a diplomatic dinner—according to importance. Only those accused of fraud got to sit up in the criminals' dock; lesser lights, merely charged with the illegal reception of millions, were down on the benches usually reserved for the public. There was no room for the public. There was no room for the prescribed two Republican Guards to each prisoner; some Guards squeezed in, but most were huddled indignantly in the lobby. Though cleaning women had been up all the night before, removing superfluous furniture from the court, there was hardly room for the safe containing the twelve-hundred-page Act of Accusation, check stubs totaling the equal of $15,260,000, and other incriminating sheets, though there had been space enough to lose the safe's key just before the trial opened. In the prisoners' dock, there also, apparently, was no room for the many ex-government officials and other big men formerly, according to rumor, implicated in the government-backed Stavisky swindling. Obviously the greatest court of justice in all France is too small to hold such big leaders of Radical-Socialist democracy.

Experts now estimate Stavisky's swindles at the equivalent of $18,130,000 over a period of three years, with an extra near-swindle of $54,600,000, on Hungarian agrarian redemption bonds, which came within three months of being successful. There is a rumor that Prime Minister Laval may be tipped out of office any time now, and that Daladier-the-Killer, so-called for being Prime Minister during the 1934 February 6 riots, will be the new chief. If he gets in, one hopes that the public, with such a grand show as the Stavisky trial on, won't foolishly organize a rival spectacle of riots again. For some of the public would be killed in the riots, and then they would never know how all the exonerations in the Stavisky trial turned out. That would be a shame.

Marian Anderson

A most enthusiastic reception has been accorded the Salle Gaveau recital of the American singer Marian Anderson. Toscanini calls her an artist; she was rated a triumph as a singer of Brahms in the summer season at Salzburg; her Paris performance called out an audience that filled not only the hall but the stage. Miss Anderson's figure, especially in black sequins, is superb; she still sings too much with her eyebrows; her forte is still her magnificent contralto. Her German diction, Negro spirituals, and Swedish pronunciation are excellent; her good Schubert was less appreciated here than her badly chosen English encores—"Will-o'-the-Wisp" and the like. It is hoped that at her approaching New York concert, both she and the city get a worthier program. Miss Anderson is from Philadelphia; was educated at the Girls' High there; and was given her foreign musical training, at first in Sweden, through the support of the Philadelphia Colored Baptist Church and the enthusiasm of the widow of the late Bishop Coppin, of the African Methodist Episcopal Church. For two years, she has had the most remarked musical career of any American now singing in Europe.

Politics

Laval is the only man in France behind the enforcement of sanctions against Italy; ° every other Frenchman is eating spaghetti and drinking Chianti in Italian restaurants to show where his heart and stomach are. The Right journals say the sanctions are barbaric, and the Left press says nothing, as a sign of civilized agreement. The Croix de Feu clubs threaten to take things into their own hands if the Communist groups don't stop beating up the Fascists, and the Communists threaten to beat up everybody if the Fascists take one more thing (and it looks like a gun) in their hands. There seem to be too many helping hands here and not enough heads.

° For Mussolini's aggression in Ethiopia.

1936

Stein—Human Nature

If French books have evaded the political question recently, one book written in France is going to go into it. This will be Miss Gertrude Stein's new volume, entitled *The Relation of Human Nature to Human Life; or the Geographical History of the United States*. The new volume, Miss Stein says, will be pretty long—about two hundred pages—and will be something in the style of her little-known essay, "Composition as Explanation," or very clear. She explains the new book's material as follows. "It is a discussion of the fact that human nature isn't very interesting and that that's why politics are what they are, since they deal with human nature. The book also deals with masterpieces; what they are and why they are so few." Thornton Wilder has annotated the MS with marginal queries and explanations which Miss Stein hopes will be included in the printed version. The book also contains a small play about identity which was written for the marionettes of Donald Vestal of Chicago. He has already made the marionettes who will play Human Mind and Human Nature, plus two other marionettes, who will play Miss Stein. Miss Stein adds that her new book is also "about money and romanticism; it's about many things." France could do with a book like that, even in English.

Jacques Bainville (1879–1936)

Most historians only write history. The late Jacques Bainville, historian, made history—in a small, posthumous way—by having his funeral procession interrupted by a Paris street battle between middle-aged Léon Blum, the Socialist, and adolescent Royalists. It was not a battle in which M. Bainville would have been interested, since his specialty was Napoleon and his favorite war site Waterloo rather than the Rue de l'Université, where the recent Parisian fracas took place. Royalist by political conviction, Bainville spent forty laborious, maladive years writing up the non-Royalist periods of French history. His famous work on Bonaparte is, despite its bias, considered a straighter report than that of Taine or Michelet. Bainville's *History of Three Generations,* which covers the nineteenth century and what he saw of the twentieth (being a pulmonary invalid, he saw little, and thought less, of it), is a remarkable, documented, prejudiced picture of great utility, especially to those who disagree with it. His last book, *Dictators,* dealing with figures antique and modern, is a disillusioned scholarly compendium which could comfort no one, not even a Bourbon, let alone the author, though it ranks as his mature final testament. Bainville detested "shock and adventure," and as a Royalist "spoke severely" against what he called the Civil War of 1789—the French Revolution. His funeral almost started a Civil War of 1936.

There was little adventure in it, except, perhaps, for Léon Blum, who nearly had his throat cut—or, as one of the Royalist journals put it, "received a scratch behind the ear." There was some adventure for a Dr. Gelse, Royalist district leader, who lost one eye in the fray. Blum's hat also suffered; it was finally found, damaged, on the editorial desk of the *Action Française,* Royalist newspaper. The Royalists can't imagine how it got there. A Communist office boy, probably.

Murder among the Lovebirds

Maybe our grandmothers were right and female standards are, on all sides, not so high as they used to be. Certainly an eclectic comparison between the mediocre murder recently committed by the nineteen-year-old Parisian flapper Mlle. Violette Nozière and the stylish assassination achieved by the consummate Mme. Germaine d'Anglemont, aged forty-eight, indicates a deplorable decline in the younger generation. Mme. d'Anglemont shot her lover like a lady, because she was jealous; Violette Nozière killed her father like a cannibal, because she wanted to eat and drink up the savings that were his French life and blood. Even in their private lives—or as private as could be, considering that both females lived on love for sale—Germaine d'Anglemont cut the grander figure, since, though an uneducated foundling, in her long life she had learned to dine with royalty, own a smart house, accept diamonds, and take such an intelligent interest in politics that senators and deputies had been her slaves. And even the gentleman she finally shot was a chief magistrate.

Though her doting parents had educated her over their heads and means in a Paris private school, in her brief career Violette Nozière had learned merely how to drink bad cocktails with penniless collegiates, was at home only on the Boul' Mich', gave her mother's engagement ring to a lover rather than received any gem from him, and certainly never met any member of the government until, on trial for parricide, she made the acquaintance of her judge.

Germaine d'Anglemont was the last of the silk-ruffled, scented, hard-lipped, handsome prewar courtesans, and she made a fortune. Violette was, one fears, not the last of the fake-silver-foxed, hard-toothed, modern young monsters of mediocre looks and without any sense of the business of life. Being up to date, her crime cruelly lacked the grand manner.

Since she was faintly intellectual, Violette Nozière characteristically chose poison and patience as her weapons. Though she did not succeed till August 1934 in putting her father into his grave and her mother into the hospital, she practiced up on murdering them in March by giving them, "as a nice new tonic" with their evening coffee, six and three tablets of veronal, respectively, which they hungrily swallowed, since both were passionate patent-medicine gourmets.

At shortly past midnight after the March evening, contented with their coma, their daughter set fire to the flat's modest parlor curtains, walked across the hall, roused a neighbor with a scream of "Fire!" and a brainy afterscream of, "I think the electricity must have short-circuited." The local fire brigade was called, and the next day M. and Mme. Nozière made the second page of the Parisian newspapers for the first and last time—thereafter they were unfortunately to be front-page stuff—for being unconscious from suffocation in what was called "A Bizarre Conflagration." Murder in an odd form was on its way to the Rue de Madagascar, where the three Nozières dwelt till they started on their separate paths toward cemetery, clinic, and prison.

In the five months which followed, the immodest Violette did nothing unusual—for her. She continued her afternoon and evening life on the large sidewalks and in the small hotels of the Boulevard Saint-Michel where, from the age of fifteen, she had been playing hooky from the costly female seminary for which her parents had scrimped so that she might star in mathematics. But though majoring in geometry, Vi knew less about Euclid than about a lot of other men. At her trial, it was brought out that she was not only a nympho- but also a mythomaniac—or a natural tart plus a born liar.

On the Café d'Harcourt terrace, she picked up men with a dual purpose, the second being to tell them fantastic fibs—that she was an heiress, that her grandmother owned a château, that an aunt had millions, an uncle billions, that she herself was noble, that she was a trigonometry professor, and that her father was a director in the French railways. He was, in a way. He was the locomotive engineer on the Paris-Vichy fast train; her grandmother's country place was a cottage where, after her granddaughter's arrest, the old peasant humbly died of shame among her cabbages. Indeed, only two things unusual were performed by Vi during those fatal five months. She continued to try to kill her mother occasionally: at any rate, whenever the girl prepared breakfast for her, *maman* was deathly sick after, so Vi must have been putting something into the coffee—besides chicory, that is. (Her father, having just fallen out of his engine cab onto his head, was momentarily in the hospital and so drank his bad coffee without ill results.)

Violette's second odd act was to fall in love: the emotion was great, since she eventually killed for it; the object was slight—an eighteen-year-old gigolo law student with sleek hair, slack morals, and American horn-rimmed spectacles, worn like a foolish foreign trade-mark on his French phiz. His name was Jean Dabin; his father, in Vi's mythology, was also probably a railway director—i.e., in reality, a whistle-blowing petty stationmaster on the Paris belt railroad.

Violette's love for Jean was the only true passion in her life, except that for murder. To him she gave all she had—herself plus one hundred francs a day, which she got from other men by night. She also promised to give him a secondhand Bugatti and a first-rate September holiday, for, as she said, she was shortly expecting to inherit one hundred and eighty thousand francs, or the exact sum her father had saved up from a lifetime of driving the Paris-Vichy express.

On August 23, her patience and poison and passion finally focused. Violette Nozière repeated what she had tried out in March, except that she increased her father's dose to twenty powdered veronal tablets and her mother's to six. This time she also gave herself a small dose of milk of magnesia, as she was feeling liverish. Then she curled up in a chair for a nap by her parent's couch while they died—she hoped. At two a.m., when she called the same neighbor, she this time screamed—since she had turned on the kitchen range without lighting it—"Gas!" and, as a new addition, "I think the pipe has burst."

The neighbor was, of all men to call in twice, an electrician and gas fitter by trades. Whatever he had failed to smell in March, this time he smelled not only gas but a rat. So did Vi, at dawn in the city hospital, sitting tenderly by her mother's bedside; the authorities had refused to let her sit tenderly by her father's slabside in the morgue. Sensing danger, she calmly rose and walked out into the new Paris day and what for one week seemed limbo, since no one could find her. By dinner, her news photo as "Wanted for Parricide" was posted all over Paris. Police hunted her everywhere, except at the Bal Tabarin (where she spent the first night after her crime gracefully waltzing) and on the Boulevard de la Madeleine, where a white-faced, neurotic, not very pretty young creature plied her trade while whispering crazily to her customers that her father was a railway director, her grandmother owned a château, and that she herself was an heiress . . . to one hundred and eighty thousand francs . . . oh, yes, she was surely an heiress by now. . . . On the sixth day she was trapped into a second rendezvous by a gallant young male who had recognized her face on the pillow from his newspaper he'd tossed on the chair. Arrested, she told the truth, probably for the first time in her life. At any rate she said she was glad she'd killed her father, who, she claimed, was a satyr, though her relief at hearing that her mother was yawning back from the jaws of death may have been a lie.

Her trial for murder in the autumn of 1934 was melodramatic.

It opened in the Paris Assizes with a five-minute silence for King Alexander of Yugoslavia, who had also just been murdered in Marseilles. In the three days which followed, Violette fainted frequently, was occasionally nearly lynched by angry crowds, and was constantly hectored in court by her mother, who was sentimentally suing her for damages for having robbed her of the sweetest husband woman ever knew.

In addition to other details, the jury was swayed by the fact that Violette had also robbed what she thought was her mother's corpse of a thousand francs pinned to the maternal corset. With lust for money to spend on her lover in cafés (for bad Martinis) accredited as her miserable motive, the jury judged her guilty of the uncivilized crime of parricide, whereupon the judge read what remains the most medieval death sentence preserved in modern French law: "She is to have her head cut off in death upon a public place in Paris. She shall be taken there barefooted, clad only in her chemise and with her head covered by a black veil. Before the execution shall be done, let the clerk in a clear voice read aloud this Judgment." Though women are no longer guillotined in France, and if they were, no matter whom they had killed, they would be allowed to die dressed and with their boots on, the rare sentence was followed by unusual silence in court, suddenly broken by Violette's vulgarly shouting, "Curse my father, curse my mother!"

To the outraged gendarme who dragged her away, she shouted in one of her illuminating afterthoughts, "Fetch my handbag with my powder, rouge, money. I must have dropped it in the prisoner's box." What was most precious she had clearly left behind her in court. Thus passed from youth into lifelong imprisonment the best-educated, worst-mannered young murderess in French annals. But it was the fact of the girl's having rudely slept in the intimate presence of the dead and dying that caused the French jury to cut her off from civilized society as long as she might live.

The jury in the same Paris court which had just tried Germaine d'Anglemont for having shot her late love, Causeret, had only cut her off from civilized society for eleven months. And even that period of sequestration was a cultivated *passetemps*, since she spent it as prison librarian; both before and after murdering, dear Germaine was ever the bookworm. Her crime, trial, sentence, were all as cynical and sociable as her origin. Born a love child humbly named Huot, whose father only made her acquaintance when she was aged eleven, at twelve Germaine had won the catechism prize in her orphan asylum, at fourteen had her first flirtation, at fifteen her first carriage and pair and the stylish name of D'Anglemont, which she picked out of a dime novel. The week before Mlle. Huot became Mme. d'Anglemont, she had been noted—pretty and shabby—in the then famous Jardin de Paris Café, the noting being done by a tableful which included Catulle Mendès, the poet; Henry Bernstein, the playwright; Prince Fouad, now King of Egypt; and other gentlemen of the 1905 *belle époque,* one of whom asked her how she got there.

She said she had run away from home penniless and had got into the café by pawning her umbrella for three francs with the *vestiaire.* The gentlemen handed her five hundred francs (one hundred dollars in those lovely days) to get some decent clothes, three francs to get her umbrella, and invited her to dine. Her second lover, according to the list the Paris judge indelicately read out at her murder trial thirty-four years later, was a Dutch millionaire named Van Horschoot; the third was an Argentine tutor the Dutchman had hired to complete the girl's education—though she seemed to know a great deal already; the fourth love was the Prince Franz Josef of the royal house of Bavaria, who died of a broken heart because she wouldn't marry him.

Among the innumerable others she did not marry were the Polish Count Wielsinski, who, instead of a wedding ring, could give her only diamonds and pearls; the Agha Khan, who merely gave her a diamond (though it was eighteen karats); Camille Picard, today Deputy from the Vosges; a M. France, who was seventy and in sugar; a M. Astruc, at whom she once threw an expensive Gothic statue of the Virgin; and a Dr. Morgilewski (whom she never saw again for thirteen years, till the fatal day when she telephoned him to come round professionally as she seemed to have shot one of his successors). The mass of Parliamentarians she also enmeshed finally dwindled down, in her forties, to the late-lamented Chief Magistrate Causeret, young, promising politician, fickle, married, father of children—and what was worse, son of the pious Rector Causeret of Clermont University.

"If I've omitted any of your lovers, pray excuse me, Madame," the Judge said ironically at her trial. "The list is already so long. You were a *courtisane de haut vol*—a highflier; you are also, alas, a good shot." It was her custom to practice in the shooting gallery near the Rond-Point where Ivar Kreuger bought his fatal suicide gun; she kept two pistols in her boudoir alongside the statue of Sainte Thérèse—all three useful as weapons to a woman in a jealous rage. For it was for jealousy that she murdered Causeret. She had him followed through the streets of Paris by a hunchback female detective (a masseuse, when spying was scarce), who reported that he had gone to a department store to buy suspicious silk pajamas, instead of going, as he had announced, to talk politics with an old gentleman.

At noon, five minutes after Causeret had returned to her smart Place Beauvais flat to lunch, there was still nothing to eat on the dining-room table, but there was a corpse with only a bullet in its stomach in the boudoir. As Germaine later admitted to the jury, she had been a little hasty—the handsomest apology a murderess ever made.

At her trial the jury also was hasty; in one minute they saw it would be useless to condemn her, since they also saw, all around the court, the visiting politicos who would demand and obtain her pardon. The jury therefore judged her guilty but with a cynically strong recommendation for mercy, which to the judge's mind meant a sentence of eleven months. Thus the quality of mercy was for once strained, since six years is a normal clement "stretch" for French female killers. Along with her eleven months, Germaine d'Anglemont also got bouquets of flowers in court, and her male friends shook hands, kissing hers.

In her trial, justice was not done. Yet injustice would have been accomplished had not a D'Anglemont's punishment been infinitely less than a Nozière's. For in a way these two were test cases, illustrating the modern French attitude toward murder, which can be summed up thus: the manner of killing is as important as the manner of living.

Léon Blum

Léon Blum, France's incoming Premier, is an odd man. He is now chief of the Socialist party, and was formerly legal adviser to the Hispano-Suiza motor firm. As a brilliant youth, he took his first degree in philosophy, his second in law. He became a popular Parisian theater and literary critic; was author of a book on Goethe, and another on Stendhal, which infuriated Beyleists; can recite Victor Hugo's verses by heart, also good kitchen recipes; loves Ravel's music; buys modern paintings; and adores cats, flowers, and fine *objets d'art*, with all three of which his beautiful apartment in a beautiful eighteenth-century mansion on the Quai Bourbon is always full. He has an odd gait, since he turns his toes far out; he wears spats and thick spectacles, is myopic and absent-minded. He is Deputy for the Narbonne vineyard district, and just misses being a teetotaler. His family were well-to-do Alsatians, his grandmother was an enthusiastic Communard, his brother René is art director of the Monte Carlo Russian Ballet, other relatives run the family fine-lace shop on the Rue du 4 Septembre. Blum, who has been married twice, is a strong Judaist but not liturgically orthodox. His political god is the martyred Jaurès. His mind is subtle and dialectic; his speeches are lucid, fluid, and delivered in a flutelike tone. For years he has ranked as Parliament's master maneu verer; till now, he has even been able to maneuver his party out of taking responsible power—no small feat. His most important pre-Premiership speech was that he made to the American Club here. The speech's tolerance pleased Blum's Moderate European enemies and angered his French Communist friends. His reference to the harm done by France's not having paid her war debt was supposed to please Americans. The last time Blum had referred to the French debt was when Premier Herriot wanted to pay it. Blum's lack of support was what caused Herriot's parliamentary fall. That was in 1932. This is 1936.

1937

Jules and Edmond de Goncourt

According to a recent journalistic literary squib, the Goncourt brothers' house at Auteuil, for twenty-six years the rendezvous of Parisian writers, is today inhabited only by a charwoman. Jules and Edmond de Goncourt bought this mansion, "*ce grand joujou de goût,*" as their *Journal* describes it, for eighty-three thousand francs. Jules died before his bric-a-brac was even in place; Edmond followed him in 1896. A widow then bought the edifice for sixty-three thousand francs, and sold it in 1920 for one hundred and fifty thousand francs to a M. Georges Liger, who sold it for eight hundred and twenty thousand francs to the city of Paris, as a future Goncourt Museum. He reserved the privilege of inhabiting it until his death, which occurred last year. The Ligers' old servant now lives in it, with no one's particular permission, and chars for her livelihood in the neighborhood. The ceremony of the Goncourt Prize award is held not in the Goncourt house but in the Restaurant Drouant, where the oysters are excellent. There is nothing excellent today in the Goncourt house but its memories. The rest is definitely dust.

Les Verts Pâturages

The intellectualism roused in French appreciators of American films must already have confused simple souls like Mae West, if she has heard of intellectual reactions anywhere, and will no less daze the talented Negroes who appeared in the film version of *The Green Pastures*, which is signally the intelligentsia's cinema sensation of the winter here. After comparing *Les Verts Pâturages* to the Anglo-Norman mystery play *Jeu d'Adam*, Pierre Laspeyres of *Comœdia* writes that the Marc Connelly film is "one of the most eminent mortal works since the Occidental Middle Ages, a renaissance of the ardent, allegorical religious spirit. It will influence art, music, methods of thinking. From now on the black people take a position in the balance of the spiritual world because they possess youth, the most convincing poesy, and the gift of representing humanity as a whole." After adding that Negro spirituals are technically similar to the Gregorian plain chant, the critic details the play's seventeen plantation melodies "which have autonomous themes. The fourth is very choral, with soft counterpart. The twelfth, 'Joshuah Fit de Battle of Jericho,' is a fast fugue. But the seventeenth is the loveliest—'Alleluia King Jesus,' a bursting suite of infant soprani with three voices developing in diatonic canon." French journalistic writing of this sort is what de Lawd called "passin' a miracle."

Gide—U.S.S.R.

It is because of the acute feeling about Spain's Civil War that André Gide's booklet *Retour de l'U.R.S.S.* has made such a stir here. These hundred and twenty-five little pages describe the author's major disappointments in Russia, where, as the pontiff of intellectual Marxism in France, he was recently invited with honors, and where he doubtless won't be asked to come again. Though he is famed as a thinker, most of Gide's comments are the materialistic observations of any visiting fireman. He found the Soviet vegetables mediocre, the beer passable, housing conditions bad. He discovered that state production, without competition, made for inferior goods; that the Stakhanovites are workers who are now producing in five hours what they were not able to produce formerly in eight hours. He found everywhere stultifying conformity, a desire not to think individually but to agree along the prescribed Marxian lines. He found a mentality more checked and terrorized than anywhere else, even in Hitler's Germany; an intellectual apathy alternating with a superiority complex; a complete ignorance of the rest of the world, which is considered too inferior and wretched for happy Marxists to know about; and the conviction that Moscow is the only city on earth that possesses a subway. He found the hopeful spirit of the people wonderful and moving, and that everything done for youth was done splendidly; he found that with the recent theoretical return to the family as a unit, to unequal wages, and to the right of inheritance, the basis of the revolution has been lost in what he calls *"embourgeoisement."* He found that Stalin was an icon. He found what visiting firemen always find.

Occasionally, though, the fine psychological writer breaks through. Gide notes that because of the emotions which Communism arouses, the truth about Russia is usually told with hate, and the lies with love. In speaking of the loss of the original Communist doctrines, he wonders whether the practical passage from the *"mystique"* to the *"politique"* may not always fatally bring with it a degradation. He no longer believes; now he only hopes.

French Films

French films used to be films which the French rarely went to see, American movies being their favorites. Celluloid has been changing lately. The movie that French fans are now queueing up for is the Ciné Marivaux's *Un Carnet de Bal*, which is not only one of the major films the French have ever made but also one of the grandest films Hollywood never made. Previous to its première here, this movie won a prize at Venice's International Biennial Cinematographic Exhibition, at which, it must be admitted, everybody good got one first prize, and some of the bad got three, as consolation. However, *Un Carnet de Bal* alone walked off with the Coupe Mussolini, which, as the name implies, is the highest award Italy can give these days. Mechanically, the story is built on the same structure as *The Bridge of San Luis Rey;* i.e., it uses an object, once associated with a group of people, as a focus for pursuing the tangents of their various lives. This film's focus is the girlish, first-dance program of a rich, ripe widow who traces the scattered lives of eight young waltz partners who had once sworn to love her forever. Owing to the brilliant all-star cast, these partners turn out to be some of the greatest male actors of France—Louis Jouvet, in the superb role of a cynical night-club owner and thieves' mouthpiece; Harry Baur, as a musical monk; Raimu, as a Midi mayor about to marry his cook; Fernandel, as a barber with a passion for card tricks; and Blanchar, as a one-eyed abortionist on the waterfront of Marseilles. Two of the waltzers have already died, one leaving a crazed widow, played by Françoise Rosay in the truest, least truculent enactment of insanity the French screen has ever recorded. The sum of the plot sounds sinister, literary, and melodramatic. Because of the energetic, dry directing of Julien Duvivier (who made *Poil de Carotte*, which you may recall), this movie bulges merely with excitement, surprise, and adult, humane humor. *Un Carnet de Bal* will probably be shown in Philadelphia and New York exclusively. Provided you don't live west of the Rockies, it will be worth the trip to go see it.

A second surprisingly fine French film is *La Grande Illusion*, starring Jean Gabin (who starred in *Pépé le Moko*, which is a third French surprise for those who didn't see it in London, where it was last spring's foreign hit). With Gabin are coupled Pierre Fresnay and Erich von Stroheim in this curious, unified, and exalted film of three Frenchmen and their attempted escapes from German prison camps during the war. The great illusion of all these soldiers, Boche or poilu, is the brotherhood of man. *Pépé le Moko*, now showing in its second season, and also directed by Duvivier, the number-one French studio chief today, could have been modeled on any American gangster film—except that the gangster is a Frenchman whose underworld is the murderous hill streets of Algiers. This makes the gang activities exotic. All of these important French films show a definite new, and perhaps unconscious, quality—a Gallic romanticism which has everything to do with intellectual modern man's emotional relation to all of life, and nothing to do with the single thing called love. Indeed, the often light, usually lunatic mating theme of the more maudlin French movies seems in process of being inspissated, leaving, on its evaporation, some heavier sensitive reality. If the French studios can just patent this, they'll be one up even on the elaborate equipment of Hollywood. Already in the past year, with this list, French films have moved to the top of the European class.

Edith Wharton (1862–1937)

The aristocratic Mrs. Edith Wharton was born Jones in a fashionable quarter of New York, arriving appropriately during the quarrel between masters about servants known as the Civil War. The parents of the novelist were without talent, being mere people of the world. From them into her veins ran Rhinelanders, Stevenses, early Howes, and Schermerhorns intact. Her corpuscles were Holland burghers, colonial colonels, and provincial gentry who with the passage of time had become Avenue patricians—patrons of Protestant church and Catholic grand opera as the two highest forms of public worship—a strict clan making intercellular marriages, attending winter balls, dominating certain smart spots on the Eastern seaboard, and unaware of any signs of life farther west. In blood they were old, Dutch and British, the only form of being American that they knew. As a child among them, little Miss Jones started living in what Mrs. Wharton later entitled their Age of Innocence—a hard hierarchy of male money, of female modesty and morals.

Moving in high society at this time meant moving but little indeed. Space, outside of Newport for the summer, had not yet been discovered, though stately trips abroad were occasionally taken by bridal couples or dowagers headed for Worth. Fortunately for the impatient authoress, she was repeatedly sent as a child to the Continent, where governesses taught her French, German, and Italian. Something very close to English she had already learned in her correct American home. Thus the future Mrs. Wharton of the book reviews was launched. Thus at an early age she often returned from Europe to her native land, her critical eyes already seeing her New York as America indeed. And thus by her elders she was, in turn, already seen as "that handsome, disagreeable little Pussy Jones, always scribbling." Her first manuscript to reach the outer world was a poem sold at a church fair when she was fifteen.

In the succeeding fifty years, according to her harshest critics, she moved with unerring failure between two careers—that of a great woman of the world and a great woman novelist. Repeatedly redomiciling herself with elegance in various garden cities of the world, she always suffered the disadvantage of being an outsider—even in the city of her birth, after she became a popular novelist. For if Boston, the city of her marriage, never forgave her for having been born in New York, her New York never forgave her for having been born in New York and writing about it.

As a talented pioneer of professionalism among the domestic women of her class, absolution might have come with the dignity of her fame, had not Mrs. Wharton discovered her sinful skill at sketching from life. Though Thackeray's *Vanity Fair* was the supposed model for her *House of Mirth*, many of her contemporaries felt they had unconsciously sat across the space of years for too many of her portraits. And in *The Age of Innocence*, certain of the leading innocents connected with the novel's adulteries and banking intrigues were decried, in Four Hundred society, as being this pillar, that pretender, or that *déclassé*—anyhow, all drawn as large as life. The only positive identification which the book afforded, and which, while it gave society at large no more comfort, afforded it even less doubt, was that of Mrs. Wharton herself altered into the sad, charming, chaste hero, Newland Archer.

For like many novelists, Mrs Wharton herself was her works. The presence therein of her friends or other characters was only a promenade for principle. They were mere illustrations of her historical report on a manner of living and thinking, often enough (for she was a moralist) discouraging. She and her characters in her wake seemed too ably to have followed the unfortunate advice of Henry James, once tendered her in a letter of consolation for her domestic infelicities: "Continue making the movements of life." All her heroes and heroines, meeting and sometimes mating under her eye, kept up this pantomime, as perhaps she did, without pleasure. Her books were filled with smart people whose capacity, according to her, for wit, wealth, and divorce, was sheer tragedy. Their activities in her day were regarded not as necessary symptoms of transitional psychology or even news, but as mere decay. She spent her early talents proving that the wages of social sin were social death, and lived to see the grandchildren of her characters comfortably and popularly relaxing into open scandals.

Though the first to utilize the breakup of the American mold,

Mrs. Wharton was still the last to understand it; she saw the plot but never the point. Born for ethics, she ignored the senses. Thus even her most famous character, Lily Bart, though a drug fiend, was not the victim of her vice. For no irresistible Baudelairean visions did she swallow her nightly quota, but as one taking an aspirin tablet, to bring on sleep or ward off a cold. Mrs. Wharton described a trained-nurse murderess, but she was one who killed the wife for professional ethics, not as a passionate means to obtain the husband illegally loved. She even took up the labor problem, but as a banker takes out his typist to dine —a mere excursion out of one's class.

It was this emotional emptiness that gave her a success which was half polite incredulity when *The House of Mirth* was translated for the more passionate French as *Chez les Heureux de ce Monde*. But *Ethan Frome*, after its American triumph retitled as *Sous la Neige*, was justly hailed abroad as a chef-d'œuvre of sufficient quality to merit a cheap edition and rank with the agrarian tragedies of Balzac and Zola. In this New England tale, small as a chance and tragic rural snapshot which the rich summer visitor leisurely enlarges for her album on returning to town, the worldly Mrs. Wharton gave something like immortality to the sadness of snow, which it is likely her nature understood too well. At the age of thirty she was remarked as already cold and handsome. She was then spending her years at fashionable Lenox, where the earth, under the many winters, retains a feeling of ice that no spring can thaw. And the rest is under glass.

Though she spent another forty years writing about human relations, it was in her friendship with Henry James that she really attained her literary height. Their Platonic amity lacked none of their style, and contained all the warmth of which she never wrote. As if preparing herself for her own future expatriation, she first fell under his distant tutelage, then under the personal spell of her country's greatest prose exile. He selected her, at the expense of Mrs. Humphry Ward, as his choicest female pupil. When distant in Rye, he addressed her in letters as "Dearest Edith," and, when present, introduced her to his London on the precise parabola of his pompous arm. To the literary, correct, meticulous Mrs. Wharton, the affection and approval of the literary, correct, meticulous Mr. James were the

real bay leaves which she humbly wore (one imagines him helping adjust them) in her beautiful blond coiffure.

Their friendship, which was the greatest and worthiest devotion of her life, covered long years and included, with other
friends, Continental motor travels together, briefer always than
the interminable charming letters which prepared for, discussed,
delayed, and finally concluded them. There was even a house
party of Whartons, Jameses, and other select souls at the grandiose Villa Medici outside Florence. And when after even that
ripe man could ripen no more and so disappeared, there was
still, for her, her famous round library in the Rue de Varenne,
with its mounting tier of his works and, amidst them, the marble
bust of their friend and author, the master American, James.

It was in this aristocratic Parisian quarter that Mrs. Wharton,
more than a dozen years ago, began her permanent expatriation.
Twice only she returned to America, once to witness a marriage,
and once for a ten days' retreat at the Hotel St. Regis, where she
prepared to receive her honorary degree from Yale. Her with-
drawal from America was her most American act. She had exhausted New York, and Boston, so it says, always refused to accept her. She had early made with one of its scions what in
those inept days was regarded as a brilliant, or suitable, marriage (of the type which subsequently has to be legally dis-
solved). Mr. Edward Wharton was the handsomest man of the
class of '73, Harvard, a group which was graduated in virile side
whiskers; but his wife had been born a Rhinelander almost in
her own right, wrote books, and had lived in Paris. Boston considered her fast.

So from the Rue de Varenne she finally started her frigid conquest of the *faubourg*, in company only with her mother, who
had been Lucretia Rhinelander, and an iron hostess in her day,
but was now disgusted with the way Newport was going. Mrs.
Wharton was perhaps too formal even for the *faubourg*. As one
duchesse complained, "*On est trop organisé chez elle*. One can't
so much as forget one's umbrella at Madame Wharton's with im-
punity."

Later, still pursuing her policy of Continental expansion, she
purchased a charming Cistercian monastery near Hyères, on the
Mediterranean, where she summered. Finally, for permanent
residence, she acquired an eighteenth-century villa, the Pavillon

Colombe, at Saint-Brice-sous-Forêt, about eighty motor kilometers from Paris. It was here that she collected her half-dozen adopted war orphans, left from the six hundred she housed during the war when she gave her property to the government, and devoted herself to France and little Belgian refugees with a patriotism of which only an expatriated American who dislikes children is capable. For her splendid war work she was decorated by the King of the Belgians and was made an officer of the Légion d'Honneur by France.

During her last years, she was a handsome New Yorker of mature age and immense dignity who had retired into a French country house and solitude. Her pavilion was not without suitability for one who had lived in contemplating the passions of others; the edifice was of the French type lovingly called *une folie*, erected by an amorous banker to house his mistresses, two sisters whose dovelike tenderness gave the property its name. The structure itself was exquisitely and correctly restored; Mrs. Wharton knew her periods, and architecture had long been one of her hobbies. In décors, she was equally exacting; she spent twenty years searching for some eighteenth-century Chinese Chippendale wallpaper of which she originally possessed a fragment.

In all details of life she demonstrated an accuracy of which she alone was capable. Her days were scheduled. The mornings were devoted to writing. The afternoons were given to walking in company with small dogs and to gardening, at which she was an affectionate expert. In all her properties, her flowers were notable. Her White Garden at Lenox was famous. Moneyed in her own right, she was able to spend her royalties on her blossoms. She traveled. She saw France, Italy, and Spain from a limousine, and the Parthenon from a yacht. She was smartly but decently dressed by Worth, who, when she once demanded of him a suitable, chic, black tea gown, offered without hesitation a model called Resignation. She was civil rather than cordial as a formal hostess. She finally gave up smoking, but in the old fashion urged upon the gentlemen their after-dinner cigars. The viands at her table were perfectly served and chosen, though the wines, for which she cared little and which were selected by her butler, were less choice—according to the cigar-smoking gentlemen. Her old French housekeeper, who had been Mrs. Wharton's nurse, dominated below stairs and even influenced her mistress on the floor above. All of the domestics, legend states, rigorously addressed each other as "Monsieur" and "Madame."

Her friends were few but of long standing. It was in her character to support the old amities with loyalty. In the closing years of her life, many of her New York familiars were either dead or gone to Southampton. Her closest connection with her own land was represented by her sister-in-law and lifelong particular friend, Mrs. Cadwalader Jones. After taking up her residence in France, her affections included the Princesse de Poix, the Paul Bourgets, certain of the noble Noailles, and—after the war—the Comte and Comtesse de Beaumont; also certain odd pedants in archaeology and horticulture of whom her appreciation was touching and logical. She was herself an omnivorous reader. Among the younger minds, she enrolled the late Geoffrey Scott, Berenson, the Florentine art critic, Percy Lubbock, and others. She also spoke appreciatively of Scott Fitzgerald. Her last retiring years' circle was expanded to receive Louis Bromfield, with whom, as expatriate neighbor, gardener, and writer, she enjoyed a finally three-faceted friendship.

On the whole she found herself living in a generation in which conversation was lost. She was a dignified little woman set down in the middle of her past. She said that to the greener growths of her day, she must have seemed like a taffeta sofa under a gaslit chandelier. Certainly she was old-fashioned in that she reserved her magnanimity for special occasions. In belief she was nothing of an iconoclast, but she had become liberal through reflection. Hers was the grand manner which triumphed over a situation where another woman's might have saved it. With years of living abroad, her anecdotes tended to deplore her tourist compatriots who mistook the baptistery at Parma for the railway station.

In her long career Mrs. Wharton published half a hundred short stories, translated Sudermann, wrote books on Italian gardens and art, a work on Morocco, a trio on France including one of the best on its war, a volume of verse, and more than a dozen novels. She won the Pulitzer Prize with *The Age of Innocence* and was the only woman to receive the gold medal of the National Institute of Arts and Letters. In writing of the sins of society, Mrs. Wharton gave the great public what it wanted, and ever since the appearance, in 1905, of *The House of Mirth*, each of her novels remained a best seller for the period of its commercial life, a remarkable financial triumph. Her earnings were estimated at approximately seventy-five thousand dollars yearly, of which a goodly slice would have come from serial rights to magazines with whose feminine readers she was always a heavy favorite. In 1929 she sold the play and screen rights to her old gold nugget, *The Age of Innocence*, which was envisaged as the most important Broadway revival of the year; her then current new novel, *The Children*, was also sold for a cinema, was the Book-of-the-Month Club's selection, and reached two hundred thousand copies within a month of publication.

At her death she was working on a larger-scale novel than she had ever before attempted; it was to be called *The Buccaneers* and was a story of the seventies and the assault upon English aristocratic society by four American misses, led by an Anglo-American governess, Laura Testvalley by name. Governess Testvalley was apparently a genuine historical character, since she was described as a cousin of the Pre-Raphaelite painter Dante Gabriel Rossetti. After her death at Saint-Brice, August 11, 1937, it was found that Mrs. Wharton had left her correspondence and biographical material to the University of Yale Library, since she had counted the doctorate the University conferred upon her as the most welcome of her many distinctions. The Wharton material will not be accessible until 1968.

In thirty years of writing, Mrs. Wharton's enormous output, with one exception, was published by two houses, Scribner and Appleton, she not being one to make changes hastily. Her publishers always found her an enemy of publicity, and her standard press photograph showed her in pearls and *décolletage*, dressed for her public as for a ball.

Mrs. Wharton's real excellencies were never marketed. Even those who loved her most came by accident upon her golden qualities. She was regarded as cold. Yet a chord of Bach once recalled to her a moment passed half a century ago with a woman who was ever after to be her fondest companion. And to the same woman she wrote, after clipping her garden's roses in the summer dawn, that the ripe sweetness of the flowers personified and brought their amity endearingly to mind. Mrs. Wharton had the tender and reserved sentiments of the truly literate.

From many she earned the title of Dearest Edith, and for herself, long before her death, she had gained what she hoped would be her final epitaph—"She was a friend of Henry James."

L'Aiglonne

L'Aiglon, in opera form, with music by Honegger and Ibert, has had its première here at the Opéra, featuring the formerly famous Fanny Heldy as the sad little Duc. This Napoleonic stunt was aimed to be, and is bound to become, popular, since the name Reichstadt even said, let alone sung, brings tears to a Frenchman's eyes.

Furthermore, the great-granddaughter of Louis XVII (provided he didn't die as a child in the Temple) has put in an appearance in the person of a young woman formerly known as Mlle. Cotillon, and well mixed up in the blackmailing gadgetries which were the funnier part of the tragical mechanics of the Stavisky scandal. Mlle. Cotillon, who till recently ran a Montmartre grocery shop, has been formally recognized by Princè Charles-Louis de Bourbon-Naundorff as his natural child and has taken the title of Princess Elisabeth. Her Highness, who is pretty, has the Bourbon nose. Her title, though legally adjudicated last spring, only just came to light through her filing suit against a girl friend for stealing what must now be regarded as the royal jewels. History isn't often so good as to provide us commoners with such jolly new Bourbon scandals.

Bread

In Europe, when bread becomes costly, beauty becomes cheap. Because France has always been a bread- and book-loving land, ink now sells the way biscuits used to. A complete set, with full borders, of the nine precious plates engraved by Israel Sylvestre of "Les Plaisirs de l'Isle Enchantée ou les Fêtes et Divertissements du Roy" (with Louis XIV portrayed as participating, on horse and foot, in his own ballets; date, 1664) can today be picked up here by a patient collector for three hundred francs. From the eighteenth century, the great Prussian de Cahusac's classical *La Danse Ancienne et Moderne*, three volumes, dated 1754, can be had for another ten dollars. From the nineteenth century, fine etchings by Whistler or Zorn go for the same price. In the history of art there are periods when bread seems so beautiful that it nearly gets into museums.

1938

Maurice Ravel (1875–1937)

With the death of Maurice Ravel, France has lost its greatest *petit maître* of modern music. He was still a prodigy pupil at the Conservatoire when he composed two of the three works for which he was most famous—the "Pavane pour une Infante Défunte" and "Jeux d'Eaux," regarded as the most perfectly pianistic piece since Liszt. The hypnotic Iberian quality of "Boléro" is partially explained by his having been born at Ciboure, near the Spanish border.

He was a slender, skeptical, creative little genius with a small private income which allowed him the slight superior standing of an amateur and the great privilege of composing slowly, uncommercially, and conscientiously. He usually wrote but one piece a year, if only a noble, sentimental waltz. He was *recherché*, literary, modest, had a dry wit, mistrusted musical bohemianism, frequented salons, and was a dandy. He designed his own shirts, wore exceptional evening waistcoats and precious buttons, and liked to have them admired and commented on. His autographs were much prized, since they included delicate pen pictures or illustrated anagrams to enrich his signature. In his late forties, he discovered *chic* night clubs, which he frequented with polite persistence, and then suddenly abjured them for his final retreat in the country town of Montfort-l'Amaury, where he lived in a small-sized house with small-sized furniture, which he preferred. He was perpetually gracious, never too busy or important to play for friends on their parlor pianos. Fauré was his music master; Satie, Chabrier, and Debussy his great musical influences. Ravel was more played, all over the world, than any of them. He was the only serious musician of our epoch popular with the common people, of whom he was no member. For the past four years he had been unable to write music, or even his own name unless a copy of it was set before him. As a result of an automobile accident, he had suffered an obscure injury to the brain. He died as a result of a neural operation, which he feared could not help him but hoped might aid science.

Art (Commerce)

With European monies and industrial values ruinously fluctuating, important modern art, if bought early and modestly rather than belatedly and dearly, is still the gilt-edged investment here. Of the twenty good Renoirs now available for purchase in Paris, a "Baigneuses" is priced at forty thousand dollars and a small study of peaches is offered for eighteen thousand, which is a lot for fruit. There are only four important Cézannes on the private market, the finest being "Les Stacks" (a study of chimneys), which Cézanne's son asks one million and a half francs for. Cézanne's son is known as just that—Cézanne Fils—and lives with his children and grandchildren in a nice bourgeois flat across from the Montparnasse station. The grandchildren have installed an electric train on the *foyer* floor, which makes it difficult for visitors to get in and see the treasures. These are some large early panels painted by Cézanne at Aix and apparently never exhibited: a "Self-Portrait," a "Picture of a Mountain," and a splendid "Portrait of Cézanne's Wife" by Renoir. Outside the front door the Cézanne grandchildren have put up a homemade sign which says in French, "This Is Not Where the Dentist. Lives." The other family joke is that old Cézanne's grandson, who is a painter, paints not like his grandfather but like Renoir.

Panama Al Brown

Panama Al Brown, Negro boxer, and the only one of any color to be the world's champion bantamweight for eight years, on a recent Wednesday here stepped into the ring after a two-year absence and retained his title—and the following Thursday morning was engaged by the Cirque Médrano to tap-dance, sing, lead a black jazz band, and skip the rope to swing time under the big top. On the Friday night he opened, it didn't look to us as if the audience were going to let him last through to the Saturday matinee. Jean Cocteau, the poet, wrote charmingly of his dark friend in the pages of the circus program, citing Al as "a miracle who refuses to cease being a miracle . . . a phantom, a shadow, more terrible than lightning and the cobra." Unfortunately, he ceased being both a miracle and lightning in his singing and dancing, one being slow and the other off the beat. Only the late Battling Siki, the Senegalese, who was equally popular with the white Parisians, ever had anything so dark, delicate, and deft as Brown's naked dancing legs when blows and sometimes blood were falling in the French boxing ring. But in his circus act, Brown's anatomy was hidden beneath incredible white broadcloth evening clothes. So very little was visible—least of all the reason retiring fighters ever think they can do anything else but.

King George VI and Queen Elizabeth

The visit of the King and Queen of England to Paris was the biggest and most popular public event since the armistice. What was dryly planned as a necessary, expensive, and elaborate diplomatic gesture, a last-minute motion to help preserve European peace, irrationally turned into a wholesale good time for all concerned, as if no one had a care in the world. Paris went on a four-day spree of cheering and sidewalk dawdling, and swarmed the streets at night in crowds that produced the most involved traffic jams seen here since the invention of the automobile. Governments never know what will catch their populaces' fancy. The Parisians' delight in the presence of the English King and Queen exceeded any demonstration London has produced, even during the Coronation.

In planning and executing the royal entertainment, the French showed, after a lapse of decades, their genius for royal fetes. For years they had failed to give themselves a good time. In giving it to someone else, democratic Parisians ironically gave themselves more entertainment than they had had since Louis XV died. The show Paris put on was superbly organized; it had imagination, humor, taste, and above all, perfect details.

It was so good that the public, which saw little of Their Majesties and less of their entertainment, nevertheless had the time of its life. For those four days, no one did a lick of work except the Garde Mobile, the police, the soldiers, the sailors, the Sûreté Nationale detectives, and the firemen. These were worn out guarding the royal line of march. Being the most agile, the firemen were stationed on the roofs of the buildings; reserve officers were posted at the windows. Down in the street, the helmeted Garde Mobile faced the crowds; the police, soldiers, and sailors faced the royal limousine in a solid armed line wherever the King and Queen moved. In the narrow Rue Royale, Maxim's, Weber's, and Larue's were ordered to sweep clients from their terraces before Their Majesties rode by to the Opéra. On the mansard roof above Rose Descat's hat shop, policemen flanked the chimney pots. After the assassination four years ago of Alexander of Yugoslavia at Marseilles, Paris was taking no chances.

The Queen is quoted as having said that she wished she could have seen the King and herself coming down the Champs-Élysées that first day, since the procession must have looked fine. It did. From the top of the Arc de Triomphe, the cortege looked like a diminutive, diapered pattern of swift-moving red, white, and blue—the blue and white of the galloping Spahis and the red and white of the galloping Republican Guard who escorted the car from which the Queen waved and the King saluted. The whole thing was over before the Arc de Triomphe pigeons, frightened into the air by the cannon salutes and the loudspeakers' "God Save the King," had had time to circle back to their nests on the statuary.

Disappointed at the brevity of the spectacle, Paris took its time about its enjoyment that night. After dinner, you could have walked till midnight from the Place de la Concorde to the Étoile on the tops of the immobilized taxis and cars. All Paris and a quarter million of provincials in to see the sights possessed the center of the town. Superb synchronized fireworks were shot from the top and bottom of the Tour Eiffel, the multicolored fountains of last year's Exposition were revived to play in the Seine, searchlights at the Grand Palais crisscrossed geometrical patterns in the dark sky. Paris's finest architecture was floodlighted and trimmed. The Crillon and its twin Admiralty building were draped in cloth of gold and their façades were hung with scarlet Beauvais tapestries woven for the coronation of Charles V. The Chamber of Deputies' portico was nobly swathed in giant tricolors, and the lighted gold dome of the Invalides could be seen across the town.

The royal couple probably had the most fun the next morning, when they went down the river from their private pier to the Hôtel de Ville. Their pier was fantastic. It bore a white Venetian tent on fancy poles, topped by a golden crown; the *quai* was decorated with red, white, and blue cement arabesques; a priceless Louis XIV Gobelin tapestry was tacked on the embankment wall; along the royal carpet stretching to the waterside there was a double line of marine apprentices carrying antique halberds. The boat was a tourist-carrier left over from the Exposition and smartly streamlined. Below the Institute, a comic marine garden had been jocosely erected in the middle of the river to make the royalties smile. It contained two Loch Ness monsters spouting water from all points, spitting hippocampi, dolphins, and a forest of miniature trees.

At the Opéra gala, the King and Queen were escorted up and down the marble staircase by liveried torchbearers; the fountains outside were illuminated and their water was sprinkled with gold dust. On one side of the royal box sat the Prefect of Police, on the other side the Chief of Judicial Police, as the two most trustworthy persons in the house. The guests, as was the case with all the functions, were chosen exclusively from the government itself.

The military review at Versailles, during which fifty thousand French soldiers passed before the King, was of course the real point of the visit, despite all the lovely fuss and feathers. For patriots and militarists, it was a splendid and picturesque sight. The often criticized French army did France proud. It looked disciplined, virile, and well tailored, and it put on a stunning show which the colonial troops—the bloomered Zouaves, the horn-blowing Senegalese, the Moroccan mounted regiments, with their *chéchias* and silver stirrups—stole as usual.

The luncheon served that noon at the Palace of Versailles was the grandest meal of the visiting royalties' lives, since the menu was like those of long-dead French kings. There was Egyptian quail, out of season; for the King and Queen, two magnums of champagne bearing the dates of their births. The viands were presented heaped on silver salvers borne by four hundred costumed footmen so carefully liveried that even their white wigs had been made to order.

Diplomatically, artistically, even humanly, the royal visit was a roaring success. Trained for more than a century in democracy, the French prefer the shout of "*Bravo!*" to the old troubling cry of "*Vive le Roi!*" but they learned the British anthem for the occasion—phonetically. For four friendly days, republican Paris resounded to the loud singing of "Godd Saive ze Kinng."

Susanne Lenglen (1899–1938)

For fifteen years Suzanne Lenglen, the champion tennis player, was one of the few female public figures of France. She was respectfully admired as being typically French—hard-working, frugal-living, obstinate, given to making occasional scenes, authoritative, capricious, expert at her job. Her premature death was regarded here as a national loss, as if she had been a general, or an *homme d'état*, or a big man in science. Tennis is historically a French game; in modern times it has been the only sport in which the French have showed genius. For a while the regular victories of French players satisfied the national pride. The tennis school which Lenglen had conducted at the Stade Roland-Garros since her retirement will be officially named after her—a redundant honor, since it was always called L'École Lenglen anyhow. Being an intelligent, constructive woman, she saw that what French tennis needed was trained adult instructors and a trained younger generation. She founded her school specifically to develop coaches and to teach youngsters under fifteen.

For a sportswoman, she was a curious creature, with the artist's rather than the athlete's attitude toward her profession. She felt about a love set as a painter does about his masterpiece; each ace serve was a form of brushwork to her, and her fantastically accurate shot-placing was certainly a study in composition. She was never physically strong, except in her nerves and endurance. As a child, she was trained by her shrewd father for hours each day. "Tennis was for me," she later said, "a matter of sheer horror. I used to cry with fatigue and boredom. My father [whom she described as her only friend and the one human being who intimidated her] was an iron disciplinarian." In 1914, with her hair still hanging down her back, she became a world champion at the age of fifteen. She had to renounce piano-playing, which she loved—"velocity of fingering being incompatible with the stiff wrist required by tennis." "My favorite pastime," she wrote to an admirer, "was always reading; a yearning for culture made me prefer intellectual to sporting pleasures. I play some golf, swim, drive my car without enthusiasm; I prefer a concert or going through a museum. I've had few men, fewer women friends. I dislike violent sport. I always sought to create an elegance of movement, a general equilibrium in a gesture, rather than to set any records. I never had much physical resistance; I won my matches on courage and nerves of steel. My victories gave me satisfaction but little joy, since I'm proud but not vain. I always loved nature, dogs, and storms." She had storms all her life, but she died peacefully.

Stein Art Collection

Since Miss Gertrude Stein's collection of pictures practically ranks as one of Paris's private modern museums, it is of interest to report that she and her canvases have moved from her famous Montparnasse salon on the Rue de Fleurus to a remarkable seventeenth-century Latin Quarter flat formerly occupied by Queen Christina of Sweden and still containing her original wall *boiseries* and her reading cabinet. The move was a good thing, since the moving men had to count up for Miss Stein what she had never bothered to inventory. Her collection today includes one hundred and thirty-one canvases, including five Picassos which are still in the china closet. Ninety-nine of the pictures are hung. The salon alone contains four major masterpieces—a Cézanne, Picasso's portrait of Miss Stein, Picasso's "Full Length Nude" (rose period) and his famous "Girl with Basket of Flowers." It also has two *natures mortes* by Braque and nineteen smaller Picassos, including four perfectly matched heads of the 1913 Cubist period, rare in their unity. The only new painter whose works Miss Stein is enthusiastically acquiring is the young English artist Sir Francis Rose, who has been recently working in China and is now in New York.

[*Actually I and not the moving men made the inventory of Miss Stein's pictures the day they were moved into the new apartment in the Rue Christine. I came to bring her a pot of white flowers (she always liked them that color) to decorate the new apartment, and she gave me a pencil and paper and said, "Put the pot anywhere and make me an inventory of my art here," which I did. J. F.*]

Chevalier at the Casino

Paris must be back to normal, since it has just launched a rather good new Casino revue. If Paris had launched an extraordinarily good new Casino revue, with satire, wit, and mirth as well as winsome wenches, that would have been abnormal. However, *Amours de Paris,* the current offering, contains the nude demoiselles; it features forty-five tableaux illustrating everything from the love life of the rose to the parlor existence of the famous courtesan Cora Pearl; it offers two imported dancing troupes, one called "The Sixteen Red and Blond Greasely Girls," the other "The Eight Exciting Skibine Ladies"; and, above and beyond all, it stars Maurice Chevalier in what amounts to a straight concert recital of his best songs, past and present. He is the hit of the show, and the German love ballad which he renders in the voice of Hitler hating democracies is the hit of his act. Chevalier still has more *métier* in his lower lip than any newcomer can offer. Unfortunately, he also still has the knack of offending his Paris devotees, as he did at the Casino's première, when, after having kissed Marlene Dietrich and Grace Moore, who were in the audience, he only shook hands with Mistinguett. His devotees, by their devoted booing, made him kiss her, too.

Georges Bizet (1838–1875)

Georges Bizet, the composer of *Carmen,* would have been one hundred years old last month if he hadn't died at the green age of thirty-seven—of "an insidious and undefined disease," which was a broken heart. Bizet's centenary has just been celebrated at the Opéra-Comique in a gala 2,271st performance of *Carmen*, attended by President Lebrun, Emma Calvé, and governmental, literary, and musical bigwigs. The night Bizet was dying, the opera was fighting through its thirty-third performance, for *Carmen* was then regarded a failure; in the fortune-telling scene, Mme. Galli-Marié (the original Carmen) read Bizet's death in the cards and fainted. The music critics, who succeeded in killing Bizet, had nearly killed his work. *Le Siècle's* critic wrote of the new opera, "M. Bizet's heart, blasé from too much trying, needs to refind its virginity." The then all-powerful *Revue des Deux Mondes* said, "M. Bizet's melody produces the effect of one of those lights inside dull opaline glass." *La France* sniffed, "Don José's offstage song is harmonically pretentious." Fortunately, the critics also added that the plot of the opera was immoral, so the public flocked to the theater, though schoolmistresses addressed indignant letters to the management asking how nice girls could be taken to a spectacle of harlotry set to bad music.

Bizet's father, a singing teacher, discovered one day that his little son had learned *solfège* while sitting outside the music-room door. Sent to the Conservatoire at a tender age, the prodigy promptly won the first prize in sight reading and piano; later, at the age of nineteen, he won the Grand Prix de Rome and spent three years in Italy, where he composed unceasingly, unequally, and usually unluckily. One of his Rome pieces, *Don Procopio*, finally had its first performance in 1906, at Monte Carlo. Offenbach's and Halévy's *opéras-bouffes* were the rage in Paris when Bizet returned and married Halévy's daughter. He kept her poorly by doing musical hackwork—copying, transcriptions, anything. He even tried to support her by writing a Biblical opera about Noah. *L'Arlésiene*, considered a fountain of pure melody today, was rejected by the vulgar 1872 opera public but went down all right with the wiser Pasdeloup Concerts audiences. *Carmen* was written in 1873. At that time there was no such word as "toreador." Bizet made it up by combining *torero* and *matador* because he needed four syllables for his musical march beat. It makes Spanish bullfighters angry to this day to be called toreadors, as they usually are.

When he was a musical student at the Villa Medici in Rome, Bizet wrote to his parents, "The artist doesn't take his proper place till one hundred years after his death. Sad? No, it is only stupid." Bizet was wrong. He took his place one hundred years after his birth.

[*Maurice Sachs, who was a member of the family, I think through his grandmother, told me that the Bizets had always considered* Carmen *a very common, lower-class opera. (I think it's a honey of an opera, don't you?)* J. F.]

Peace in Our Time

OCTOBER 2

There is only one person in Europe who is competent to tell what really happened during the past week, and that is Prime Minister Neville Chamberlain, who has already told it all—or as much as the world may ever hear—in his at first heartbreaking, at the last heartwarming, Wednesday-night speech before the House of Commons. Up to that time, Paris knew only that the problem of saving Prague had been replaced by the problem of saving democratic Europe; that two and a half million Frenchmen had been mobilized; that communiqués communicated nothing, since nothing was known; that calm was demanded in the face of approaching torment; that war seemed imminent. Now all the French know is that there is peace. In their curious calm, they don't want to know anything else. It is the only thing worth knowing; that and the new knowledge which is exciting the whole population of Europe today—that statesmen can think everybody's way out of war. Treaties have plunged into disfavor, and the four talkative national chiefs are expected to start a diplomatic cleanup and rearrange the Continent into some sort of United States of Europe. France's ten days of mobilization cost her ten million dollars a day. A mild sort of treasury inflation is already taking place. Lots of the French feel that no matter what it all has cost them and however much the franc drops, the solution has been worth the price.

Hundreds of thousands of Parisians lined homecoming Premier Daladier's route from Le Bourget to the War Office, where he laid down his burden of peace. At the sight of him, many wept. Mothers held their children up to see him, so that they could always remember something of the happy day. Absent from the cheering crowd were several hundred billposters, at the moment sticking up extreme Left and extreme Right political placards demanding the downfall of Daladier and his government. He displeased the Flandin defeatists by promising to go to war for Czechoslovakia and he angered the Communists by failing to do so. On Saturday, L'Humanité declared, "We take no part in the brigade of cheerers. The Munich accord is a diplomatic Sedan." Blum, though he and his Chamber majority forced Daladier to vote for war after first declaring for peace, has been more poetic and humane. In his Saturday editorial, he gave to Chamberlain and Daladier "their just tribute of gratitude. War is averted. Man can take up his work again, can again sleep at night, can once more enjoy the beauty of the autumn sun."

Unlike London, which made elaborate preparations for air raids, Paris during the week of anxiety offered its citizens nothing but sand to extinguish incendiary bombs, the advice that all inhabitants should dive into their coal cellars when the sirens screamed, and plans to scatter the population throughout the countryside. All that the government tried to do was move two and a half million men under arms in three days up to the Franco-German border. The government did it. All men who were fine artisans and under sixty were drafted. There was hardly a skilled mechanic, blacksmith, plumber, or carpenter left in civil life in the land. They were all up at the front, twiddling their thumbs. The calmness of the excitable French, as compared with the emotional mobility of the phlegmatic English, was fantastic. This would not have been a popular war; the political issues were too confusing. But the French, without enthusiasm, marched off in complete calm, amidst calm on the streets, in the churches, in the home, and even in the newspapers.

Only the radios were excited and caused excitement. They gave the shouts and opinions of men from all the lands concerned. As the crisis deepened, efforts were made to pour information into censored Germany. The London B.B.C. gave nightly news in German; Russia announced broadcasts in four languages; the French station at Strasbourg was used as a key information-giver in German. We heard the Munich station haltingly translate into German Chamberlain's melancholic but determined Tuesday-night speech. We heard the translator omit Chamberlain's reference to having received German letters imploring for peace, to his belief that Hitler's attitude was unreasonable, to the English conviction that oppression would have to be resisted, and to the final fact that England was arming. On Thursday night, while all Europe waited for news of the Munich peace conference, the Sudetens and the Czechs each put on a radio atrocity hour. The Sudetens broadcast stories of Czech eye-gouging, reported through a Hamburg station by an American voice with a Southern accent. The Czechs responded from Prague with a Brooklyn accent which gave accounts of Sudeten rapes and tortures. Suddenly, around ten-thirty, in the midst of the playing of a German phonograph record of "Dinah," an excited Frenchman in Munich shouted into the microphone, "*La paix semble d'être sauvée.*" It was the perfect bedtime story. France slept that night for the first time in a week.

During the crisis, there were fourteen thousand Americans in Paris. For their protection and evacuation, the American Embassy had in readiness stocks of food, gasoline, fleets of motorcars, and shipping arrangements which included temporarily parking refugees in Madeira. Two cruisers waited to take off American nationals at Brest; two more waited to take off European gold at Gravesend. During the week, *évacués* from the Maginot Line region rolled by the thousand into Paris, and Paris *évacués* rolled out along the best highroads, their automobiles piled with beds, bicycles, statuary, and perambulators. In view of the gasoline shortage, motorists put reserve supplies into anything handy—champagne bottles, even teakettles. Food staples and dollars were bought to be hoarded. American banks hauled bales of foreign securities, roped like old packages of wastepaper, to the vaults and then hauled them to the center of France, since it was thought that the government, in the event of war, would be set up at Vichy or Clermont-Ferrand. On the great sky route between Le Bourget and Orly, the heavens were empty of planes: the French army chiefs were wasting no men or material before the zero hour.

Were the French children not so wise, they would have

cheered at the news that fear of war had postponed the opening of the autumn school term. They did not cheer. In small towns, where newspapers were precious, President Roosevelt's great second message, in fine French, was pasted on shop and house windows so that passers-by could read, reread, hope, and remember when once the Yanks were coming. In Paris, nothing is now left of the fear of war except the hooded street lights at night and the minute blue flames of the curb lanterns to be used during air raids. With danger past, the dimmed streets look very beautiful indeed.

Peace in Our Time

OCTOBER 12

No sooner was the Munich accord made than the critical parliamentary locusts both in Paris and in London began nibbling at the peace laurels. The laurels were sad and sparse to begin with—as ragged as an army coming home from the worst war in history. It would have been that kind of war, so it is that kind of peace.

Since 1918, everyone has known what war costs. Since Hitler's Godesberg demands, the democracies have been learning what peace costs. It is a price which the French on the whole still seem glad to pay. Few, except the unmathematical and the feverish, think that war could have cost much less than annihilation, even in victory. Many stale truths have become painfully fresh in the past fortnight. One is that democracy is not geared to meet crises. To save what remained of the peace of Europe, Premiers Chamberlain and Daladier were forced to act like dictators, indifferent to constitutions, legislators, and the voters. The practice of democracy dates from the last part of the eighteenth century and the time of the stagecoach. The functional speed of democracies is still that of the vehicles that bore the first argumentative democrats around liberty-loving lands. Fascism dates from the first third of the twentieth century. Like all startling political innovations, it reflects its period, and thus takes its tempo from the airplane. Though the recent European crisis has been an agglomeration of human evils and weaknesses, fundamentally the two leading democracies, France and

England, found themselves in a bad way because practically everyone else in Europe was not a democrat. A democracy is the only entity with which another democracy can, with its inefficiencies, effectively compete. Like it or not, Herr Hitler is the head man in Europe today.

Maybe democracies, by being as unprepared for war as they are uneager to slaughter, are preserving themselves. Maybe the German people's recent unregimented jubilance at escaping war —a joy apparently as great as that of the democratic nations— indicates that, by one of those folk movements of which humanity is at times capable, they may escape taking a nationalistic pride in their present foreign conquests. What is more certain is that only the German people can conquer the German people. Defeated by many nations and with great difficulty in the last war, the Germans have reassembled under Herr Hitler as the same sort of belligerent warriors who fought under Kaiser Wilhelm, under Bismarck, under Frederick the Great. Their notion of what is the goal of a great nation differs, by several hundred years, from the ideas of France and England, superior to the cynical about conquest now. It is this difference in aim that is pulling Europe apart. If the democracies could, by a miracle, conquer Germany tomorrow, they still couldn't, from the outside, change a point of view which can be altered only from within.

The change for the democracies will have to be more immediate. They will have to decide at once what they are voting for, and they had better be right. Otherwise "in our time," as Mr. Chamberlain said, referring to peace, we may see what we still refer to as democracy and liberty slip into mere history.

France is now a second-rate European power; England is a first-rate-minus one. Reflecting the new ratio, the French newspapers are paying less attention to France's reaction to the recent crisis than to the way the English are feeling. No criticism or praise of Daladier in the Chamber of Deputies was as constructively realistic or as blindly humane as the comments on Chamberlain's program expressed in the House of Commons. In London, the Labour M. P., Arthur Greenwood, drew from Shakespeare's *Henry IV* an apt quotation: "What, ho! chamberlain!" In the French Chamber, the Socialists quoted nothing except the orders of their chief, Blum, who commanded them to "benevolently abstain" from voting, although they are France's majority party and the vote was to be on the greatest issue in postwar French life. Their Communist political allies' voting en bloc against the government marked the official demise of France's famous Front Populaire. The government is now definitely moving from the extreme Left to that Center, which in France is called the Right. All France now knows what was hitherto the knowledge only of a few special Germans and Frenchmen—that while France's fortifications, artillery, and infantry are so good that her men could have stayed in the Maginot Line, like military moles, forever, German planes, like birds of prey, could have flown over the Ile-de-France almost unpursued, for France's air force will be utterly inadequate until her new motors start appearing next month. Since the Front Populaire's stay-in strikes of 1936 in the automotive industry and the Front's idealistic forty-hour-week program are now held responsible for France's unpreparedness in the air, and since it has been the Socialists and Communists who have demanded aid for Czechoslovakia (which France could not fight for, since she had no planes to fight with), popular feeling is now against the defunct Popular Front. As a reform, it came high; peace will cost a fortune in further armament, and France is in more money difficulties, as usual.

The newspaper *Paris-Soir* is collecting a fund to buy Prime Minister Chamberlain a French *maison de paix* and a trout stream; *Le Journal* wants to give the local British hospital a Neville Chamberlain Peace Bed, where "anyone even remotely related to" anybody English could be ill; the *Populaire* and *L'Humanité* want to give money to "our German and Czech comrades in the Sudetenland, victims of the '*diktat*' of Munich, and of Chamberlain and Daladier." *L'Œuvre* wants to give "a souvenir" to Daladier, Bonnet, and Madame Neville Chamberlain, and would further like to give the Nobel Peace Prize to Czech President Eduard Beneš. All the French feel that they have already given their prestige to Herr Hitler, but that if war is evaded, their helpless generosity was worthwhile.

Peace in Our Time

OCTOBER 25

Time here appears to have been standing still ever since the near-war fright of a month ago, because peace is standing still. No steps are being taken, there seems to be no motion among the English and French men of power; there is hardly any talk, even for gesture's sake, and there is certainly no uncensored information. In what was announced as an effort to prohibit false rumors, the French Republic's present government has suddenly taken to telling the public not what is news but what isn't news. The newspapers are now forced laconically to state, "We are officially informed that it is inexact that the Gestapo has been installed at Prague, that Berlin has demanded the extradition from Sudetenland of fleeing Germans, that Marshal Göring will visit Paris," etc. This is hard on the newspapers, which the day before had published these inexactitudes as gospel truth. The situation of the Daladier government is even harder, since, as it candidly stated in its communiqué concerning rumors, "The multiplication of news of this sort tends to feed polemics prejudicial to good international relations, and to nurture an unhealthy interior climate unfavorable to the financial market." And so the real news emerges—that France's finances are in a terrible way, and that Paris, once leader of Europe, dare not risk even verbally offending neighbors whom she formerly deigned to insult by battle.

One thing which has come out of the so-called peace is a Voyage de la Paix, a five-day, 1,175-franc junket from Paris to Cologne, Godesberg, Coblenz, Frankfort, Nuremberg, Munich, and Berchtesgaden. The excursion is being advertised by the Compagne Française de Tourisme. Some of the French feel it cost them so much to send Mr. Chamberlain to Berchtesgaden that they can't afford to take the trip themselves.

1939

Peace in Our Time

CONTINUED

JANUARY 12

No one knows if Daladier is intelligent and strong-minded or just lucky and obstinate. In any case, the military flourish which surrounded his trip to Corsica and Tunis, as a gesture of nonappeasement to Mussolini, delighted the French nation, skeptical of an umbrella's ever again looking as powerful as a cannon.°
Paris is becoming more than ever a refugee camp. The post office has installed a service by which telegrams in German, English, Italian, or Spanish, but not French, can be given over the phone to *les opératrices polyglottes*. The new identity card for all foreigners must carry a profile photograph of the bearer, showing his or her right ear. In special cases, fingerprints are required, too. Lots of ladies would as soon be fingerprinted as submit to the new high hairdo.

Suez

Owing to the superinstability of European affairs and the supersensitivity of Europeans just now, the Suez Canal and Hollywood are suddenly in trouble. Italy is demanding more Italian directors for the Canal, and France and England are protesting against the Darryl Zanuck film *Suez*. The London *Daily Telegraph* complains that Hollywood has taken an important chapter from Empire history and "treated it as if it were a fictitious story of a job of large-scale plumbing." The French weekly *Match* acidly asks if *cinéastes* can thus travesty reality, pointing out that when de Lesseps was twenty-five (about Tyrone Pow-

° The umbrella carried by Chamberlain as part of his daily costume was a popular cartoonists' symbol for Great Britain's appeasement policy.

er's age), the future Empress Eugénie was a tot of four, hardly
ripe to rouse romance. Furthermore, it wasn't Emperor Napoleon who sent de Lesseps to Egypt, but King Louis-Philippe.
And what is worse, as the many de Lesseps descendants cry,
their distinguished ancestor, far from being in love with the Empress, was happily married twice, had seventeen children by his
two devoted wives, and was sixty-four when he and Her Highness met—to open a canal, not to conclude a flirtation. By the
de Lesseps clan here the film is considered "an offense to the
memory of a great man"—and to a big family, since it puts de
Lesseps's children in the awkward position of apparently never
having been born.

In London, an indignant cinema critic wrote: "What would
Americans think of a British film of old Kentucky, with Lincoln
as a plantation owner courting Harriet Beecher Stowe to the
theme-song of 'Alexander's Ragtime Band'?" Lots of Americans
would probably think it was grand.

Cyrano de Bergerac

We are a month late in reporting on the Christian Bérard art
work for the Théâtre-Français revival of Rostand's *Cyrano de
Bergerac* because it took us a month to get a ticket, so great are
the crowds at the box office. Bérard's costumes, always an item
of important European theater news, are individually, rather
than en masse, as rich in imagination as in fabric; looking at
Roxane's battle dress is like scanning poetry. The Gothic décor
for the climactic balcony scene is as touching as any medieval
house still standing in the Bergerac countryside. However, the
significant thing about Rostand's chef-d'œuvre is that at this precise troubled moment in French life Cyrano's Gallic logic, cyni-
cism, courage, civilization, wit, and literature should be what
the French most want; that they should, indeed, have remained
so much a part of the national education that night after night
the theater is filled with young and old, rich and poor, murmur-
ing the lines along with the actors. It is this fact which furnishes
the true critique of the play, which supplies a complete editorial, more exact than a dozen daily newspaper dispatches, in

the atmosphere of Paris right now, with Munich behind and heaven knows what lying ahead.

Pablo Picasso

For the first time in three years a representative show has been held of Picasso's latest paintings, and for the first time in his career the show, which is at Paul Rosenberg's, is full of pretty Picassos. Critics are in a stew, for this time the public doesn't have to be lectured on modern art, since any ignoramus can see it's full of beautiful flowers. Except for one canvas, which features a frying pan, and two that depict Picasso's window-casement theme, most of the twenty-odd pictures displayed concentrate on flowers in a vase. No other great European painter could risk so much on still lifes. Everything about the new Picassos is new to Picasso: the luscious palette of purple and white, the upholstered romanticism, even the composition. Rumor says that what Picasso has been privately painting for the past three years is wonderfully ugly roosters, and that he painted the pretty flower pictures only to please Rosenberg, who is selling them at one hundred and fifty thousand francs each, probably only to please Picasso.

War Clouds

FEBRUARY 2

With each week's accumulation of diplomatic news, it becomes increasingly clear that Europe is now permanently divided into two camps of conviction, which differ fundamentally on one thing: war. For historical and material reasons, France and England today consider war a *summum malum;* for biological and material reasons, Germany and Italy consider war a *summum bonum.* You could talk all night—and lots of worried citizens here are doing it—and you'd get no further than this approximation of how far apart these two attitudes toward life and death are, and how distant tangible peace appears. For the net result of these diametrically opposed convictions is that, even if the French and English were at this minute so adequately prepared for a war that they could win it, they still wouldn't want to fight it because they have passed the period of eager belligerence in their history and now regard the battlefield as vain, not glorious. The Italians, whose heroic conquests are so ancient that Caesar is only a classic bore for schoolboys, and the Germans, who lost the last great war only by a margin of massacre, are, on the other hand, animated by a fresh ardor for military victory, though their high regard for war, which their opponents loathe, is no proof that such love will have its reward.

In other words, no one alive today can know which side's dead men will win the war, if there is one, and anybody can see that people who don't want something are less likely to get it than people who do want something. The setup in Europe today is a struggle between the active and the passive. Everything else —wheat, oil, bluffs, insults, territorial expansion, *Blut Heil,* iron rations, self-sacrifice, state visits to weakened countries—is simply a trimming.

The fall of Barcelona has brought home to Parisians the closeness of the German flying field below Irún, from which Biarritz is ten minutes and Paris only three hours away by fast bomber's flight. Owing to tension, the political pantomimes in the Chamber of Deputies have been wild. When the non-airplane producer Cot, former Air Minister, accused the Right benches of being victims of Hitlerite propaganda and they called him an agent of Moscow, the liveried Chamber stewards, their silver chains of office rattling, had to separate the brawlers; desk tops were banged in the traditional boyish racket the Chamber uses to express fury and Speaker Herriot was forced to don his top hat, official signal that the sitting was suspended. However, the Chamber voted as one man against ceding an inch of French soil to Italy, and a majority voted against the Spanish-intervention motion of Léon Blum, who ironically fathered French nonintervention when he was Premier in 1936 and the tragic Spanish war was young.

Exodus (Spanish Civil War)

MARCH 1 °

There has never been anything in modern history like the recent flight of the Catalonian army and civilian population into France. Since the exodus was without precedent, nobody was prepared to take care of it. When the French frontier roads were finally opened, about three hundred thousand Spaniards —soldiers, civilians, women, and children, all hungry, exhausted, and in a panic—swept down on the two hundred thousand French inhabitants of the Pyrénées-Orientales, who, though they were at peace and at home, found themselves living in what was practically occupied territory. The Spaniards, entering as a horde of homeless guests, found themselves living largely as prisoners of war. The discomfort and confusion for both French and Spanish have been bitter.

Certainly the Spanish militiamen believed that if they stayed in their own land they would be killed. They are now alive— behind barbed wire—in France. It would seem that between the two extremes of life and death everything else to them is relatively unimportant.

In Perpignan, there are two hundred thousand refugees, mostly soldiers, in the two largest concentration camps on the sandy wastes of Saint-Cyprien, and Argelès, and about sixty thousand, more lucky, in smaller camps such as Amélie-les-Bains. The little camps are better situated, mostly have hills for protection and trees for firewood, and are, naturally, easier to run. In the three sectors of the Amélie camp we saw about twenty-five thousand men, of whom six thousand were milling on a football ground in what looked like misery but was the envy of the other camps. The men were under the surveillance of the Garde Mobile, who shooed them around like chickens when they spread out too thickly on the highroad. Mimosa was blooming on the hillside, but the air was cold. Most of the men had brought a blanket, their sole possession, and wore it all day draped like a giant scarf over their shoulders. There was no

° This was a month before the end of the war. On April 1 Franco made his formal victory announcement.

shelter. The refugees sat, slept, and waited on the brown ground. The camp, being near the snow-topped Canigou peak, afforded pine boughs for firewood; smoke hung like a flat, low second sky over the scene. The French government was giving two pounds of bread daily to every twenty-five men, who, as a unit, were cooking their stew, beans, and rice soup when and how they chose or could in washboilers, buckets, or iron pots. Much of the food was contributed by the Front Populaire or by neighbors. Some of the meat lying in newspapers on the ground came from Spanish cows or horses which the refugees had brought with them and butchered. Amélie is ordinarily a watering place, favored by modest English visitors. One elderly British lady with an anachronistic parasol came daily with baskets of raw mutton chops for the soldiers, and also daily complained that she couldn't cook properly on a slab of sheet iron balanced on boulders.

Behind the football ground is a little rocky river, where the men, stripped to the waist, were washing when we were there. During the first three dreadful days, the refugees, out of fear of pollution, were driven away from the river. They stood in line all day waiting to get water from a spigot with a trickle as wide as your thumb. Now bad water is general and dysentery is commonplace in all camps. The main hospital tent at Amélie was full when we visited it but seemed well run and didn't smell. It contained about seventy patients bedded on straw pallets, each wedged into a sort of window frame set on the ground. Most of the men had minor wounds. One grizzled Goyaesque peasant with the ague shook all four patients boxed around him. The pharmacist, doctors, and internes were picked from among the refugees. Fifteen days after the camp opened, it was excellently run by the Spaniards themselves, the manager being a former Barcelona impresario. While there, we watched three contingents of the younger and bolder men march off, singing and shouting, to join the French Foreign Legion—if they weren't shipped to Franco, as one officer predicted they would be.

In the arid countryside between Amélie and Saint-Cyprien, the refugees have left three tragic traces. First are the ruined valley vineyards, where, before the Spaniards were dispersed to camps, they helplessly rested; burned whatever came to hand, to keep from freezing; and wrecked the land. Second are the thousands of abandoned jalopies, battered trucks, and semi-smart sedans. And finally there are the tens of thousands of slowly moving, deserted Catalonian horses and mules, herding together in hunger, idleness, and misery, and constantly edging, with strange sociability, toward human habitations. The day we were there, a vast troop of these beasts attracted to the Saint-Cyprien camp, were being rounded up by the unpopular Spahis, who waved their sabres and shouted Arabic from their squealing little stallions—men and animals all rushing in a dark cloud of wind-driven sand and dust that turned the pale sun into a red harvest moon. Inside the barbwired camp we saw the hated, surly Senegalese guards, with their scarlet fezzes, rubber truncheons, and unfraternal faces. In general, what we saw was a maze, miles long, of dun-colored shapes which, when viewed close up, turned out to be white men—walking, standing, sitting on sand, sleeping on sand, breathing and eating sand as it blew on food and faces, men living by the thousand on a treeless beach, on the edge of a muddy, soiled sea. Because of the flying sand, all Saint-Cyprien refugees have, in addition to their other troubles, conjunctivitis. From the camp center, a loudspeaker called the names of men who had mail, gave orders, asked questions. Some men who had been issued sheets of corrugated iron were laying them out on the sand and digging holes underneath to form a home. The latrines were unsheltered, saucer-shaped declivities scooped in the sand; the kitchens were any spot out of the wind where a man could find wood. The whole scene was an unforgettable one except to those living in it. They had been in the war itself and seemed to notice nothing. The one bright feature was the intelligent, unsentimental work being done by the International Commission for the Assistance of Child Refugees, largely an English and American Quaker group aided by Swiss volunteers.

In the International Brigade sector at Saint-Cyprien, a German soldier asked us to mail a postcard to his home, written in French. It began, "Dear Family: Since several days I find myself in France and I find myself in good health and now I find myself in a concentration camp."

Itinerary

It is now taken for granted that everyone will have to brush up on geography to be competent to follow the elaborate and gloomy voyage of annexation Hitler has laid out, in which no picturesque rich small country will be missed. Rumania, Yugoslavia, maybe Ukrainia, snippets of Holland and Belgium, and finally a grand tour through Switzerland, en route to the capture of Lyons, are the supposed itinerary. It is less fancifully taken for granted here that somewhere on this too perfectly planned voyage there will be an unexpected stop—a long and terrible stop, if terribleness can't be avoided. But precisely where and of what nature that stop will be is just what the geography books as yet don't show.

Modern European history has been made from the rise and fall of empires. Over the past few hundred years there has been almost a fashion in power, with half a dozen states in succeeding seasons being all the rage. Usually, as one has gone up, another has gone down. In turn, Spain, Holland, and France have mounted and descended. Only England has remained in a permanent position as a great empire. Whatever may happen to France will only be incidental to the main struggle lying in some form ahead. That struggle will be between the old empire of England and the new empire of Germany.

State Visit

APRIL 1

While Herr Hitler was taking Memel, paralyzing Poland, and capturing Rumania's oil trade, President and Madame Lebrun, as guests of the King and Queen of England, were in London on a state visit which British diplomatists dared not defer lest the delay encourage Herr Hitler to try to take Memel, paralyze Poland, and capture Rumania's oil trade. The French newsreels of the visit were exceptionally fine. They featured the Queen's diamond diadem, Madame Lebrun's Worth gowns, the gorgeous Guildhall, the beautiful Duchess of Kent, and the Windsor

Greys, and appeared in all the first-run Paris movie houses—along with newsreels showing the entry of the German troops into Prague.

For the first time in many centuries, there is no anti-English sentiment audible in France, no shrugging reference to perfidious Albion, no shifting of past French errors onto the shoulders of British politicians and milords, dead or alive—in brief, no criticism of any sort. It would seem as if, so far as England is concerned, the faculty of criticism had suddenly left the French and been replaced by a concentrated curiosity—by a state of absorbed, intent observation, as of a *rara avis* whose queer reactions to danger, whose slow gait, apparently without goal, whose caution, whose quaint, proud, meaningless motions all bewilder the beholder. This is a moment—one of the worst in both French and English history—when the French mind can make neither head nor tail of the English mentality.

In the meantime the French have been busy understanding themselves. By Daladier's decree, Frenchmen on the dole who refuse to work for pay in armament factories don't get any more dole; by decree, the garrulous French press is now censored; by decree, the French Army has been partially mobilized. Without any decree, the French have accepted as one of today's new political laws the fact that democracy is for fair weather, not for foul.

Comte de Paris

The question of what to do with what remains of Louis XVI's family has just been raised. The Bourbon Pretender's son, the Comte de Paris, has written to President Lebrun asking permission to serve in the French Army for the duration of hostilities, if they should come. And since Article 4 of the law on exile specifically states that "no member of the families which have reigned over France may join the Army of the Earth and the Army of the Sea," the Comte suggested that he join the Army of the Air, which certainly wouldn't be against the law, since airplanes hadn't been invented at the time the exile decree was made. "I insist," says the Comte, who is a licensed pilot, "on my aptitude for aviation." He seems pretty talented as a lawyer, too.

Because anything about any Pretender always makes good newspaper copy, and because the Comte de Paris is more energetic, rational, and dramatic than most such historical anomalies, and above all because France is in an emotional patriotic state, the Comte's request has been brought before the Air Commission and will be presented to Premier Daladier in Parliament, along with questions about the desirability of revoking the exile law. Unfortunately for the Comte, L'Action Française, official royalist newspaper, whose noisy, troublesome devotion to his cause he deplores and can't do anything about, has just been cited by Herr Hitler's Völkischer Beobachter as Germany's unique anti-encirclement French friend. This places L'Action Française at the head of the Fifth Column here and puts the anti-Nazi Comte in a bad spot. However, if France is to have a new political leader, what she needs anyway is just a simple man of genius, not genealogy.

Tourist

The late Jean De Koven was an average American tourist in Paris but for two exceptions. She never set foot in the Opéra, and she was murdered. In the first four July days of her initial visit to the capital of France, her routine had been classic: she had settled in a quaint little Left Bank hotel near the Place Saint-Germain-des-Prés, she had seen the boulevards by night, had attended the Folies-Bergère, admired the Louvre, and bought a ticket, ironically enough, for Dukas's Ariadne and Bluebeard. But when the opera's red-and-gold curtain rose, her seat was empty—for she was dead and probably already buried under the front porch of a cottage in Saint-Cloud.

The relation of the murdered and the murderer is the base of any assassination. The relations between Jean De Koven, professional dancer from Brooklyn, and Eugene Weidmann, practiced criminal from Frankfurt am Main, were merely social. Sociability with strangers was her personal weakness and his professional stock in trade. Urbanity (until it was interrupted by her strangulation) marked both their brief meetings—the first at the Hôtel Ambassador, when Weidmann, presenting himself with what Miss De Koven's aunt, Miss Ida Sackheim, afterward de-

scribed as the most gracious smile she ever saw, offered to inter-
pret for the two ladies, who were with difficulty trying to locate
a friend in the building. "I have just met a charming German of
keen intelligence who calls himself Siegfried," Miss De Koven
wrote that day to an American friend (though to the aunt, anyhow, he had called himself plain Bobby). "Perhaps I am going
to another Wagnerian role—who knows? I am going to visit
him tomorrow at his villa in a beautiful place near a famous
mansion that Napoleon gave Josephine."

While Miss De Koven must have been disappointed historically in the villa—French house agents' standard euphemism for
three rooms without bath—the Bonapartian and Wagnerian talk
probably satisfied. Her Siegfried was well read, having been
prison librarian at Saarbrücken while serving five years for robbery. He loved *The Ring*, and in the weeks after she had gone
used to leave his house (over her buried corpse) to go to his
next-door neighbor's and listen to Wagner on the radio. In the
brief hour spent with him before Miss De Koven went to her
new operatic role, sheer sociality reigned; they smoked, she took
pictures of him with her nice new camera, he kindly refreshed
her with a glass of milk. When, five months later, his unfortunate guest was disinterred, she still summed up (except for the
murderous cord tight around her throat and the awful action of
time) the sartorial elements of the sociable summer tourist. She
was still wearing her cute brown sports hat, her gloves, her blue
dress with its red Scotch plaid top, her new patent-leather shoes
—still had with her her white handbag (empty of four hundred
and thirty dollars in American Express checks and about three
hundred francs cash), still had at her side her nice new camera
containing snapshots of her murderer.

The De Koven case started the next morning, Saturday, July
23, 1937, when her aunt received a telegram stating that all was
well and not to worry (which she had done all night). That evening a letter came, mentioning "Chikago" gangster methods but
assuring her that the girl was sound and safe, kidnaped, and
held for ransom five hundred dollars, the Teutonic phrasing and
spelling being illustrated by the Gothic shaped j's, the triangular
t's, and the general Nordic slant of the handwriting. Miss Sackheim went immediately to the American Consulate and the police. But the case didn't get seriously under way, owing to the

constabulary's cynical laughter. One of the rare gaieties of the Sûreté Nationale in Paris is provided by the missing Americans and English who later turn up, abashed, repentant, or still dazed after their first foolish fling in gay Paree. Furthermore, as the police pointed out, Miss De Koven was twenty-two years old; she was (the aunt had shown the police an overflattering press photo of the dancer) beautiful; she had departed voluntarily with a man whom the aunt described as handsome and Swiss; her disappearance was probably a publicity scheme; the kidnaping was an American *truc* that couldn't happen in France, and anyhow Saint-Cloud (if she'd really gone there, which she probably hadn't, since her aunt had heard her say she would) was lovely in summer *pour un beau couple d'amoureux.*

Still smirking, the police nevertheless kept an official eye on the contact messages which the aunt, at the kidnaper's request, was running in English in the agony column of the Paris edition of the New York *Herald Tribune:* "Jean, please come back." "Jean, everything ready. Why did you not answer?" "Jean, do not understand your way of acting. Want proposition immediately." The police also had their eye on the two rendezvous mentioned in notes from the kidnaper. One was the Jardin du Luxembourg, where the password was to be "Jean," spoken three times; the other was in the church of Saint-Sulpice, where the word was to be simply "Baby." Indeed, the police kept such an obvious gaze fixed on these places that the kidnaper never turned up, sending instead a final, angry, ungrammatical post card. "Remind," he said on it (though he meant "remember"), "the least sign we have of the police and we don't send nobody to get the money."

It was the money that finally sobered the French Sûreté, for the girl's ten-dollar American Express checks began coming in, execrably forged. Honest voyagers like you and me may have difficulties in cashing our modest traveler's checks, aided by our proper passports, our unimpeachable calligraphy, our respectable faces, and the backing of bourgeois friends. With perfect ease, two hundred and forty dollars' worth of Miss De Koven's checks had been cashed by what, judging by various cashiers' descriptions, was a motley pair of men, one big and maybe Austrian, one little and French, and, apparently, two local women, one blond, one dark. These four had among them one passport—Miss De Koven's. The most respectable Parisian houses were accepting the forged paper—Guerlain's perfumery, two French banks, Lancel's leather shop on the Place de l'Opéra, and the French Bureau de Tourisme. When the Trocadéro gateman of the Paris Exposition turned in a forged De Koven check, the police changed their tactics and the De Koven "kidnaping" (the sarcastic quotation marks are the Paris *Herald Tribune's*) was for the first time made public on August 7, fifteen days after the American girl's "disappearance."

The reaction was immediate and twofold. No more checks were cashed, and Jean De Koven, once her photograph was published, was reported as being seen all over France. A sharp-eyed M. Poo, headwaiter at the roguish Réserve at Saint-Cloud, saw her lunching on his terrace *en flirt* with a handsome French athlete; a taxi driver said she had screamed, in his taxi, to be taken to the American Embassy but that her two gentlemen escorts had preferred he deposit them all at the Closerie-des-Lilas café in Montparnasse; a fortuneteller in Nancy saw her in a trance, by the ocean somewhere; a cruel M. Tarashkoff telephoned five times in one afternoon to the aunt's hotel to give his name and announce "in a frightful voice" that the girl was dead; some crooks offered to sell clues to her whereabouts for six hundred dollars. On August 16, Henry De Koven, brother of the girl, arrived in Paris, made a touching, dignified statement that "in our modest family my sister is considered a serious-minded girl, incapable of the acts which have been insinuated, either any escapade or publicity stunts," and offered in the name of his father, Abraham De Koven, a ten-thousand-franc reward. The brother was convinced that his sister was dead and so were the police.

The faithful aunt, "Sacky," as the niece always called her (the kidnaper's first telegram had been oddly addressed to "Secky," which had convinced her that the criminal was that smiling Swiss "Bobby" she had met), was too loving to believe the girl had been done away with, too sensible not to know that tragedy of some sort seemed affirmed though it could not be defined. Despairing, she and the brother sailed for home on September 18. By the Sûreté Nationale of Paris, by the French Police de l'État, by the American Embassy, by the American Consulate in Paris, by Secretary Cordell Hull, who had been appealed to for

G-men's aid, by Governor Lehman of New York, by all on both sides of the Atlantic who had by this time been drawn into the unprofitable search, the De Koven case was considered closed, unsolved.

As a matter of fact it was just beginning to open. Unfortunately, it needed five more murders to be complete. On September 7, a Parisian chauffeur named Couffy was found dead, robbed of twenty-five hundred francs and his car, and with a bullet in the nape of his neck, in a forest near Tours. He was driver-owner of a luxurious limousine, ordinarily stationed for hire near the Opéra, and had started in it for Cannes with a client who was Anglo-Saxon, or at any rate spoke English fluently. He was a cool client. When a passing Touraine peasant named Blé saw, just after lunch, a rotund recumbent figure on the grass with a newspaper over its face, he called to the stranger sitting nearby and whistling, "Aren't you afraid you'll wake your friend?" and received the reply, "No danger. He's sleeping soundly." This was true. Beneath the newspaper covering his bloody face, Couffy was sleeping the sleep of the dead.

On October 3, though the police did not then know it, a Strasbourg cook, Mme. Jeanine Keller, who had come to Paris in response to a help-wanted ad, was killed in the Fontainebleau Forest by a bullet in the nape of her neck, and robbed of fourteen hundred francs and a pitiful little diamond ring. On October 16, opposite the cemetery of Neuilly, a parked car was discovered to contain the corpse of M. Roger Leblond, who had been shot, robbed of five thousand francs, and then wrapped in a green-and-brown curtain, laundry-marked M. B. Leblond's latest mistress said he was a press agent, that he had gone to meet a business-advertisement correspondent named Pradier about a new cinema agency. The seven hundred Pradier families of France were vainly questioned by the police, and three hundred Parisian laundries were vainly consulted about the M. B. tag. On November 22, though again the police were not then aware of it, a German-Jewish youth, Frommer, who for his anti-Hitlerian political views had once been incarcerated in the prison at Saarbrücken, was robbed of three hundred francs, murdered by a bullet in the nape of the neck, and buried in the basement of a villa near the famous mansion which Napoleon gave Josephine at Saint-Cloud. On November 27, only five days later and also at Saint-Cloud, a house agent, Monsieur Lesobre, was robbed of five thousand francs and murdered by a shot in the nape of the neck by the pal of a client with a foreign accent to whom Lesobre was showing a three-room villa more than usually euphemistically called Mon Plaisir.

It was at this point that what began and ended as the De Koven case entered into the peripheries of a master detective story, transferred, for once, from the folly of fiction into grim, real life. It was at this moment that an unusually intelligent and lucky criminal began to be tracked by an unusually intelligent and lucky detective. Into the hands of a Commissaire Primborgne, a detective *sous-chef* of the State Police at Versailles, county seat of the Saint-Cloud district, fell a bloody visiting card found beside Lesobre's body. The card was that of Arthur Schott, traveling salesman of the Rue Parc-Impérial of Nice. From Nice the detective traced Schott to Strasbourg and summoned him to Versailles, only to learn that the cards had been distributed to thousands, including, among six other recent recipients, Schott's nephew Frommer, the young anti-Nazi.

Primborgne's search for Miss De Koven now began by his hunting a man he'd never heard of alive and didn't know was dead. All that Frommer's meager Idéal Hôtel in the Rue Saint-Sébastien knew was that Frommer had walked out on November 22, leaving his belongings and no explanation. The municipal registration offices for furnished rooms, for prisons, for hospitals, and for foreigners knew even less. However, in the Île de la Cité's *carte d'identité* files the detective discovered that Frommer's application blank gave, as resident reference, one Hugh Weber, 58 Rue de Clichy. Weber had moved, leaving no new address. Through the neighborhood police, the detective discovered he now lived somewhere in the Rue Véron, and there he found Herr Weber—and found, too, that Herr Weber spoke nearly no French. However, the patient Primborgne gleaned that Weber was another of Frommer's uncles and was worried because the youth had failed to appear for the usual family Sunday dinner. He was even more perturbed at his nephew's occasional luncheons with a criminal compatriot apparently named Sauerbrei, whom Frommer had known in Saarbrücken Prison.

Sauerbrei lived, Weber thought, under the name of Karrer in the woods around Saint-Cloud.

Primborgne knew that, wherever Leblond had been murdered by that bullet in the back of the neck, it was near trees, for their leaves were on the soles of the dead man's shoes; he knew also that Lesobre had been killed by the same sort of shot, and, *parbleu*, near trees, since he had been murdered at Saint-Cloud. He was sure that Jean De Koven had also disappeared in Saint-Cloud. The detective was by now nearly sure of certain things but didn't know where in Saint-Cloud to set about searching for them. Inquiring always through house agents and garages (Weber said Frommer said Sauerbrei said he had a car), Primborgne at last located Karrer's landlady, Mme. Marie Binder. Though she didn't yet know that her best green-and-brown curtain, laundry-tagged M. B., was gone from Karrer's cottage, she had another complaint: for all his charming smile, good manners, intelligent air, and excellent neighborhood reputation, Karrer had been late with his October rent—hadn't, indeed, paid it till November 29. On November 27, Lesobre had been robbed of five thousand francs.

Nobody being at home in the Karrer villa, the methodical Primborgne set off to telephone the villa's house agent for further details, leaving two men to watch the house. Within five minutes of his departure, Siegfried-Bobby-Sauerbrei-Karrer-Pradier-Weidmann walked through his front gate, playing with a neighbor's dog. The watchers, interrogated, said they were tax collectors; were politely requested to show their proofs and showed their police cards instead. Weidmann's last courtesy consisted in begging them to precede him into his house. Thinking of the backs of their necks, they refused. Weidmann entered first, but once over the threshold wheeled on them and fired three times, wounding them both. Being economically unarmed, as are all French State Police unless they choose to buy guns at their own expense, the men fell on him with their bare hands. One of them, tumbling in their struggle upon a little hammer (Weidmann had been doing some small household repairs), knocked their host unconscious. By the time he came to, in the police station, Couffy's automobile and Lesobre's had been found, neatly parked, and with a light covering of December

snow, in the villa's back yard. The day had been unlucky f
two lucky men. The lucky murderer had finally been caught,
and the lucky detective had not been present when the capture
was made.

The next morning, with a cigarette which the police put into
his manacled hands and a brazier which they put at his feet
(the French Sûreté believe comfort brings better results than
American brutality in grilling), Weidmann started on his orderly confession. Saying that there was one thing he couldn't
say, but could write, he wrote down the name Jean De Koven.
For her he then shed his only repentant tears. "She was gentle
and unsuspecting," he said. "I enjoyed speaking English to her,
which I learned in Canada. When I reached out for her throat,
she went down like a doll."

Eugen Weidmann was born in Frankfurt, February 15, 1908,
of respectable parents—his father is still agent for a small ex-
porting business at Frankfurt, where his son went through grade
school. At the age of sixteen, he served time for his first theft
and was afterward imprisoned for robbery in both Canada and
Germany. He was a model prisoner, a favorite with German
wardens, who considered him remarkably intellectual and well
read; they have said since that they can hardly believe he killed
five times. He spoke, besides German, fluent English, French,
and some Portuguese. After his final arrest, in France, he spent
his time in his cell reading Aventures de Télémaque, by
Fénelon, and writing his memoirs; indeed, he had so little time
for working at the regular paid prison labor, brushmaking, that
he lacked the money to pay the prison barber for a shave. Before the investigating magistrates, his uncouth appearance hu-
miliated him, especially the fact that, having caught cold in a
chill cell, he had need of a handkerchief, denied him lest he
hang himself with it.

Weidmann was an exceptionally handsome male in the medieval manner; his features were those of an etching by Holbein of
some German moyen âge merchant, with an alert, inquiring, virile, hungry eye, with a well-cartilaged nose terminating in a
cold, curious ball like that on the end of a thermometer, and a
large, amply delineated classical mouth with adequate lips. The
hair rolled free from the forehead in tidy artistic profusion. He

looked and acted like a man who, if he hadn't had in his make-up the criminal compartment, would have made a good Gothic citizen.

He was scrupulously veracious with the police. "I never lie," he truthfully told them in relating the murder of Leblond, which, on his terms, they could hardly believe. "Here is the proof," he said, and flipped open his coat to show Leblond's suspenders, which he was wearing. He had also saved the press agent's incriminating cigarette lighter, watch, and gold pencil, the baldish Mme. Keller's blond wigs, and Lesobre's useless small shoes, which he neatly preserved on shoe trees. He was also obligingly helpful to the authorities, who otherwise certainly never would have been able to find the grave of Mme. Keller in a subterranean grotto in the Fontainebleau Forest, though he never explained why on earth his photograph came to be found by her side. Because she was also discovered without her shoes on, the theory of an erotic fetishism was raised, principally in a brilliant article by Mme. Colette in *Le Journal*. Certain of the official investigators were at first also inclined to a belief that his emotional nature must be peculiar, largely because, outside of his terrible crimes, he seemed so sensible. The court interpretess assigned to him—he had fits of saying in German that he had forgotten all his French, and usually consulted with his French lawyer only in English—bluntly said she thought, in his collecting instinct, that he was less erotic than plain practical. To Mme. Tricot, mistress of his assistant, a novice French gangster named Million, Weidmann gave Mme. Keller's imitation fur coat and one of her wigs. They were useful when a disguise was needed for check cashing.

Contrary to his name, Million's part of the four months' swag —including his reward for having practiced up on murder for the first time by killing Lesobre under Weidmann's tutelage with what Weidmann called "the shot in the back of the neck that never fails"—netted him only a fourth of the paltry twenty-two thousand francs which the six murders brought in from July through November. For there was a fourth in the Weidmann combine—clown-faced Monsieur Jean Blanc, of good middle-class family and with a private income from a doting widowed mother. The previous summer Blanc backed Weidmann with thirteen thousand francs, apparently just for the thrill of being in on big crime. He and Million had already been arrested in Germany for some trifling illicit reichsmark transactions and had indeed first met Weidmann in prison, where sure enough they all met again.

Probably the most esoteric feature of the whole case was that while hundreds of officials were searching for what they thought was Jean De Koven's coy hiding place, seven people knew she was dead, and where the body was, and never told. Outside of the murderer, the six others were Million; Million's father; Million's father's café boss, and his boss's wife; Million's mistress, Mme. Tricot; and her innocent cuckolded husband, M. Tricot, to whom she told all. Jean Blanc was evidently such a bourgeois boob that he was told little and allowed to pay the big bills. It should be noted that Weidmann gave away none of these accomplices to the police—categorically denied, at first, that anybody had helped him. He admitted they existed only after the police caught them. As the police said, he was chic.

The Weidmann case was the biggest murder trial in France since Landru, whose cell at Saint-Pierre Prison the German occupied. Like the other so-called Bluebeard, the new mass murderer was tried in Versailles. His chief defense lawyers were Maître Henri Géraud, who had failed to save the neck of Gorguloff, the assassin of President Doumer of France, and Moro-Giufferi, who had failed to save Landru; assistant counsel was a lady lawyer, Maître Renée Jardin, assigned to the case by the court. The granddaughter of George Sand, the novelist, was the defense's handwriting expert in the affair. Together it was not thought they would be able to save Weidmann's head. The French are still a rational-minded race and their law courts show it. In France there is little legal nonsense such as pleading insanity for a man who had an exceptionally high I.Q., as Weidmann showed.

His trial turned out to be not only one of the most important and popular, but also proved to be, psychologically, the strangest *procès* recorded in French criminal history. That he would escape the death sentence was expected by no one, not even Weidmann, who in one of his two sensational Rousseau-like confessions said to his judge, "I am guilty, terribly guilty. I offer all I can offer—my life." He also offered a truthfulness so impressive and solicitous that he, the criminal, gradually assumed the role of a judge and became the arbiter in the desperate conflicts among the three other prisoners, the regiment of bibbed lawyers, and the crowd of weeping, bereaved, black-swathed relatives, all of whom (whenever it was useful to them) accepted the murderer's "Yes" and "No," or even the taciturn nod of his head, as gospel. "Give me the final consolation of believing in the sincerity of my sentiments," begged Weidmann of the court during one of the dramatic moments, when his devotion to veracity led him to declare that while he had murdered five times, Million, his petty-gangster confederate, had made the sixth kill. As a futile Faustian character whose power of speculation on good and evil was profoundly revealed—if a little tardily—in the prisoner's dock, Weidmann appropriately inspired some of the best newspaper literature Paris had seen since the trial, in the same courtroom, of Landru. Le Journal's, and France's, star crime reporter, Geo London, and L'Œuvre's crack man, Pierre Bénard, both turned out pages of that mixture of malice, insight, libel, philosophy, and inaccurate reporting that constitutes the genius of the fourth estate here. And as a special reporter for Paris-Soir, Mme. Colette, in a brilliant appreciative essay on the murderer's spiritual capacity for truth, honored Weidmann with fine writing such as she has hitherto bestowed only on nature and animals.

It is indicative of the rational attitude of the French, during this particular moment of acute nationalistic tension, that Weidmann's being a German was not considered an additional crime. Indeed, as a Gothic cruel criminal, the French more than gave him the benefit of their curious international-minded sympathy. Million, like Weidmann, was condemned to death but was later pardoned by the President of France and permitted to look forward to life imprisonment. That the murderous Frenchman was allowed to keep his head while the even more murderous German lost his was a source of acute dissatisfaction to the average Paris man in the street. "It didn't look right," he said. "It had an air of giving the Boche the worst of it."

Weidmann's decapitation was more important than he could have dreamed. Ever since Dr. Joseph Guillotin, Parisian professor of anatomy, imposed his instrument "for decollation" in 1792, executions, as part of the murderer's awful punishment, have taken place in a public place in France. Weidmann will go down in modern French judicial history as the last to lose his head while morbid crowds gaped at dawn—at a criminal whose popularity was so great that it changed the law. Within a fortnight of Weidmann's death the French Minister of Justice passed a new decree, ordaining that in the future French executions would take place privately behind prison walls. The *kermesse* scenes in Versailles the night before Weidmann's punishment were considered too scandalous; cafés were given an all-night license extension, wine flowed, around the little prison blared jazz on radios whose previous announcement of his approaching death the prisoner had already overheard. The new Monsieur de Paris, or high executioner, nervous at only his third performance, insisted, against the Procurer of the Republic, that Greenwich rather than summertime dawn should be the official hour. Weidmann was, contrary to custom, thus executed—and clumsily to boot—in broad daylight. He met his end bravely. That is to say he shut his eyes when he saw the guillotine and walked to his death like a somnambulist.

Only a typical Frenchman like Million, accustomed to the old apprentice system and his country's gerontocratic policy, by which the young always work (and at low pay) for their elders, would have participated in such a poor proposition as the Weidmann murders. Only a typical postwar German like Weidmann, unfamiliar with the value of money as the rest of the freer world knows it, would have killed so many people for so little. And only a typical American, like poor Miss De Koven, would have been so sociable, so confidential, and could have seemed so rich. The De·Koven case was a small and sinister European entanglement.

Anatole Deibler (1863–1939)

Anatole Deibler, grand high executioner of France, recently fell dead of a heart attack in a Métro station while en route to his four-hundred-and-first guillotining. He was seventy-six years old, dapper, quiet-spoken, looked like Poincaré but was handsomer, liked to go fishing alone, and was the last to bear the name of his family, which was of Bavarian origin and provided France with headsmen for a hundred and ten years. He was known as Monsieur de Paris, since for centuries French executioners have taken their title from their city of residence. Until Napoleon III cut down expenses by naming a national decapitator, each province had one of its own. Deibler's father, Louis, who was the last guillotiner to wear a top hat when performing his duties, was originally Monsieur de Rennes, executioner for Britanny. He married the exotic Zoë, daughter of Rasseneux, chief of another famous headsman family. Rasseneux operated as Monsieur d'Alger. Anatole Deibler leaves no male heir (as serious a lapse to a decapitator as to a king, both professions being dynastic). Deibler's only son was accidentally killed as a child by a careless drug clerk who made up a poisonous prescription. The new Monsieur de Paris is André Obrecht, Deibler's valet (as the assistant is called) and nephew. He wanted to be a son-in-law of Deibler, but Mme. Deibler said she'd rather see her daughter dead than married to an executioner. Mme. Deibler's family is related by marriage to the Desfourneaux, an even older clan of headsmen than the Deiblers. She and her husband first met at the Auteuil Velocipedic Society's meetings. Deibler was an ardent bicycle rider and rode for his club in the sprints. When he died, he had been the state's executioner for forty years. His last salary rise gave him eighteen thousand francs a year, or about four hundred and eighty-six dollars. Since his job carried no pension, he said he could not afford to resign.

Diaghilev's Ballet

With the present so disagreeable, a pleasant lapse into the past has been furnished by the Louvre's magnificent and meticulous "Ballets Russes de Diaghilev" exposition, organized by Serge Lifar and covering the years from 1909 to 1929, when the great impresario died. In those two decades, as much was done for modern art as for classic legs. A list of the painters who made curtains or costumes during the Ballet's twenty years' utilization of the talents of all Europe contains what are now the most famous, and were then some of the least-known, names on earth. Bakst, Benois, Jacques-Émile Blanche, Bonnard, Braque, Chirico, Cocteau, Derain, de Segonzac, Max Ernst, Gontcharova, Juan Gris, Jean Hugo, Larionov, Marie Laurencin, Matisse,

Modigliani, Picasso, Pruna, Rouault, Sert, Tchelitchew, Utrillo, and Van Dongen make up the major group which Diaghilev patronized, presented, and helped preserve for fame. The stage curtains, which in the old days of frantic first nights here were as essential to the excitement as the music and the choreography, figure in the exhibition as touching antiques today: Utrillo's limpid, urban backdrop for *Barabou*, Pruna's postal-card painting for *Les Matelots*, Chirico's architectural disarray for the waltzing in *Le Bal*, Picasso's silhouettes for *Tricorne*, Max Ernst's proscenium curtain for *Romeo and Juliet*.

The balletomanes who attended the exposition's opening assembled for the joy of recollection but became its melancholy victims. More than any other spectacle, Diaghilev's Ballet has come to symbolize what are now called *les beaux jours*, the days of civilized, uncensored pleasures, of new musicians and artists, and their new notions, which formed fresh pictures and gave new sounds to a familiar world—the days of the curly nineteen-twenties, when politicians as well as hedonists thought a permanent, pleasant, peaceful age had been born.

With such memories in mind, it's not strange that balletomanes were saddened by the show. It was enough to make the angels weep.

"Peace in Our Time"

France now thinks there is a good chance of peace, though of uncertain duration. Unquestionably there will be peace until Herr Hitler addresses his Reichstag. There can be peace till the beginning of summer, when he may have his small sub-Axis states frightened into his fighting line. There may be peace till August, when the Balkan wheat harvest is in. There may be peace till 1940, or even long after that. Maybe Europe is in for a Hundred Years' Peace, like its Hundred Years' War and looking much the same—years of threats, conquests that are small measured against the disruption of men's minds, peace in the manner of war and with almost the same costs, until everybody goes bankrupt from being so well armed that nobody dares fight the big fight. Certainly Herr Hitler's chances of winning the big fight have declined in the past week. France and England, after first acting as if they would fight for anything and then as if they wouldn't fight at all, have finally made it apparent that they will fight for only a few things, but for them will fight to the death. In the last war against Germany, America came in late, but now all Germans angrily believe (whether Americans are pleased to or not) that America would be the first to pour its money, if not its men, into an anti-Nazi ideological war. Against these three nations, German treaty ties with the smaller states are mere diplomatic bowknots.

For the first time since last September, the European landscape can be clearly seen. At the present moment, peace no longer essentially rests on what the democracies will cede but on how much the Germans will risk. If Germany is willing to risk Germany in order to destroy England, there will be war. Otherwise there will be this thing we now call peace.

Gaieté Parisienne

Paris has suddenly been having a fit of prosperity, gaiety, and hospitality. There have been money and music in the air, with people enjoying the first good time since the bad time started at Munich last summer. There have been magnificent costume balls and parties, with dancers footing it till early breakfast, hitherto a dull meal people got up on rather than went to bed after. There have been formal dinner parties in stately houses; there have been alfresco fetes held in the *salon* because of the sunspot storms; there have been garden parties that couldn't be held in the garden but were not dampened in spirit by the rain. The expensive hotels have been full of American and English tourists. The French franc is holding up fine; Finance Minister Reynaud's speech on his recuperation policies, before the powerful Anglo-American pressmen's luncheon club, apparently pleased the foreign pressmen and certainly pleased the French peasants when they read about it. French workmen are working; France's exports are up; her trade balance continues to bulge favorably; business is close to having a little boom. It has taken the threat of war to make the French loosen up and have a really swell and civilized good time. The gaiety in Paris has been an important political symptom of something serious and solid, as well as spirited, that is in the air in France today.

The great costume ball of the summer was given by Comte Étienne de Beaumont, to which his guests came dressed as characters from the plays or period of Racine, whose tercentenary is now being celebrated. Mme. Marie-Louise Bousquet went attired as La Vallière, wearing a chiffon mask painted in the likeness of that eventual nun. Maurice de Rothschild, garbed as the Ottoman Bajazet, wore the famous diamonds of his mother on his turban, and on his sash the rare Renaissance jewels which are a part of his family's Cellini collection. At Versailles, Lady Mendl gave an international garden party for seven hundred and fifty guests and three elephants, all three of which refused to be ridden, by, among others, Princesse de Kapurthala. The most inventive and best big party was that of Mrs. Louise Macy, who hired a long-disused historical mansion, the Hôtel Salé, for the night, put in temporary furnishings and plumbing, a mobile kitchen, and several thousand candles, and requested her guests to wear diadems and decorations, and no nonsense about their not having any. Elsa Maxwell said it was one of the most successful parties she never gave.

There's also been a lot of suave diplomatic wining and dining. The President of France and his wife gave a dinner in honor of their young Majesties, the Emperor and Empress of Annam. After all, Annam is still one of France's vital spaces. The Polish Embassy gave a desperately brilliant diplomatic dinner. After all, Danzig is not yet one of Germany's vital spaces. Ambassador Bullitt gave a huge ball for the visiting Yale Glee Club boys. Male youth is vital all over the world these days.

Preparation for War

AUGUST 26

General mobilization, expected this weekend of the crisis, hasn't yet taken place. For three days Danzig has been in military readiness for the arrival of the German fleet. It hasn't yet sailed in. Despite the disappointing Henderson-Hitler interview, diplomatic circles believe that Roosevelt's insistent messages may have made an impression. For these three reasons there is today a faint hope of peace which didn't exist on Thursday or

Friday. However, everybody in France—government, soldiers, housewives—continues to prepare for war in case war is to be an inevitable part of history. During these last three anxious days the people in Paris have remained completely calm. As they say, "*Maintenant nous avons l'habitude*—we've had March, 1938; we've had last September; now we have August." The greatest emotion has centered around the Gare de l'Est, the railroad station where thousands of soldiers have entrained for the northern frontier fortresses. Mostly they have been in uniform and steel helmets, but carrying the family blankets and little bundles of clean socks and handkerchiefs they were ordered to bring from home. Also, mostly their mothers, wives, fathers, and sisters have shed no tears till the troop trains have pulled out. While the majority of the men have been called to the colors by the official poster entitled "*Appel Immédiat*," which has been pasted on walls all over the cities and towns, the government has telephoned to many of them or has sent private messengers to their houses, apparently so that enemy agents can't figure out precisely how many soldiers France is mobilizing. Thus in any house where a male of military age lives, the phone may ring and an official voice say, "*Allons*, Monsieur So-and-So, you are mobilized. Report at once at such-and-such a garrison." There are no flags, flowers, or shrill shouts of "*Vive la patrie!*" as there were in 1914. Among the men departing now for the possible front, the morale is excellent but curiously mental. What the men say is intelligent, not emotional. "If it's got to come, let's stop living in this grotesque suspense and get it over with once and for all." Because French soil has not yet been violated, patriotism has not yet come into play. Few Frenchmen are thrilled to go forth to die on the Somme as usual—this time for Danzig. Yet all the French seem united in understanding that this war, if it comes, is about the theory of living and its eventual practice.

Besides the military call-to-arms poster, on city and village walls there are two other official announcements. One, entitled "Passive Defense," warns the people that "enemy bombs may be redoubtable" and tells them what to do in case of gas attack. The second poster is an *avis à la population* and instructs civilians what to do with automobile headlights and public and private lamps during blackouts. In the villages of the Ile-de-France the town crier appeared today with his drum balanced on the handlebars of his bicycle, beat out a roll, and announced that tonight no lights should be visible in any house or on any road. Last night, most of Paris was only partially illuminated.

Since the French government has requested everyone who can to leave Paris, evacuation along the big south and west highroads has begun, with automobiles piled high with babies' cribs, luggage, pets, bedding, and food. The Louvre and other state museums are closed; the art treasures are being shipped off to the provinces. As art objects, the palaces of Fontainebleau and Versailles are also closed, but unfortunately they can't be moved. The American Hospital at Neuilly is packed and ready to be transferred to Étretat, near Havre, at the zero hour. While Poland's citizens have been urged to buy a hundred and fifty pounds of potatoes, flour, etc., so they won't become state charges in case of war, the French are being asked not to hoard, since they are thrifty anyhow. In consequence, sugar, flour, and rice, already unavailable in large quantities, can still be bought by the kilo. Candles, however, are being sold by the candle, not by the box.

The air-raid sirens, which are usually sounded for a full minute at noon every Thursday to make sure they're in working order, on this Thursday blasted only for a few seconds, for fear Parisians would think the warning was suddenly valid. In the little suburb of Chatou, because of defective wiring the air sirens suddenly went off in the middle of the night. Chatou turned out with courage in its nightgowns and pajamas. With even grimmer fortitude, the powerful Left labor union, C.G.T., has just declared itself against the surprising pact made by Communist Russia with Nazi Germany. Upon learning of the pact, Léon Blum wrote in his *Populaire*, "I shall vainly try to dissimulate my stupefaction." Premier Daladier made no effort to hide his and promptly suppressed the two Communist dailies, *L'Humanité* and *Ce Soir*. *L'Humanité* had hailed the pact with the headline "The Pourparlers in Moscow between U.S.S.R. and Germany Will Aid the Cause of Peace." In general, what Russia has done has been summed up by the French in one classic French phrase, "*Nous sommes cocus* (we've been cuckolded.)"

The radio has been less significant and informative than in the crisis of last September because news has been so slow and scant that even European newspapers, with their one edition a day, could catch it all. And while the propaganda on the radio was a vitally important verbal battle front last September, for the past two days Germany and Italy have oddly continued their regular music hours; last night, Stuttgart broadcast the ironically dulcet Mozart "Nachtmusik." The argumentative violence of last autumn's day-long radio propaganda has in this autumn's crisis been concentrated by the Germans in their so-called news announcements. Thursday nights, the Hamburg station's English-language news commentator sarcastically quoted previous editorials from both the London *Observer* and the London *Times* in favor of the abolition of the Polish Corridor. But on the whole one of the dreary agonies of these past three days has lain precisely in the fact that there has been little relieving excitement—nearly no news, no discussion, no facts, no arguments; nothing but waiting and watching men march off to what may be Sunday's, Monday's, or Tuesday's war.

War in Our Time (Declared on September 3)

The special nature of this war demanded as a primary condition a victim state. Last September, the sacrifice state was to have been Czechoslovakia. This September, the martyr was Poland. The ultimate result would have been the same no matter what the date or the name of the country. Instead of for the theoretical liberty and salvation of Czechoslovakia in 1938, the Allies have gone to war in 1939 for a Poland already in ruins, and so distant that France and England could not fire a shot in Warsaw's defense. The cannons now occasionally rumbling on the Western Front are too far off for the Poles ever to hear the avenging sound. It is these geographic elements, as well as the time now being taken by diplomats traveling like drummers back and forth between Moscow and Berlin to haggle over last-minute concessions, threats, and dickerings, which make this seem an unnatural war. As a matter of fact, it is really a commonplace war, since it is simply a fight for liberty. It is only because of its potential size that it may, alas, prove to be civilization's ruin.

INDEX